"About the nature and content of faith and morals, Jana Novak asks both the basic questions and the hard ones; and her father fields them well. He is direct and clear about the intelligibility of existence, the possibilities and limits of human knowledge, the interaction of knowledge and religious faith, and the problem of evil."

—William F. Buckley, Jr.

"Prominent Catholic philosopher Michael Novak and his daughter Jana have written a thought-provoking book. They ask the most important questions in life: Is there a God? If so, what is he like? And why does it matter? They are answered with seriousness and a disarming honesty. Read this book, ponder it, grapple with it. It is well argued and well worth arguing with. There are not enough books like this anymore."

—Michael Cromartie, senior fellow,
Ethics and Public Policy Center

"Michael Novak is a national treasure, and this book reminds us once again why. In the finest tradition of C. S. Lewis and other great defenders of faith, TELL ME WHY is a stirring and stimulating discussion of every person's need for a relationship with God and His church in a secular age."

—Ralph Reed, Jr., President, Century Strategies

"Why hasn't this been done before? Obviously, it was an idea awaiting Michael and Jana Novak. Parents and children all over America should turn off the television, read this book, and then embark together on a similar conversation into the things that matter most."

—Richard John Neuhaus, editor in chief, *First Things*

"Both believers and nonbelievers can profit from the study of Mr. Novak's touching exchange between himself and a beloved daughter, in which he responds to questions she has raised. They are all ancient, of course, but they still occur afresh to each new generation of young thinkers . . . [Against the many absurdities or our time] there stand certain noble souls such as Michael Novak, whose arguments do not ravage reason and whose will is warm and good. Since even within his own family there are those who do not fully agree with him, the same will obviously be true of his readers. But it is important to continue the great debate, the magnificent ongoing attempt at civilized discourse, the respect for the noble ideals of truth, reason, love and social justice."

—Steve Allen

"A scintillating dialogue between father and daughter on the philosophical underpinnings and social ramifications of Christian faith. Both provocative and perceptive."

—Fr. Ellwood E. Kieser, C.S.P., Paul Productions

"Michael Novak takes on the honest and probing questions of his daughter, whose doubts are those of many young and sophisticated Americans. His answers—sympathetic, wise, and lucid—exemplify an unflinching faith that is hospitable to reason and argument. The book adds a new milestone to the tradition of dialogical apologetics."

—Avery Dulles, S.J., Laurence J. McGinley Professor of Religion and Society, Fordham University

"People of all faiths should read this honest and beautiful book. *Tell Me Why* talks equally and powerfully to the mind and to the heart."

—Dennis Prager, author of *Happiness Is a Serious Problem* and *The Nine Questions People Ask About Judaism*

A FATHER
ANSWERS
HIS DAUGHTER'S
QUESTIONS
ABOUT
GOD

TELL
ME
WHY

MICHAEL NOVAK
AND
JANA NOVAK

POCKET BOOKS
New York   London   Toronto   Sydney   Tokyo   Singapore

For
Karen Laub Novak
Wife, Mother, Friend

POCKET BOOKS, a division of Simon & Schuster Inc.
1230 Avenue of the Americas, New York, NY 10020

ISBN: 0-671-01885-X

First Pocket Books hardcover printing September 1998

10 9 8 7 6 5 4 3 2 1

Text design by Stanely S. Drate/Folio Graphics Co. Inc.

NOTE TO THE READER

As far as possible, we have tried to keep our conversation open to all persons of good will, and to stress things held in common. This is not because some of the issues that divide consciences are not important. It is because the larger issue is whether the religious side of human nature deserves cultivation, or should be allowed to lapse into desert.

Further, we have inserted throughout the book favorite prayers of men and women of many faiths down through the centuries, and a few challenges from nonbelievers. The former show how other generations thought about God—and spoke to God. The latter express doubts. Challenges from both directions aid us. While believers sometimes doubt, nonbelievers sometimes speak or act as if they believe.

At some places, Jana (pronounced "yaw-nuh") wanted us to spell "god" in lowercase, to keep the discussion neutral for her sake. This departure from normal usage seemed appropriately provocative.

This book is written so as to be read in either of two ways: either straight through to grasp the overall argument, or in daily reflection on one of the short sections into which each chapter has been divided.

Jana wishes to add that some troubling pages fell into focus for her on the second reading, after climbing to the top. From there, the view is different, and you can see how the "roundabouts" fit.

She did her best to fight the argument.

M.N., J.N.

CONTENTS

On a huge hill,
Cragged, and steep, Truth stands and hee that will
Reach her, about must, and about must goe.

—John Donne (1572–1631)

JANA'S CHALLENGE ARRIVES

In the early summer of 1996, my daughter Jana asked me to lend her some books on religion, and then we got to talking and one thing led to another. I was about to leave for Kraków, Poland, to take part in an annual seminar. She borrowed the books and then a few days later sent me a long fax that began with a fascinating comment and ended with a long series of questions.

The Hollywood writer and actor Ben Stein once saw Jana in high school (she is now in her twenties) and said she reminded him of the young Ingrid Bergman. She is stubborn and tough, and she told me when she was nineteen that I would not have to worry about her having a delayed rebellion because she had always been in rebellion and had more or less gotten over it. And in a way, but not entirely, she has. She does not like to be told anything she can figure out for herself, which has sometimes left me out of it and not a little perplexed.

That is why I leapt to respond when I received a fax full of questions from my very own daughter. An unprecedented event. Not that she has not sent me faxes, but usually they are about things she thinks I might want to see or something I am not supposed to forget. (She never asks for money. Her mother always was a very cheap date—hates to spend money—and in this and many other attractive ways, Jana follows her mother.) This time, a whole series of questions! A father dreams of this. In fact, the hardest part of being a father is feeling, from the first moments in the delivery room onwards, especially with my daughters, utterly useless.

In fact, Jana even agreed, when I tentatively brought it up, that we could write a book together. She is a born writer but shy about writing, although she had a by-line on an article in *The Washingtonian* when she was only a college sophomore and a research assistant. Recently, she enjoyed an eighteen-month stint as assistant editor of a magazine in which she wrote a number of things, including several departments of her own. This editing job expired at the end of 1996, so perhaps she figured getting some writing in would help during the transition to something new; she now writes for a prominent national leader. I'm just glad she agreed, because it helps me enormously.

In 1965 I published *Belief and Unbelief*,[1] a book that sold more copies (in paperback) than any other book I have ever written. Once a customs officer at Kennedy Airport asked me if I was the one who wrote it, recalling the title from his required readings in college. I began to apologize for it being forced on him but he said, No, it was okay, he liked it a lot, at least the parts of it he could understand. Which left me with mixed feelings. But it was nice to be recognized. Jana's fax showed me that the questions young people are asking today are very different from those asked back in the sixties. I had sensed that difference but, on my own, I don't have the touch that I had then. (At that time, I was just finishing graduate school myself.)

---

[1] Third edition, Transaction Press, 1994.

New questions are in the air, after the busyness of the last swift decades. The secular city seemed fresh in the sixties; now it is old and stale, and not very satisfying. The young have experienced a thoroughly secular life, and now have a budding desire to study about religion, while being quite put off by many actions of religious organizations. It's a funny time. Not hostile, not even exactly skeptical. Curious isn't the right word either. Maybe even inquiring gives the wrong idea. Being at least a little religious seems as natural as liking music. The desire to explore the religious quest, at least when it is not being forced on you, is again becoming natural. Anyway, young people have a lot of questions, and not many opportunities to ask them.

There is one thing I'm still uncertain about regarding how Jana and I should proceed. It's been my experience (at least at dinner parties and other casual gatherings) that people have special questions about the Catholic Church. Maybe it's so public, or photogenic, or so countercultural and always coming up in discussions, or maybe it's just so much a part of Western civilization that everybody bumps into it, and usually has feelings about it. Jana and I are Catholic—although at this point she may wish to say that she just happened to be born Catholic and is keeping her options open—and so a bunch of her questions come up in Catholic form. We want to write for people in all religions, but there's no gain in avoiding the Catholic part. Quite often in moral matters that means "Christian, full-strength" (although evangelicals have been remarkably jealous of the straight teachings of the gospels, too). So it is some gain to find out what Catholics believe, and then to adjust that for other denominations. For sure, at dinner parties Catholics come in for more than their share of "Can you tell me why?" questions. Sometimes, these are even not unfriendly.

Usually, Catholics themselves haven't inquired into all the corners of their tradition, and since the Second Vatican Council in 1965 the nuns aren't what they used to be, and Catholic religious instruction hasn't even come up to "lite." Anyway, I hope Jana and I aren't making a mistake in including so many "Catholic" matters. Maybe readers will be kind enough to chalk these up to things they probably should have gotten in Western Civ anyway, for general knowledge. They happen to be life-and-death matters for me, and are clearly important to Jana since she brings them up. In my responses, I try to be fair to other traditions, for her sake as well as truth's sake.

It makes me happier than I can say to be able to write about these matters with my daughter. She is giving me a great gift. Fathers want so badly to be useful. Maybe we don't recognize all the opportunities daughters are always offering us. It seems harder with daughters, though. Fathers and sons seem to have a long tradition of fighting and kidding, disappointing and hurting one another, and being in silence together. It's somehow easier between them. Rich (Jana's older brother, the eldest of our three) and I have had our bad moments, but his achievements have made me very proud, the last decade or so between us has been a joy for me, and the wife and the children he has brought Karen and me—our first grandchildren—are precious jewels.

She will hate me for saying this, but Jana is our youngest, our baby. Ever since eight-months-in-the-womb she almost died with her mother (her mother was wading innocently in the ocean off Miami Beach, stepped into a hidden sinkhole, and was swept away by a powerful, errant wave until a providential rescue), she has seemed to us unusually a gift of God. Each child is special in a special way, but Jana is precious because we came so close to losing her, and for years we held her with that in mind. I think she doesn't realize—no child does—all the things that go through her parents' minds when we look at her. But, then, we often don't pick up on what she is thinking, either.

Probably the first thing I should do is let Jana speak for herself. Here is the fax she sent that started things off. She telephoned afterwards to say that she hadn't had time to correct mistakes or polish it. It is blunter that way.

J A N A : *My random thoughts on religion:*

The problem with religion for many of my generation, as well as for those who grew up during and after the 1960s, is that we are constantly looking for fulfillment. It is as if we have all grown malformed—with a piece, a very small piece, yet an integral piece, missing. It is a cycle whose beginnings I don't think I can pinpoint.

Our lives, particularly as teenagers, were chaotic and we wanted something to enforce order and fill the void, but not in a confining, cold, overbearing way—we wanted someone to hold our hand and comfort us. We were unable to find what we were looking for in the church. Religion we found to be patriarchal, distant, and unsatisfying. Quick fixes are in, patience is not.

Rebellion flourished and religion was neglected as a sym-

bol of—no—as "the" establishment. Where once people felt bad, alone, and guilty, now there was a momentary sense of yes! That must be it. We have shaken off the shackles which bound us to misery. But the void—originally felt because of religion—only grew. It was like a paper cut that seems so tiny yet continues to fester and sting for weeks. At first, admonishment and dredged-up proof of wrong-doings were relished as justification for overturning and rejecting religion. Eventually, though, my friends and I noticed that we needed something in our lives to give it meaning. Some then turned to Asian religions such as Zen Buddhism, and Zen and The Art of Motorcycle Maintenance became a best-seller (heaven forbid anyone actually spend time reading the real Buddhist texts—we all relied on the Cliff Notes versions). Then New Age mysticism and other such endeavors.

For years religion has been mocked as the opiate of the masses—but has it really been used to control, or is it merely that the people have chosen to be happy? It slowly began to dawn on rejecters that it was not the former but the latter. While religion did have the added bonus (to a leader) of maintaining a "weaker" populace, that is really not the reason that religion has survived thousands of years, and is now at the cusp of a new renaissance in America. The simple fact is, people desire religion. They desire the succor it provides, the effort it requires, and the discipline it instills. And so now we see people flocking back to the churches, the synagogues, the temples. Is it ironic? Nah. It is only ironic that returnees seem to be so set on introducing their children to religion.

Okay, here go my questions:

1. Why is religion, any religion, important?
2. What is the difference between one Christian church and another? Does it matter which one anyone chooses?
3. How do you explain the existence of other religions, especially non-Christian religions such as Buddhism?
4. Is there leeway to say "I don't agree with everything the Christian church teaches" and still be a Christian? Is this true of Catholics, too? For example, I disagree with the Church's stance on contraception, etc.
5. Sex? Is it a sin to enjoy it (if you're married)? Is it really solely for procreation?
6. Why doesn't the Catholic Church have married priests? Couldn't there be two tracks for the priesthood? One where the priest could marry and one where he could not? I just believe a married priest could relate to others so much more. For example, he would understand the difficulties of adolescence (through watching his own children), love, and marriage. He would be able to serve as a better counselor (above and beyond being just a Father Confessor) and he would relate better to the temptations of life and how to avoid them. He would also be able to be more of a role model to children.
7. Homosexuality? I know many people do not approve of homosexuality and I know that part of this disapproval stems from the fact that homosexual sex is always just sex for physical or psychic pleasure. But does this mean that those very conserva-

tive Christians who take this to heart have a right to discriminate against gays? Or wouldn't Christ say that we must treat gays equally and not discriminate against them—Christ always looked out for all outcasts and minorities, such as lepers—although we still shouldn't sanction their behavior. What if two gays are a completely committed and monogamous couple who truly love each other? Is it still wrong if it is more than just sex? Does the Church believe homosexuality is a mental disease to be cured? Or is it merely natural human desires that we are supposed to control and not act on?

8. Children? Are we supposed to focus our life around having children—around having a lot of children?

9. Abortion? What if the woman's life is in danger?

10. Birth control? What about in the case of a woman whose period is very irregular and for health reasons her gynecologist/doctor prescribes it? (I believe I was told at a Summer Institute in Theology at Notre Dame—which Mom and I attended together—that in that case it was okay.) What if one's spouse has some sexually transmitted disease, such as having received AIDS from a blood transfusion? Is the uninfected spouse allowed to request a condom to protect herself?

11. AIDS? I know some hard-core religious people believe this is God's will to destroy the "evil" in our community: in their mind, gays, drug addicts, etc. But isn't that similar to people's reactions in biblical times to such diseases as leprosy, when it was only Jesus who stood up to them? Shouldn't the Church

be running AIDS hospices, etc? Doesn't it not matter how a person contracts any disease—only that we are all God's children and as such we must all be loved and taken care of?

12. *Infertility/adoption? I thought I remembered having once heard that if a family was unable to conceive, they should focus on God, not on infertility drugs, in vitro, surrogate, or adoption.*

13. *Bible? Is this considered truly the word of God or merely human interpretation and embellishment on events—in other words, just a story? Do Christians need to be literalists? Can you be an evolutionist and a scientist and still be Christian? Are those people who are literalists/fundamentalists wrong or deluded?*

14. *Volunteering, etc.? Do you need to be a Mother Teresa to be a good Christian? Do you need to forsake all material comforts? Or can you go about your business and be fine as long as you act in a Christian, moral, and ethical manner?*

Jana's fax led me to plunge into the beginnings of a reply right away, sitting there in the medieval city of Kraków. Here is what I started to write:

In reply to your memo, Jana, a lot of what follows is not going to be very chatty. Some of the things you've asked me are more important to me than anything else in the world. So expect me to get carried away sometimes (I'll try to put a brake on). I want to do the best thinking and writing I can, because as far as I'm concerned this is your inheritance, or the most important part of it. We are not wealthy

9

people and, God knows, we do not descend from nobility but from very humble roots.

Those roots are not far away from where I'm typing this, maybe not two hundred kilometers south of Kraków, across the Dunajec River where our seminar went rafting Saturday. The Dunajec forms the border between Poland and Slovakia and cuts through fairy-tale mountain passes where tall silent pines rise to peaks in the sun and a rare black crane big as an eagle strokes gracefully on the upper wind. Just over the mountains there lies Brutovce and, just farther, Dúbrava, high on the ridge over the valley of the largest castle in Central Europe, on whose wooded grounds the Novaks once labored for a Hungarian count.

I received nothing more valuable from my mother and father—and their mothers and fathers, and so on back to (as near as I've been able to research it) the twelfth century in those villages—than the life of God through the sacraments of Jesus Christ: baptism, penance, the Eucharist, the gift of the Spirit, matrimony, orders, the rite of the dying.

What I have to leave you, Jana, is the inner life of our faith. It has kept our family going through wars and peace for perhaps a thousand years, in the invisible lustrous chain of God's love. (Our God has an odd way of showing his love: through suffering, borne with grace.)

I won't get to everything in one sitting, but let me begin with those parts of your inheritance that you have asked about.

I

FOUNDATIONS

"Person" signifies what is
noblest in the whole
of nature.

—St. Thomas Aquinas
(1224–1274)

1

WHY DOES RELIGION, ANY RELIGION, MATTER?

As at the entrance of the church on Sunday and on the feast days,
When we go to Mass,
Or at the funerals,
We give each other, we pass each other the holy water from hand
    to hand,
From neighbor to neighbor, one after the other,
Directly from hand to hand or from a blessed branch dipped into
    the holy water.
In order to make the sign of the cross either over ourselves, who
    are alive, or over the casket of the person who has died,
In such a way that the same sign of the cross is as if carried from
    neighbor to neighbor by the same water,
By the ministry, by the administering of the same water,
One after the other, over the same breasts and over the same
    hearts,
And the same foreheads too,
And even over the caskets of the same deceased bodies,
So from hand to hand, from finger to finger,
From fingertip to fingertip, the eternal generations,
Who are eternally going to Mass.
In the same breasts, in the same hearts up to the death of the world,
Like a relay,
In the same hope, the word of God is passed on.

—Charles Péguy
(1873–1914)

JANA: *For myself, and my generation as a whole (I believe), deciding to have faith, to believe in God, is not as hard to accept as it was for your generation. For this reason, Dad, I think we need to start at the concept of religion and then work backwards to God. I find making the leap from believer in God to practitioner of religion much harder. With my own experience, I realized this very quickly. After having spent many years not believing in anything or anyone, let alone some higher being that is all powerful and supremely good, the comfort that having faith in God provides was a welcome relief; at least someone out there is watching over you and caring what happens to you. Yet it is still possible to feel like something is missing, something concrete. Believing in God is such a matter of faith that it would be nice to have something to touch, hear and smell. Logically, I would guess that something is religion. As in, "I've got religion." Well, I don't—at least not right now. (Although I have very much enjoyed the times Mark, my boyfriend, has taken me to his Presbyterian Church with its very traditional minister and his wonderful, thick-as-molasses Scottish brogue.) Part of the reason I don't "have religion" is that I am not totally convinced that my lack of religion is the problem. Question one: Why is religion—any religion—important?*

Organized religion superficially appears so contrived— and so controlling. Its structure—so bureaucratic with its layers of priests, ministers, etc., and its large, imposing temples, cathedrals—seems to physically reinforce the charge that religion works to put a greater distance between the individual and God, rather than to bring them closer. For example, organized religion often comes across like a gate-

keeper or bodyguard: unless one does this *or bribes it with* that *on earth, it won't let you in, or recommend you, to see the celebrity that it's so possessively guarding—that is, God. Psychologically, I have often felt this way—that I could not hear God for the noise of his "bureaucrats."*

I even wrote a poem years ago at a crisis point in my life when I wanted to turn to the church and to God, and yet felt alone and abandoned, like a little girl lost in the wide, cavernous darkness of an empty, cold cathedral.

Of course, I have always had hope—hope that the alienation I felt from the church would be rectified when it awoke to its distance and tried to recapture its spirit.

I am still not completely clear about the purpose of religion per se. *Question two: Why is it necessary to believe in a religion? Is religion just a means to an end? In other words, does religion merely act as a paved path to God (as opposed to forging through the jungle, perhaps even without a machete)? If so—question three—does the existence of many, many different religions only illustrate the variety of paths to God without specifying or implying that one is necessarily better than another—that it is merely a matter of finding a good fit between you and the religion?*

Finally, based on the fact that we are, after all, human and always want to know what's in it for us, my fourth question: What is religion supposed to offer or accomplish? Personal peace and fulfillment? I can understand that one certainly should not be asking for anything personal and superficial from God—that would be audaciously presumptuous (although I do still turn to him and pray for assistance and favors anyway). But if one can believe in God without truly needing to believe in religion, then why bother believing in religion unless it offers you something?

DAD: Why, you ask, is religion, any religion, important? My simple answer is: Because it is true. If it isn't true, you shouldn't accept it. You wouldn't want to turn to religion merely for comfort, security, or peace of mind (although that's what atheists say religion is for). Because if religion isn't true, you wouldn't find peace of mind or comfort or security anyway.

Besides, if the religion you now accept isn't fully true, the longing for truth—the longing to get reality right—will drive you to pursue the evidence wherever it leads, however arduous that exploration (that "pilgrim's progress") may be.

If God is God, it cannot be impossible for him to have given us sufficient evidence to come to where he wants us to be. We have to look for it. That is the greatest detective story of all times. (All detective stories are parables for finding God.)

There is no other reason for counting yourself religious, except that it says something true about your place in the world.

There is no other purpose in joining a religious communion except that it is a communion bearing the truth about God, human destiny, and yourself. Keep your eye on the question of truth.

In some ways, a church or synagogue makes your way to God more difficult, not less. Every social institution is a clumsy thing. Some days, the preaching is not simply poor, but offensive. The music may be poor. (It may even be too beautiful: Søren Kierkegaard, the Danish philosopher, says that paganism often begins just when the music soars—just when your soul turns toward the bodily thrill of gorgeous sound. Music is lovely and good in itself, a gift of God, and yet it can quickly become a distraction from the presence of God. Kierkegaard believed in keeping first things first, with a fierce purity of purpose.)

A church group may be too cold and impersonal—or too cozy, coy, and chummy. So I don't think a church "paves" your way to God; it may throw boulders in your path. I remember the English novelist Evelyn Waugh writing about the agonies he often endured attending public worship. Even some religious persons, left to themselves, prefer solitude and minimal involvement with others, especially institutions; they would prefer being hermits to enduring community.

In America especially, where "choice" reigns, many persons choose a congregation because they prefer its minister's preaching, the superior friendliness of its people, or the beauty of its worship services; or because they feel more "at home" in it than in some other. These are not unworthy motives. But neither are they *religious* motives.

To the extent that they are not rooted in conscience and a serious pursuit of the truth, such motives might be described as "social" motives, akin to those that might govern one's choice of a private club. Such motives eventually diminish the intellectual content of a religious body.

In fact, many American church groups might just as well join together as one religion of "the American way of life," a religion of gregarious sociality and individual choice. The basic commandments of this religion would be: Be open and friendly; give no offense; do the decent thing; be kind. As world history goes, these are not trifling virtues.

By contrast, just before his conversion from one Christian church to another, I have seen a grown man cry because he knew that he would miss his old friends at worship, and would feel ethnically and intellectually lonely in his new congregation. Yet conscience demanded that he go where truth is, not where for human reasons he preferred to go. Similarly, C. S. Lewis recounts how for years he felt uncomfortable in church. He went out of duty, because Christianity is a communal, public religion, not a solely private one. It is "the Body of Christ," a public organism as well as a fellowship of spirit. But for a long time, Lewis found churchgoing painful.

I hope you will forgive me, Jana, in stressing so much the pursuit of truth. Read, study, pray—involve your whole soul (mind and will) in your decision. Do not make a religious choice for lighter reasons, even though, perhaps, most people do.

At least for Christians and Jews, religious faith is very heavily invested in the integrity (however wounded, however weak) of reason. For Christians and Jews it is an almost necessary presumption that there are truths to be discovered and known, that evidence matters, that reasoning is not in vain but attuned to the way things are, even though creation's secrets are far vaster than reason's repertoire.

Jews and Christians trust the instinct that humans were made to inquire, to understand, and to exercise judgment, since they were conceived and created by One who understands, chooses, and loves everything that he has created, enjoys the lot, cares for each detail of it. Pluck a tulip, a blade of grass, a bit of purple clover, and study the detail. It will *repay* study, everything will, everything is made with intelligence and care and love. Commit your life to intelligence; love your studies; devote yourself to science—such love will never disappoint you. Realm beyond realm of sense will open itself before you. However far you go the Light has been there.

If I were an evangelical Christian, I might tell you here to think of your sins—the deeds you are ashamed of, convicted by your own conscience—and to recognize that Jesus by his death and resurrection offers you forgiveness. He is the only source of forgiveness, forgiveness to the depths of your soul, in the world. For myself, loving the Catholic tradition as I do, let me call your attention to the opening of the Gospel of St. John:

> In the beginning was the Word: and the Word was with God, and the Word was God. He was with God in the beginning. Through him all things came to be, not one thing had its being but through him. All that came to be had life in him and that light was the light of men . . .
>
> —John 1:1–4, The Jerusalem Bible

I take this to mean that we learn about Jesus, the Word, in two places, first and most vividly in the gospels, but also in all the things that are made. All are made to reflect him. We can approach the whole of creation as another "book" about our Creator and Redeemer. This is the greatest detective story.

Jews and Christians trust the intuition that there is a Creator, not way back when, but *now*, holding in existence—making the world stand out from nothingness (*ex*—out from + *sistere*—to stand), to be, to occur at all. It takes energy to raise concrete things out of nothingness and to hold them in existence for the appointed time; then they slide back into the nothingness. The First Cause, so to speak, is working all the time. We can feel each staccato second racing by, our life dissolving like the hill of sand in an hourglass, quickly, quickly. Yet here it is. *Being* (in the sense of existence) can almost be tasted. The wonder of it all is that there *could* have been nothingness. Instead the world came to be—this is the first of wonders! Those who say that there are no miracles overlook existence. They who deny that there are miracles, they are the miracle, every bit as much as those who breathe thanks.

The first moment of religion begins in awe of truth, in fear of getting things wrong, missing the whole point, and wasting the precious and shining and rapidly filtering sands of existence.

All my life I have felt these sands slipping away. I remember distinctly—I was fourteen, in the crowded stands of Notre Dame Stadium during a lull in a game—sensing the onrushing wind of death and realizing that I had to hurry, and pay attention. It was hard for me to believe that everybody else in the stands didn't hear the same wind, seemed actually to be aware only of the game below and of one another. I know today that the two mounds of sand of my own life are pretty uneven, and that we're getting awfully close to the last rush. (As my brother Jim said before he died last year, Novaks are not afraid of death; but we do have a sharp sense of how brief and precious life is.) The point is, I know from some of your own poetry and drawings that you have sensed the same thing, and what I want to underline is that fear; in this sense, fear of the Lord, and awe, and wonder, and eagerness to hear the call correctly, whatever it is. This is the beginning of true religion.

The reason why religion is important—to repeat—is that it's first of all about *truth*. Nothing that is lying or false, even if it is otherwise "nice," is worthy of creatures such as we have been made to be. Religious people don't promote study and build universities for nothing. Judaism and Christianity are (among others) "religions of the Book"—a book to inquire into, to meditate on, to study, to put to the test of real-life practice. That should tell you something about the weight these religions put on seeking truth, in the light of evidence, especially the evidence of daily living.

You feel the pull of the evangelical Protestant denial that "religion" is a genus of which the gospel of Jesus is just one species. They insist (and so do Catholics) that Jesus is the Logos, the Word, in whom all things were made, and that he is the sole road to salvation. In this view, the other religions, however noble, miss the one crucial point: Jesus is the personal Savior of everyone. Evangelicals prefer, therefore, to talk of "faith" (faith in Jesus) rather than religion. You need to know that they are allergic to "religion in general."

This is true as far as it goes. Still, encouraged by the Catholic tradition, I like to think that "the Word in Whom and by Whom and through Whom were made all the things that are made" is partially revealed in all that is good and true in *all* human traditions. So when I write "religion," please see that I only want to include religious persons, like some of your friends who are not Christians or Jews, so that they and their parents can draw the appropriate comparisons to their own predicament in a secular age. All things human teach us to reflect on aspects of Him we might otherwise miss. This is one reason for terming the church "Catholic." *Nil humanum mihi alienum:* "Nothing human is alien to me," is an ancient Catholic conviction. The problem is to discern what, in all things, belongs to the Word.

Traditionally, therefore, we read the Jewish Testament as "prefiguring" the Christian, and study Judaism today to learn much about ourselves. (Correlatively, Jews have been much influenced in their self-understanding by interaction with the Christian world.) In a more remote way, the study of Islam and Zen Buddhism, Confucianism, Hinduism, and the rest has been a rich source of insight for understanding (not only by way of contrast) the impact and range of our creation and redemption.

JANA: *But don't forget my first question. I have more or less come to accept God, but organized religion still bothers me. It's common to read that religion has been used, can be used, and maybe even is used as a means to control and subdue the populace. Not to mention the abuses committed over the centuries by organized religion. Think of the Spanish Inquisition: fear and intimidation used for control. I don't have any personal experiences of this kind, but I still don't see why it isn't possible to have a personal relationship with God, without intermediaries.*

DAD: Look. Staffing an institution, training ministers, putting up bricks and mortar and keeping existing buildings clean and in good repair—all this is a lot of work. In a way, many people who are good at all the practical things, the nuts and bolts, the upkeep, the personnel problems, pensions and health insurance, and the rest, may not be conspicuously good in prayer or even in reflection. My friend John Cogley, an editor and reporter, used to say that some people have an ear for religion—God, prayer, contemplation—and some don't, and most of the people who staff religious organizations don't. It's easier to raise money and put up buildings than to spend an hour on one's knees every day, imploring God in the darkness and emptiness in which he dwells. For practical people, that can be tedious.

God is usually found in silence. In suffering. Wordlessly. For many, it's a lot easier to keep busy.

In my generation, and even more so when I began teaching in the sixties, there were many young people who couldn't stand silence. They'd come into their room, turn on the TV, put on the music, look for someone to call, or something to do—keep moving. Pick up the car keys, go out to look for something happening. Many were afraid of fingertips beating on the windowpane, the silent rustling in their own souls. I think that's why people liked music loud and full of motion. They needed to act out a kind of vacantness when they were "down," or a kinetic mime of passion when they were "up." Sometimes I wished I could be part of their diversions; maybe I have been, sometimes. But I always felt that that wasn't my world. To surrender to it meant letting go of my inner life, yielding to the collective. No thanks.

There were other aspects to youthful distancing, of course. It meant a kind of liberation, a clearing of the decks, a world of one's own apart from adults. No generation in history had ever been so massively programmed for years upon years of being lectured to in classrooms, sometimes beginning in preschool and stretching out through three or five or nine years after college, in law school, medical school, or various graduate programs.

After the creation of "teenagers" early in the century, we created "twentyhood"—the longest period of prolonged preadulthood in recorded history. A culture very largely without adults, without tradition, without clear guidance to command reflexes and aspirations—tidewaters swirling back and forth, loose, unformed, directionless. The culture surrounding you suddenly turned ambivalent about drugs and sex and limits. You were told you were young and vital and should be having fun: That was your moral duty—*Have fun!*

In retrospect, I see very clearly why going to church was a bore to you, a foreign experience, and even came to seem fraudulent. I do not doubt that everything could have been done better—the liturgy, the music, the sermons, the ideas, the sense of prayer and holiness and seriousness. But no one can fairly ask to be surrounded all the time by saints and prophets, shocked, inspired, fired up, through no effort of their own. I think you wanted the Church to prove itself to you, when the real task was quite the other way around. The Church can only be what it is, a thoroughly, hopelessly human organization, with all the grinding faults and unin-spiring, middling virtues one must expect from such a thing—through which, nonetheless, God has chosen to con-vey the springs of eternal life in communion with him, begin-ning right in this mediocrity. It would have been nice if he came with trumpets and angels, instead of with such people as we.

JANA: *I think it is unfair—and somewhat alienating—to lay the blame for my negative experience with the Church at my feet. I don't believe that I wanted the Church to prove itself to me (although why not?) but to simply respond to me; to provide me with not only practical assistance—such as someone to listen to and advise me during the good and bad times—but also with the explanations and guidance necessary to facilitate this constant inquiry you referred to earlier. I didn't want angels, in fact I wouldn't be able to relate to angels, but rather humans—flesh and blood that would make this God stuff and religion stuff concrete and understandable.*

DAD: Okay, I'll admit the obvious: the Church also failed you. So did I—that bothers me more. Still, I don't think you can evade all responsibility. You *could* have figured out more on your own, and read more on your own. I think you were blocked by a sense of rebellion on your part, a kind of refusal. Well, it's easily forgivable, and water over the dam.

Your cousin Father Andrew is a priest, and so was your uncle Richard, who died in Bangladesh in the missions when he was only three years older than you are now. You know the faults and weaknesses of the rest of us in our family, and every priest, every minister, comes from somebody's family in this way. I think you may agree that God showers special graces on them, and their sacrifices for us are special, like Christ's, but neither they nor we have illusions about them. What saves us and them is *God's presence in them*, not their particular talents or works.

That's why, Jana, we don't despair too much when one

of them "goes bad," makes bad mistakes, even does real evil. Isn't it bound to happen sometimes? Maybe even for a whole era in a whole culture or part of a culture. Our faith isn't rooted in *them*. Despite them, around them, using them as broken instruments (the novelist Graham Greene loved this theme), God's grace strangely abounds.

I don't think your problem is with the Church. I think your problem, Jana, is wanting to limit the ways God can act to the ways you approve of. I don't think you recognize how humbly God accommodates himself to the kind of creatures we are, in our everydayness rather than in our rare saintly best. If God was going to pass on his word and communicate his life in a human way, if news of the God of Abraham, Isaac, Jacob, and Jesus is to reach you, it had to be through a people and an institution—hence, the synagogue and the church down the everyday ages.

As Irving Kristol once said, count up the prophets and count up the rabbis—there were only twelve prophets, about one each century, and scores of thousands of rabbis, generation after generation. That's why Judaism is so practical, he says, why it lasts and lasts. It's not always pretty, but it endures. It keeps regaining vitality, like an old olive tree well pruned. The same with the Christian church. It's a pretty poor thing. Jacques Maritain resisted being converted to it, dreaded it, called it—afterwards—"that dunghill." But it's in a church community that Christ buried the pearl of great price, planted the tree of life. You don't get to tell God how to do it.

Besides, if God had made the synagogue and the church something splendid and miraculous, many people would find it superhuman and fear they couldn't measure up.

The trouble is, a synagogue and church cut to human measure depress something romantic and utopian in us. We'd really like a religion that invited us to be pure spirits, wiped away our faults once for all, allowed us to pretend we aren't our imperfect selves. That's why purely spiritual movements that deny the role of the human body and are full of disdain for existing "organized religions" are always attractive to many persons.

In all centuries, even Christians have had to fight the idea that Christianity is solely about the spirit and at war with the body. They did this by stressing humble bodily tasks—like doing laundry, keeping the kitchen clean, taking care of the toilets. This was also the point of displaying the physical crib at Christmas time—the animals, the hay: to stress the humanness of the body.

JANA: *But get back to the church.*

DAD: Organized religion is homage to the body. Organized religion is as necessary for our souls as politics is for democracy. Democracy is always in bad shape (the worst system except for all the others), but it would be in even worse shape if bitter rivals couldn't be held to elections, and forced to appeal to the interests and concerns of competing factions. Factional fights are like oxygen for the fire of representative government; no air, no fire.

A lot of people are disgusted with politics but claim to love democracy; what they really wish is that they could get their way without the work of persuading those who disagree with them. They tend to *like* little dictators who promise to fix things lickety-split. And there are a lot of people who claim to be disgusted with organized religion—for good reasons—whose secret belief is that their own inner lives are too good for the ordinary run of people who are in church. They secretly hold that if God were really smart he would have chartered a secret, noble, perfect, and purely privatized religion, such as theirs. That might have been a good idea, but he didn't.

What God chose instead is something very human and very flawed. A cross for sensitive and idealistic persons to carry, and hard at some points for everyone. But its very humanness somehow seems more consoling the older you get. If you were not made of flesh and blood, Jana, you would not need the "comfort" of a physical, human church—or, rather, the *discomfort*. In politics, you get disgusted with particular elections, candidates, or political claims, and you rebel in the name of starting in new directions. The synagogue and the church also need their rebels and their self-starters. Organized religion is not *them*, it's *us*. Only traditions alive with fresh growths endure.

You know the Commandment of Love, "Love your neighbor as yourself"? In my experience, the hardest part in that—the sleeper—is loving myself.

So I wish my children (and grandchildren) would feel at home in the human race. I really admired my brother Jim for prescribing that the reception after his funeral should be in an ordinary, tacky American Legion Hall in a small rural town outside State College, Pennsylvania. He wanted us to remember how much strength he had always drawn from plain, working people, with all their roughness, generosity, and quirkiness.

That's one reason Jimmy loved his years in the Army—

Third Armored Division, where the rough edges are and the big, dirty machines. Grunt work. He loved being the commander of ordinary guys, browbeating them, humoring them, and leading them to win the all-European gunnery championships, which the Germans or Brits had usually won. He loved doing it with a newly formed unit, that didn't even have yet the proper command structure. It vindicated his preference for the six-pack crowd, every time.

Take that as a clue to organized religion. It isn't just for the poets and philosophers, the literary critics and the commentators, the professors and gallery directors. It's for infantry and armored, too. It's for all classes and all temperaments. I really love that aspect of our poor, often wounded Catholic Church. It is not a sect, for a small cut of the human race. That makes it pretty messy. But, by God, it's *us!*

I wish I could communicate that to you. But I think you've got it. There were always signs that you had gotten it.

JANA: *I like your comments so far, but at times you've been pretty abstract and, for me, haven't given a practical conclusion.*

DAD: Holy smokes! I thought I was being very down-to-earth. I thought I was basically finished, and you want more!

Okay, if you want a church that offers something you can "touch, hear, and smell," a friendly environment, and you also want immediacy with God, you have a problem. If there are human intermediaries—preachers of the Word—their glaring faults are bound to get in the way. You can, of course, see "through" them directly to God; God does work immediately within you. But the church, any church, is always something of a stumbling block.

JANA: *I can see all that. But you still haven't told me what the church offers me. If it has nothing to offer, why bother?*

DAD: Every church, in every religion, offers a poetic ancient form by which you will be able to welcome your children into life and bury your parents. Through its local ministers, churches, and rituals, the church offers you continuity across generations. This is no small thing. Humans are historical animals, and a church places us within an historical tradition. Invariably, this tradition is replete with stories of heroes, crises, struggles, lessons learned at great cost. Invariably, too, this tradition offers nourishment to those whose spirits need study as deer need water.

Your generation is not the first to wrestle with fundamental questions. One benefit a religious affiliation offers is a wealthy intellectual and spiritual tradition, and an abundance of narratives about the heroes and the struggles of the past.

The important point for now, however, is this: Religion is important to the extent that it is true, and throws light on two questions: *"Who am I, under these stars?"* and *"Who are we?"* The test for religion is its truth.

The great German philosopher Immanuel Kant (1724–1804) added two further questions: "What may we hope for?" and "What ought we to do?" These questions, experience shows, cannot be answered without setting to rest how our existence is linked to God's and who God is.

To summarize: Your first question was, Why is religion important? My answer was: Because it's true, and teaches us something crucial about ourselves: the ground for our hope in eternal life.

Why is it necessary to belong to a religious institution? Because we are creatures made for community, and the flaws of real communities force us to confront the difficulties and joys of being humans-in-community. The community strengthens our conscience and helps us guard against becoming prisoners to the illusions of our age.

Is religion just a means to an end? Yes and no. The end is steady, constant union with God. Properly understood, a religious institution is both the means to and a participation in the end. *All* of us are made for community with God and with one another. The Church is all of us as one—past, present, future—in whom God dwells, hidden by our faults.

Does the existence of so many different religions mean that one religion is as good as another? We come to this question in our next go-around; but you can guess.

What does religion offer? If it is worth anything, it offers a true vision of who we are; an historical tradition; communal support in a centuries-long conversation; a framework for past and future through rituals of memory and expectation; and a mission in history. Most of all: it communicates to us the presence of God. And God's best name, from this point of view, is Truth: "I am the way, and the truth, and the life." (John 14:6).

Finally, when by "religion" one means "faith"—that is,

the Christian faith—such a religion offers us eternal life with God, our Creator, our Redeemer, our Love. This calling helps to explain why each human being is of imperishable and irreplaceable value; it is our ground for saying that our rights are endowed in us by God.

Others may come to different grounds for their being. Respectful conversation with them about these matters is the seed of civilization, its best promise of a great flowering.

2

WHY ARE THERE SO MANY DIFFERENT RELIGIONS?

THE KING'S THREE SONS
There is an old story about a king who had a beautiful ring and three sons. Each son wanted the ring. When the king died, he left three rings for his sons and a note that said, "My dear sons, one of these rings is real and two are fake. The way you will know who has the real ring is that the son with the real ring will be kind and generous to all people."

Each of the three spent the rest of his life being good to prove that he had the real ring. It's the same with religions. The way to show that your religion is true is not to yell and scream about it. The way to show that your religion is true is to live it.

—Rabbi Marc Gellman and Msgr. Thomas Hartman
From *How Do You Spell God?*

Grant, O Lord, to all teachers and students, to know what is worth knowing, to love what is worth loving, to praise what pleases you most, and to dislike whatsoever is evil in your sight. Grant us with true judgment to distinguish things that differ, and above all to search out and do what is well-pleasing to you . . .

—Thomas à Kempis
(1379–1471)

JANA: *Okay. So religion matters. So now what? Unfortunately, just to say that religion is necessary and important does not put the matter to rest; attempting to understand the vast variety of religions is confusing and intimidating. Furthermore, the very existence of this variety seems to undermine the argument that religion matters: that there are many answers to one question may not prove that there is any answer at all (all may be wrong), it may only show that the question is not legitimate.*

Let me explain: If religion truly mattered, it seems there would be only one religion—or at most just a few—to imply that this is the correct path. The fact that there are many religions seems to marginalize the concept of religion, for if there are many different paths to God, who is to say that any of those paths are right? Why not strike out on your own?

Is each of the religions, or paths, equally valid? Or are some better than others? Is it simply that each person is different and has a unique way of relating to God, so that the various religions arose to respond to these differences? So that, in fact, every religion is preaching essentially the same message but using different styles and emphasizing different parts of the message? Of course this answer can easily be used to explain the differing factions within Christianity, but what about Islam, Buddhism, etc.? And, why is Christianity such a factional religion?

What does the variety mean? Is it simply a reflection of a human desire for competition, for "new and improved," signifying nothing more than the very human pressure for alternatives? Are all the different religions only one more example of how we like to break into different "cliques" and stick with people who believe exactly the same way we do? Or is it nothing more than superfluous branches off the one "correct" root?

Either way, how does one go about choosing among the different religions? For some people, that may be easy: they'll just go with the religion of their childhood or of their parents. But for others, with either no heritage to fall back on, or a determination to avoid or reject their heritage, how do they "find" religion? For example, a friend of mine was brought up Catholic, but he never quite felt comfortable there. Now, as an adult, Jon has chosen the Methodist Church in which to raise his children—and he feels so welcome, he has actually become quite active and involved in the church. But the choice originally seemed so haphazard, as it came down to a recommendation from one of Jon's friends that he would like the minister at this particular church.

So how should average people—people like me, raised in one church but unsure of where I'd like to go—explore their options?

DAD: When I lose heart a little (and sometimes I do, thinking that I can't find responses that are satisfying, even to me), I remind myself that you will find your way, and that your real dialogue is not with me but with God. A father is only a surrogate for the Better Father of us all, a prop, a starting place. *"Ecclesia supplet,"* as a priest friend of mine in Poland often says, "Grace makes up for our deficiencies."

You are actually asking two different questions: *Why* are there different religions, and *How* should someone in your predicament *choose* one religion from among many?

The first question seems to be as old as prehistory, before written chronicles. The Bible itself, in a narrative dating

35

back some four thousand years, offers an explanation for such diversity in the story of the Tower of Babel:

> Hitherto, the world had only one way of speech, only one language. And now, as men travelled westwards, they found a plain in the land of Sennaar, and made themselves a home there; Here we can make bricks, they said to one another, baked with fire; and they built, not in stone, but in brick, with pitch for their mortar. It would be well, they said, to build ourselves a city, and a tower in it with a top that reaches to heaven; we will make ourselves a great people, instead of scattering over the wide face of earth. But now the Lord came down to look at the city, with its tower, which Adam's children were building; and he said, Here is a people all one, with a tongue common to all; this is but the beginning of their undertakings, and what is to prevent them carrying out all they design? It would be well to go down and throw confusion into the speech they use there, so that they will not be able to understand each other. Thus the Lord broke up their common home, and scattered them over the earth, and the building of the city came to an end. That is why it was called Babel, Confusion, because it was there that the Lord confused the whole world's speech, and scattered them far away, over the wide face of earth.

—Genesis 11:1–9, The Holy Bible (Ronald Knox translation)

At the crossroads of human destiny, Jerusalem was a marketplace between three continents, and thus the Jews of old continually encountered peoples of religions utterly different from their own. Serious Jews held fiercely to the vision recounted to them by Moses: that there is only One God, the true God, Who must be approached in spirit and truth; and all other gods are false. The One God made all the things that are made, and is our undeceivable Judge. Accordingly, the great gift the Hebrews gave to humankind was the conviction that there is only one truth for all creation, and that this truth must be painstakingly discovered, and weeded out from all that is false. The story of Babel then describes how confused humans are about truth.

Moses then recounted another crucial aspect of reality; namely, that the One God chooses to be worshiped by women and men who are free. He does not force himself upon humans, by some shattering and irresistible explosion of Light. On the contrary, he calls softly, even whispers. He speaks through every blade of grass, every drop of rain, every leaf, every pair of human eyes. God is always beating softly on the door, but the dweller inside may choose not to hear, even aggressively *refuse* to hear. Picking up on Moses, Romans 1:20–25 describes a time that you may find very like our own.

> Since the creation of the world, invisible realities, God's eternal power and divinity, have become visible, recognized through the things he has made. Therefore these men are inexcusable. They certainly had knowledge of God, yet they did not glorify him as God or give him thanks; they stultified themselves [repressed the knowledge they had] through speculating to no purpose, and their senseless hearts were darkened. They claimed to be wise, but turned into fools instead; they exchanged the glory of the immortal God for images representing mortal man, birds, beasts, and snakes. In consequence, God delivered them up in their lusts to unclean practices; they engaged in the mutual degradation of their bodies, these men who exchanged the truth of God for a lie and worshiped and served the creature rather than the Creator—blessed be he forever, amen!
>
> —Romans, 1:20–25, The New American Bible

Thus, Judaism established for all humankind the primacy of truth and Christianity followed its path. No matter how rich, powerful, or successful a human being anywhere might be, that individual will be judged in the light of truth. Truth has primacy—not wealth, not power, not personal taste.

The British author Paul Johnson has written in *Modern Times* that all through this twentieth century modern peoples have drawn a mischievous lesson from Einstein's Relativity Principle. They have fallen in love with the idea that in morals "everything is relative." Frequently heard aphorisms reflect this: "One religion is as good as another"; "To each his own"; "Your moral life is your own business"; and "Autonomy means defining your own destiny." Most educated people say such things.

But no one is actually able to live that way. They say it, but they also are constantly saying the opposite: "But that's not fair!" "You promised!" "That's a lie!" "You won't be allowed to get away with that." Very few people say, "The Nazis can't be held guilty, because they acted according to their own preferences, they showed real commitment, and who's to judge whether what they did was wrong?" And even in lesser matters, around the office, in restaurants, on television, one often hears expressions of outrage, based upon a very sharp sense of wrongs needing to be righted. "This is a no-smoking section!" "Who do they think they are?"

In a way, many people today play at relativism. They say relativism is their creed. They even use "relativism" as a justification for being nonjudgmental about themselves and others. Such relativism is little more than a form of moral laxity. For they are often quite hostile to those who differ with them about morals. This is a sign of anything but serious relativism. (If everything is relative, everybody is right, so why be hostile?)

It's often best not to challenge people about their "relativism," but instead to watch quietly in order to see whether in all things they are equally forgiving of others. Are they actually indifferent to injustices done to them, content to continue in friendship with liars and cheats, comfortable with the oppression of women and the poor? Hardly ever.

Most people act as if they actually do know the difference between right and wrong, truth telling and lying, cheating and playing by the rules, fidelity and infidelity, hypocrisy and commitment to principle. The two most common sentences heard in America are: "I'm an American, and I'm free to do whatever I want to do," and "There should be a law against that."

Thus, my answer to your first question is quite Hebraic and very ancient, and it has two parts. The first part is: Yes, there is One God, one true God, and there are many false gods. The second part is that, even in his special revelation through Jesus Christ, this God has chosen to let his light shine among humans in a humble, patient, indirect, and subtle way, respecting all the probabilities of human weakness and absolute individual liberty of conscience. This God wishes to be worshiped by persons who come to him freely in Spirit and in truth, out of the desire of their hearts. Like a kind of gravity, grace pulls at the inner lives of all; but anyone can block the attraction.

Still, people usually gain their ideas about God from particular communities. Here, too, we need two steps. The first step is that no one can make an act of faith in God for someone else. God speaks heart-to-heart to only one person at a time. As the poet Rudyard Kipling put it in the poem "Tomlinson":

> Though we called your friend from his bed this night, he could not
> speak for you,
> For the race is run by one and one and never by two and two. . . .

39

And carry my word to the Sons of Men or ever ye come to die:
That the sin they do by two and two they must pay for one by
one . . .

The second step is that faith comes by hearing; other persons are almost always the channels by which the voice of God comes to us. They direct our attention to signs of him, set an example for us, show us the shortcuts, give us the courage to press on. Before God, each is ultimately alone—and also in the presence of, and indebted to, legions of others.

You and I have no idea, Jana, how many persons (unknown to us) have prayed so that we might pause to notice God's whispering. There is all around us an invisible girdle of grace and charity, like a brilliant electronic web, an Internet of sacrifice and prayer and tears and fervent pleas by which those who love God beseech him to show himself to unknown others. They do not know face-to-face those for whom they pray. This is what is meant by that phrase you've heard, "the communion of saints"—not just the holy ones but also those who are just trying; and what Jews mean by the eternal circle of the righteous ones in every generation.

JANA: *But why are there so many different religions?*

DAD: Why so many? Because God leaves many subtle signs everywhere, but he seldom forces himself on anyone. Many humans refuse, positively refuse, to see these signs—again, Romans 1:20–25. For most of human history, God did not reveal himself directly. From a Jewish and Christian point of view, the God who made us and all things waited a long time before revealing himself in history, first of all through one chosen people, the Jews, a small and poor people in a relatively poor and harsh land. He chose to work in history as a little piece of yeast works in a large dough. Time is required for his words to become known to the whole human race.

Meanwhile, the peoples of the world are on their own. God has whispered to them quietly, through their own natures, and through the geniuses and great teachers among them. While there is but one God, the separate peoples of the world spent long eras in almost total isolation from one another. That is why one detects today both "family resemblances" and dramatic variations among world religions.

In each of the major strands of religious tradition—there are fewer than a half dozen if one thinks of the "trunks" rather than the "branches"—there are worthy and beautiful things to learn, and sometimes to incorporate into one's own life. But this does not deter us from judging that on this or that point some of the traditions are more sophisticated than others, more discerning, truer to human nature. Without intending to play God, or to be invidious toward others, we rank them, at least unconsciously. We do so simply for our own practical estimate regarding which to invest time in.

We may agree that all humans are children of one Creator, and that insofar as each people is faithful to the light given them, seeing and behaving as God through conscience directs them, God is pleased with their good will. In that limited sense, we may recognize the truth in their religion, while still holding, in view of other matters shown to us, that for our consciences it would not be adequate. We will be judged by a different standard and, we recognize, may be judged more harshly than they.

JANA: *Let me see if I understand you correctly: God planted the one seed of truth for humankind to ponder and figure out. In the intervening years, many peoples have said aha! and felt they have discovered god's truth. They then created a religion based on their knowledge of the truth. Thus, many religions were founded, scattered across the globe. The problem is that humans have not grasped—may not ever be able to grasp—the whole truth; perhaps we are too limited and God too infinite. Whatever the reason, those religions not worshiping false gods are different simply because they are based on different parts of the truth, or hold only one part of it. But then, which are the true religions (those that are based in some way on the one truth)? And which are the false (worshiping false gods)? For example, is the Buddha just another name for God?*

DAD: It is not clear to me that Buddhism is a theistic movement; it seems, instead, to be a method of meditation and human development. The Buddha is not regarded by Buddhists as god, but only as a highly disciplined and gifted teacher, a master of wisdom. The point of the method is not clarity about god but (it seems) silence and quiet in the soul.

Basically, though, you have the general idea. We can take as *false* any idea of God that simply localizes him in a great stone or graven image; but it is possible that not even aboriginal tribes ever actually did that. If they did, that would have been to confuse the idol (or the symbol) with the reality. (Sometimes nineteenth-century anthropologists attributed to their subjects their own primitive materialism.) We can take as false, as well, ideas of God that imagine him to be physical, made of matter or energy—in other words, as in some sense a *part* of the universe. For example, to the extent that the Maya identified God with the rain, or the serpent, or the water lily, or other animal or organism—as the guide books assert, although we may be skeptical of their perspicuity—we find such an idea of God far too limited. This is why the Jewish insistence that God is not an idol but Spirit and Truth is such a great breakthrough for the human race.

As I suggested earlier, few of the major religions even intend to be universal. Few are designed with all humans and the whole universe in view. Perhaps only Hinduism, Islam, Judaism, and Christianity meet this test. In this age in which there is so much aggressiveness from secularizers, I would prefer to stress what all the theistic religions have in common.

In *The Abolition of Man*, C. S. Lewis excerpts texts from the literatures of world religions (including secular traditions) under basic headings such as the law of general beneficence; the law of mercy; and others. These texts illustrate what he calls the *Tao*, the natural moral law for all human beings. Among the principles he collected under these important headings, internal resemblances are very strong. *So* strong that Lewis wonders if there is not, in a profound sense, only one human civilization. This civilization, if it exists, has had many variants, but from time immemorial these variants have interacted. They may even (he speculates) have had one common beginning.

Does it seem to you, Jana, as it does to me, that *both* the similarities and the differences among the major living cultures are very large? "Family resemblances," arising from the more or less invariant structures of human nature, everywhere the same in birth, pain, love, and death, are enough to explain the *Tao*. But different ideas about God give rise to quite different visions of the human vocation, especially along the axis of human liberty and personal initiative.

JANA: *The differences strike me most, but go back to my earlier question, How ought a person to choose a religion?*

DAD: The best I can do is a few "soundings."

Ask yourself (among other things) these three questions: Which communion has truth as its primary concern? Encourages personal holiness and the profound adventure of the inner life? Takes a universal viewpoint—has as its ambition to reach all human beings? C. S. Lewis decided, when he was an atheist, that only Christianity and Hinduism set for themselves such criteria. (All religions carry some important truths—otherwise, serious persons would not lend their support to them—but not all are equally profound or equally true.)

This matter of many different religions is tricky. You have no doubt noticed two opposite tendencies in my thought so far. First, *true is true*. To the extent that on crucial points two religious traditions are in direct opposition, one is right and the other is wrong. There are not two truths.

Second, *interaction between God and the individual that*

takes place in the deepest recesses of the human heart is sacred, beyond the trespassing of any other. The ways of God are mysterious, and so are the ways of the human heart. We do not understand our own hearts very well, let alone the hearts of others.

The first proposition is not in conflict with the second. When others differ from us—and we have grounds to believe that they are serious and mean it—we should respect the duty they owe their own consciences. We should also fasten our attention on what is good and noble in their commitments, and on what they have in common with us.

Later, we should review the reasons why we do not share their belief. If we learn something from their witness, we can appropriate it, and add it to our own store of inner resources. If we remain convinced by the reasons why we cannot completely follow them, we can await an appropriate moment, if one comes, to discuss with them the grounds for our disagreement. When this disagreement concerns an important matter, our friendship with them will prompt us to find a graceful way to discuss it with them.

Since such conversations are difficult to conduct even in the best of cases, mutual exchange of that sort best awaits a moment when all parties are ready to practice the necessary forbearance and generosity.

In America today, we need to give each other more such moments. Americans are starved for good conversations about important matters of the human spirit. (In Victorian England, religious devotion was not a forbidden topic of conversation; sex was. In America today, the inhibitions are reversed. Today you can say anything you want to say about sexual behavior, but you will have to pick very carefully any company in which you wish to talk about prayer.)

C. S. Lewis describes all Christian traditions (and for our purposes, I would include Judaism) as sharing a common hall, from which the doors to the individual wings of each tradition open out. In trying to choose which wing to choose as your own, he writes, you must initially do two things: pray for light, and then obey the rules common to the whole house.

The third step, then, is to ask, "Which door is the true one?" *not* which door pleases you best by its paint and paneling. In plain language, the question should never be: "Do I like that kind of service?" But "Are these doctrines true: Is holiness here? Does my conscience move me toward this? Is my reluctance to knock at this door due to my pride, or mere taste, or mere personal dislike of this particular doorkeeper?"

JANA: *Does this apply only to the Judeo-Christian tradition? Or can a "Christian-raised" person consider something like Zen?*

DAD: No, it doesn't apply only to Judaism and Christianity. Many Christians have benefited a great deal by undertaking the disciplines of Zen. Your mother has always been interested in the Christian mystics—especially St. John of the Cross (1542–1591) and St. Teresa of Avila (1515–1582)—and in the Zen masters. One key difference is that Jewish and Christian mystics address even the emptiness they find in personal terms, by daring to speak in the darkness to a divine Person, even if unseen, whereas the Zen masters are far more ambiguous. Perhaps this is only my ignorance, but to me they seem content with an impersonal void.

Let me return to your question about the many denominations of Christianity.

On the points that separate the Methodist tradition from the Catholic, does your friend find the Methodist path true and the Catholic false? Does he find holiness in the former that he found missing in the latter? Does his conscience support him in his choice—and on what grounds? In moving out of the central hallway, and in selecting a wing of the Christian tradition for one's residence and for the education of one's children, these (or something very like these) are the appropriate questions.

For one reason or another, some persons get off to a wrong start in the church of their childhood. The conscience of others develops in such a way that what they need at a certain stage in their development (and maybe for good) is not to be found where they started. Faith is a journey, a voyage, the ascent of a mountain—and sometimes, in moments of grace, when one is carried along, it is like the flight of a dove.[1]

The mysteries of the movements of the human soul fill an observer with awe. The drama of the inner life is spectacular, crowded with successive moments of dull pain, desperation, anguish, sudden hopes, shattering joys, turning points, loves, losses, doubts, wanderings. (I have met some persons whose public lives have been full of drama, but whose inner lives, so far as they reveal them, seem empty

---

[1]That is how I arrived at the title of my introduction to religious studies, now out of print, *Ascent of the Mountain, Flight of the Dove* (Harper & Row, 1971).

and monotonic.) One of the endlessly fascinating aspects of religious studies is the reading of autobiographies, the characteristic Jewish and Christian genre.

Take, for instance, the Bible.

Practically every chapter of the Bible focuses on a narrative, and in particular, in what happens in the human will. The inner arena of the mind and will is set forth as the axial point of human history. In one chapter, King David is faithful to his Lord; in another, not. The suspense always is, What will he do next? And *action* is always, first of all, in the secret places of the will, even more so than in outward action. Not that the latter is unimportant but, rather, that it gets its significance from the kind of fire that burns in it from within.

JANA: *Would a good comparison to the differences between the Christian churches be the United States and its citizens? Among Americans, there are many ethnicities, priorities, political views, etc. Many Americans disagree over parties and policies. Yet we are all unified by our "fiercely held" belief in the democratic system and our Constitution. Much the same way, at least among Christian religions, the varied churches disagree about operational leadership (such as bishops and the pope) and are united by their belief in God and his Son, and other fundamental issues.*

DAD: That's not quite right. The United States does have a sort of creed: "We hold these truths, etc." Yet the U.S. Constitution is a practical document and it asks only that we obey its provisions; it does not impose a *religious* creed or even one single philosophy or ideology. Thus, people of

all religions (or none) have little difficulty promising to uphold this conscience-respecting Constitution.

The Christian churches are different in several respects.
For one thing, they share a substantial number of common
beliefs—truly, an astonishingly long list. Second, they share
one baptism, in the name of the Father, Son, and Holy
Spirit, and some other elements of worship, including hearing the Word of God read aloud and preached in their as-
semblies. All believe in sin, grace, and redemption, in death
and eternal life; in the creation and the Last Judgment.

They disagree intensely regarding how to interpret the
meaning of grace, the sacraments, the ministry of the apostles, authority in the church, the appropriate structure for
the church, and other questions. After the passage of centuries, of course, the intensity around some of these differences has evaporated like steam from a boiling pot. It is
getting close to the time when a new generation (of both
Catholics and Protestants) will reconsider the Reformation,
and find some way to recognize each other's good faith, and
reunite along commonly agreed upon fidelity to God. Almost every year now, we see partial realignments among
Christian bodies. A few more generations may be required.

Whatever choice you make, make eventual reunion
with all Christians your work and prayer. The current divisions are a scandal.

Jana, I am trying to explain how from a Catholic point
of view, my own point of view, every branch of Christianity—every religious tradition in the world, every story of
every single soul—has something to teach us. Something of
God is refracted through each one. That is another part

of the force of the word "catholic," meaning universal, *truly* meaning universal, including every individual. The full meaning of what it means to be catholic is only revealed in the sum of all human stories. Historically, institutionally, a catholic church is expected to be always learning, always opening itself to other cultures and other ways, trying to discern all the workings of God's grace in the world. That is how I interpret "catholic" in "Catholic Church."

JANA: *But of course everyone has something to teach us—even evil people provide lessons to be learned by others. But that doesn't quite seem to get to the crux of the matter: What is a person supposed to do with the confusing array of religions confronting her?*

DAD: You do not think of yourself as Catholic, I know; you are withholding allegiance, drawn elsewhere. So for you the crux of the matter is different than for me.

You may be interpreting my statement that "everyone has something to teach us" as a statement of typical liberal piety. Open-mindedness. Tolerance. Understanding. I meant something different. I was trying to suggest that the Catholic Church has a unique relationship with the other Christian denominations, different from those that the others assume toward one another.

From the point of view of most liberal Protestants, the individual should follow personal conscience in making a choice. Private conscience is the arbiter. Each person has direct access to God, without mediators (such as priests or popes). The priesthood is embodied in all believers, and access to God (so to speak) is by a direct individual line to God. This is one context for the assertion "everyone has something to teach us." It is, roughly speaking, a liberal way of thinking, in the sense that it's hard to say that one denomination is true and the others, at least in part, false and deficient.

Both the Catholic and the evangelical Christian see things quite differently. The Catholic way, like the evangelical, often infuriates others. I know you well enough to know that it sometimes infuriates you.

The evangelical way insists upon a strict communal discipline under the Scriptures—with high emphasis upon certain nonnegotiable basics: salvation comes through faith alone, given in commitment to Jesus as one's personal savior, after a confession of sins, with trust that by his atonement for our sins our sins are washed away. (We Catholics join them in these basic affirmations.) And so on. Their belief in the essential given of individual conscience and direct access to God's mercy ("the priesthood of all believers"), however, does not take away from them their *communal* sense of fidelity to the Scriptures, under the discipline of the Reformation. All Protestants, but especially the evangelicals, work out of a communal tradition of their own. Individual believers are not, in this sense, "Lone Rangers," as some Protestant emphasis on individual conscience would have you believe.

The Catholic way is also to begin with conscience, but to hold conscience responsible for discerning certain nonsubjective measuring rods. It is also to protect a set of God-given checks and balances, including the roles of the bishops and of Peter. It is to hold that, while the Catholic Church is the one true church, all the other Christian churches reflect a part of that truth (sometimes better than the Catholic Church, in that respect). However, the Catholic Church is large enough—catholic enough—to include each of these parts in the whole. It often does this clumsily and not well. It is constantly in need of reform. Especially in recent generations, it has also tried to learn the lessons of the Reformation. Yet *in principle* it tries to be the "mother ship" of the whole Christian fleet, so to speak. Whatever any of them has that is validly Christian, the Catholic Church also tries to bring into its own life.

Look at it this way. (I am taking a Catholic point of view, but you could do the same from the point of view of one of the other Christian churches.) Grace is at work in the Methodist Church and in each of the other Christian communions. If you like the quiet prayer of the Quakers, the contemplativeness, even the trust in the Spirit working through consensus in the whole assembly seated in prayer at the meeting, that is a way of grace also familiar to Catholics, through the tradition of the Benedictines and other contemplative orders.

When I am moved by the beautiful liturgies of the Anglican Church and the "middle way" of Anglican theology, that stirs me to wish that we Roman Catholics would do our own liturgies more beautifully, and carry out our theological thinking with fresh infusions of common sense.

In the Orthodox churches of the East, one recovers the full experience of the great, majestic teachings of the Greek (as distinguished from the Latin) Fathers of the church, the powerful sense of God's Lordship in Christ over all of creation, and a special tenderness toward Mary as the mother of this cosmic Lord. One recovers the distinctive Eastern traditions of holiness, prayer, and long leisurely worship, and the rhetorical eloquence of the ancient Greek and Russian passion for the transcendent God. You have probably met this sensibility in Dostoyevsky, Tolstoy, Solzhenitsyn, and perhaps even in Berdyaev. (Berdyaev's book on Dostoyevsky is without peer.)

I have learned from other friends to love the sweetness of the Methodist sense of service and community, and the kindness and gentleness that spring from John Wesley (1703–1791) and the other founders of Methodism. These should be a lesson to Catholics of the importance to Christian faith of the adverbial side of religion: the manner and tone of the practice of Christian love.

The seriousness of the Lutherans, their zest for good music and solid reflection and reform of life, their intent to be Catholic until the Catholic Church reawakens to its own calling—this witness, too, and the real achievements of this communal tradition, are a spur to Catholics.

The great witness of the evangelical churches in bringing about real conversions of life in their members—getting them to change their habits and to live in a more godly way—and in nourishing daily life with Scripture, study groups, and activities built up from those studies should serve as an awakening to Catholics.

Another thing. Being Catholic does not mean uniformity. In England, in Italy, in Poland, in Mexico, in France, in Korea, in Germany—in all these and in other places—I have found different forms of Catholic life, worship, and culture. Moreover, if you live for a while in a Benedictine monastery, a Jesuit house, with the LaSallette fathers, with the Carmelites or Franciscans, or in an Opus Dei community, or with the School Sisters of Notre Dame, or Madames of the Sacred Heart, or with a multitude of other communities, you will find a quite distinctive spirit in each.

There is still one more thing, a big thing. The Catholic Church may be the mother of all the other Christian

churches, and all the others may bear important family resemblances to this mother, but in history she has been a
difficult, often sinful, and problematic mother. Pride, self-
ishness, lust, every scarlet sin imaginable has wracked the
church of Christ. Look for a long moment at the front wall
of Michelangelo's Sistine Chapel, painted in 1541, which
shows various figures in the Church—archbishops, cardi-
nals, popes—being rejected by Christ on Judgment Day,
and cast into hell.

Many years ago, I was walking through St. Peter's
Square and then into the cool air of the vast basilica itself
with two Protestant scholars. I felt, as always, an awe of
the place—from the *Pietà* of Michelangelo in the side chapel
at the rear to the baldacchino of Bramante over the central
altar—and gratitude and pride and love. But one of my colleagues mentioned quietly that the sight of all St. Peter's
grandeur made him think of the blood that Rome had caused
to be shed. The whole experience made him faintly ill (not
even so faintly). It did not seem to him that such a grandiose
building is a suitable evocation of the Christ of the gospels.

I thought otherwise.

But now we are starting to get into why I remain committed to the Catholic Church. Not everyone will follow me
in this choice. But many people, I find, are quite curious
about it. They ask many questions about it, in any case.

I guess that's only natural. Most people define themselves around the Catholics, in one way or another. The
"enlightened" define themselves as light, compared to the
Dark Ages. Jews have many reasons why they refuse to
become Christian, no matter what pressure—indirect or direct—has at times put on them to do so. Protestants owe
their beginnings to what at the Reformation they separated

themselves from. If you are brought up Catholic, you are often surprised (in movies, in books, in real conversations) by the ferocity of antagonism against the Catholic Church; it is a fact of life. "Anti-Catholicism," Peter Viereck once wrote, "is the anti-Semitism of the intellectuals." Everybody's identity seems to be affected by the Catholic people in some way or other. So curiosity is natural: changes in their understanding of "Catholic" require changes in their own self-identity, however slight.

The point I am trying to bring out is that the human spirit is various, colorful, diverse, so that even in one Christian church there are (and ought to be) many different wings.

If there is abundant variation in the Catholic Church, how can there not be even more variation in the great world of religion outside the Catholic Church? *Universality* does not mean *uniformity*. The religious life of humans is not one-size-fits-all. It is a baggy, patched garment, not a seamless one. The ways of conscience and sensibility, pilgrimage and adventure, are not laid out in advance in a neat logical pattern, but to be discovered, invented, and realized amid the ambiguities of history. In the Christian view (Catholic as well as evangelical and "mainline"), the archetype is always and only Christ and his saving work on the cross. But how that Word will come to be embodied universally is hidden from our sight and committed to the free action of human persons and communities. In this sense, Christian faith is and always will be a work-in-progress, *many* works-in-progress. Faith comes from God's amazing grace in the messiness of history, through intricate labyrinths in every soul. We accept Christ as Lord, but most of the world (as yet) does not. Our trust lies in God's patience and mercy and wonderful ways.

To review, your first question was: Are each of the religions equally valid, or are some better than others? My answer was yes and no. Some religions are true but others are not. But among those that are true, some still reflect the truth considerably better than others.

Second, you asked what the variety means. My answer: God chooses not to force himself upon us, imposing the truth about himself in a blindingly irresistible fashion. Thus, following their own intuitions and reflections in human experience, humans have generated considerable variety in trying to figure out the truth about God and ourselves. Sometimes this is out of good will, sometimes out of bad will—a refusal to heed God's whisperings in the soul.

Third, how does one go about choosing among the different religions for oneself? Through careful study, critical thought, and quiet prayer. The test is not which religion is more cozy, but which seems best to reflect the truth. Some good signs are a passion for truth and inquiry, a striving to inspire a universal viewpoint (its ambition to reach out to all human beings), a credible claim that this religion originates in God, not in humans, and an ability to foster holiness of life.

Here at the end, I thought this prayer by a Catholic saint might suit you:

> From silly devotions
> and from sour-faced saints,
> good Lord, deliver us.
>
> —St. Teresa of Avila
> (1515–1582)

3

WHAT IS GOD LIKE?

THE RABBI OF BRATISLAVA

"Rabbi," said the earnest young student. "Tell me what God is like."

"Do you see the sun?" began the Rabbi. "No, do not look at it. Hold out your arm, roll up your sleeve."

The young man did as he was directed.

"Do you feel the sun?" asked the Rabbi.

The young man nodded, still mystified.

"You think it is far away, but you can feel it on your arm," said the Rabbi, and said no more.

"But what does that prove?" the boy finally asked.

"It proves that you have a cold heart."

The young man grew despondent. "What do I do about that?"

"You must bare your heart to the sun, as you bared your arm. You must love the Lord your God with your whole heart and your whole soul and your whole mind. Then you will know what God is like."

Very slowly the young man broke into a smile.

—Anonymous

JANA: *Dad, I think we need to go back to the beginning. My biggest difficulty is religion, but I also have trouble thinking about God, in my own mind or talking with others. We have to go back to the first "leap" people need to make, that is,* believing *in god. We need to address why people should believe in god at all—in any god. Besides the fact that religions can be seen as lulling people into a possibly false sense of security, believing in a god does not necessar-*

ily make sense. After all, in this age of advanced technology and knowledge, when the need for a god or gods to explain the unexplainable is seemingly unnecessary, how can one believe in a god? It seems difficult to find a reason for god—let alone to prove he exists.

Besides, what is god? There are so many mixed messages offered about God that I'm confused about what God is like. Sometimes it seems that God is only a concept, a philosophical ideal, that has served to fill the emptiness in our world. Other times God is sketched as the ultimate role model, and the stern teacher: "Just wait until your father finds out." And other times, well, other times God is just a god. People then seem to use him as an excuse, an explanation, even the target of their wrath. I know that none of these descriptions is true, but that still doesn't get me anywhere. Also, I don't find it comfortable to get around the question of what God is just by talking about "Jesus." What does it mean to say "Jesus is God"?

I know God is everywhere, yet in truth nowhere, since he is not something we can "sense." (In other words, the five senses, such as touch and sight, are of no use when it comes to God.) Yet, if we can't sense him, then how can we know about him? How can we believe in something we can't know? That requires such a leap of faith. And if we can know him, then what is it that we know? How should we even begin to think of God?

Maybe I should say: How shouldn't we think of God? In art, sometimes pictures are drawn by shading in the background—drawing what isn't the object—rather than actually drawing the object. I think that that might be helpful here. So tell me what God is not. Perhaps between your trying to tell me what God is and what God is not, I'll figure out what God is like and why he's important.

Plus, how does one know which god to believe in? How do you explain the existence of other gods—of polytheism? Are they all just different interpretations of the same god? As if the one god stands inside a cylinder and each religion offers a tiny window to look through and catch a glimpse of the god (and some religions have managed to secure several windows). So that it ends up being like the three blind men who were touching the elephant—all three felt different parts and so thought they were touching separate and radically different animals. So in this way, each religion shows the same entity, but different facets of it?

DAD: Okay, Jana, you want me to talk first about *what* God is, before we ask *if* he is. A good instinct. If we start by imagining X in the wrong way, we could look in all the wrong places. But you've also asked me three tough questions: How do we know that there is a god? How should we think about God—about what he is not, and about what he is? And why are there so many different gods (as in polytheism and also in so many different religions)?

Let me give you three point-blank answers first, and then ask you to walk back and forth across the mountain with me while we climb, trying to see these answers from a better vantage point. It will seem like going round and round—in order to say what I want to say, I need to help you grasp several other distinct ideas or images, each of which needs to be understood in its own context. So be patient with me.

The quick answers are these: (1) We know that God

exists by learning some things about our own acts of insight and judgment, making some inferences, and trying out— testing—some new ways of grasping reality. No one sees God *directly;* you have to see that he exists out of the corner of your eye, as it were, by reflection on your own inner life. That is where he is best found. (But he allows no one to trap him like a butterfly, confine him, limit his ways of approaching others.) But we better attempt all this in a separate go-around, later.

(2) The best way to think about God is probably the way most Jews and Christians and Muslims always have: as light and as love. These terms require us to do some exploring, and we will. But I also very much like your suggestion of sketching in what God is *not.* Good idea! I'm going to begin with some negatives—how *not* to look for him, how *not* to think of him.

(3) Finally, remember that even the God of Israel and Christianity revealed himself very slowly in history. He tolerates a lot of ambiguity and has very long time-horizons (so to speak). Take your point about the three blind men and the elephant: humans have only a limited ability to see. It takes generations of trial and error even to get the questions right. God knows humans are groping to find him on their own, and making lots of mistakes; the Bible shows this. If Judaism and Christianity can imagine God in this way, we need to loosen up our imaginations, too, and not hold God to narrow expectations.

There are many ways *not* to think of God. Let me begin with three.

WAYS *NOT* TO THINK OF GOD

Nowadays, many people want to look for God only under our brightest lights, science and logic. This is a little like the drunk who lost a ring and kept searching under a lamppost, even though he admitted to a passerby that he had lost it down the street. "Then why are you looking here?" he was asked. " 'Ere's more light here!"

Wrong place. God is *not* a scientific explanation, for use when normal scientific inquiry trails off. The idea that "God" is an all-purpose explanation for what we don't yet understand is a big mistake. "God" is not a term to plug into holes that appear in scientific theory. With that approach, the more that science succeeds in explaining, the smaller the hole that God fills. A god found in that way would be a purely theoretical construct of our own reasoning, and therefore our servant. God does not explain the mechanisms of existence; he is not part of the field of scientific explanations. What God "explains," at most, is why theory is possible; why inquiry is not madness; and why this world stands out from the void, and *is*.

The second way *not* to take: You keep mentioning that the church is only using God as "the opiate of the people." That phrase is in the air everywhere; it's an invention of Karl Marx. In a close variant, you will sometimes hear people say that you "need" God. That can be a dangerous way of thinking. It puts *you* at the center of the universe, it makes God the servant of your needs. It makes you god.

It is a little different to say that your heart is restless without God, that you thirst after him, that you hunger for him. Or that in your weakness you need help—help and forgiveness. Those propositions leave open the possibility that God is a great deal more important than you are. Maybe more than you can fathom. Maybe infinite.

If you are going to think of God, or to become conscious of the fact that you are already in his presence, it is best to prepare your mind for how vast the undertaking is. As I am writing this in Delaware, for example, it is a brisk day in November, the sky is robin's egg blue after last night's furious storms, and gray-white clouds are scudding across Delaware Bay outside my window.

Out beyond Cape May, eighteen miles away across the gleaming Bay, and down along the beach stretching to my right toward Florida, lies the Atlantic Ocean, pencil thin on the horizon. Sea gulls circle. Naturalists here speak of centuries like days, and tens of thousands of years like weeks. Horseshoe crabs that lay millions of eggs on our beach in May, and then die by the hundreds if they can't catch an outbound wave, their black hulks stinking in the hot sun, are said to have been laying eggs on shores like these (only a handful in the world, here and in Japan) for more than a million years. The cold tidal waters swirl round them on the sand and recede. And have done so immemorially.

Here it is easier to stretch the mind, be quiet, and let God be present. All this reminds me how you were impressed by those lines in the play *Inherit the Wind*, by Jerome Lawrence and Robert E. Lee, that explained that the biblical term "day" isn't taken as a measure of hours, but of eras. A "day" might have been a narrator's way of saying "a hundred million years."

Let me add to this another line of thought. When Thomas Jefferson wrote in the Declaration of Independence, *"endowed by their Creator,"* his readers were thinking of a very great and vast God: Creator of all things, including all the wonders of the New World, the vastness of the ocean, and the stars above. Congress added two other words to the Declaration, *"Providence"* and *"Supreme Judge."* A fourth favorite term in the founding generation was "Governor of the universe," the model among free persons for all sound government. You need to push your imagination to the stars, beyond known galaxies, to grasp what such terms point to. These terms—"Creator," "Providence," "Judge," "Governor"—are part of an American inheritance. God is *not* therapy; something vaster.

A third way *not* to think about God: It's important not to *look for* something. God is not an *object*, like all the other objects in the world, another piece of the world's furniture. "No one has seen God," says St. John's Epistle (1 John 4:12). You don't need only the biblical word on that; you can experience it. The very notion that we have a kind of inner eye by which to espy some mysterious object of sight is bound to result in the search for an idol, not worthy of much—more like a creature than like the Creator. More like an object to categorize and file among other objects.

So here I've pointed out three ways *not* to go: Don't think of God as a part of a scientific explanation; don't seek God as a function of human needs; don't look for an object, a thing, to be seen. These are false trails, leading nowhere.

Let me add some more images that God is *not*. He is not "the Big Guy upstairs," nor the loud booming voice that Hollywood films affect for God, nor the swirling bright lights that artists sometimes gyrate against dark clouds. God is not the hectoring voice of a Superego issuing nagging words of disapproval. There are hosts of bogus pictures for God: the Watchmaker beyond the skies, the puppeteer of history, the rush of orgasm or orgiastic dance, the reeling ecstatic madness of drink or drugs, the hyperheightened consciousness of creativity or bliss, the sweet feelings induced by musical and other artistic harmonies. It is especially wrong to think of God as the inner soul of the universe, as if God were the life principle of the sum of things in the universe. That is a kind of pantheism. (Some environmentalists today are bringing pantheism back, speaking in hushed tones as they endow this fragile earth with superhuman sacredness. In the New Age version, the self dissolves into the All, like a raindrop in the ocean.) All these things make God a part of man, a surging cosmic sea, a roof-timber to the universe. They are the best images that agnostics and atheists have, since, having them, they are certain to smash them at their pleasure.

Take it as a general rule: If an idea of God is partial or petty, it is not true. If your aim is to belittle him, you will not find him. If you wish to find him, watch for him in quiet and humility—perhaps among the poor and broken things of earth. There are people, like Dorothy Day and Mother Teresa, who looked into the eyes of the most abandoned of the poor and saw infinite treasure there, treasure without price, and there found God dwelling.

JANA: *But how should I even think about what I'm looking for? For me, seeing God in the poor isn't enough. That seems to take faith first. I admire people who can do it, but it doesn't help me.*

DAD: More positively, Jana, there are many paths toward knowing that God exists outside the Bible (as the Bible itself notes):

> The heavens declare the glory of God,
> The vault of heaven proclaims his handiwork;
> day discourses of it to day,
> night to night hands on the knowledge.

No utterance at all, no speech;
no sound that anyone can hear;
yet their voice goes out through all the earth,
and their message to the ends of the world.

High above, he pitched a tent for the sun,
who comes out of his pavilion like a bridegroom,
exulting like a hero to run his race.

—Psalm 19:1–5, The Jerusalem Bible

The theologians call these ways of learning about God "general revelation," the ways revealed through the works of creation. One of my favorite authors, Jacques Maritain—you've probably noted that I own about thirty of his books—has described in his book *Approaches to God* six "ways" of showing that God exists. While this may not reflect well on me, I may be one of the few people you know who find philosophical paths to God helpful, even persuasive. Maybe you, too, *have* to go by way of philosophy, your mind insists on it.

Still, of the more fruitful paths, some you can't discover until you've snaked your way through obstacles. Some you can't map out for others, but can only point out by walking with them. After they've toiled up the mountain for themselves, they appreciate why some paths can't get you there. And how others can.

Even people who are certain that there is a God find it hard to put in words what they imagine when they think of God. Some of my Protestant evangelical friends, when they think of God, use a set of images different from mine. Some unconsciously adopt the mental image of a judge at a high bench and picture themselves at the bar of judgment, smaller, vulnerable, conscious of having done wrong. Their most powerful awareness is of being judged, knowing that they are at fault, and needing a Redeemer. One friend of mine never saw this point until a minister asked him to look at Jesus bleeding on the cross, and to recognize that his sins helped put him there. For many, to become aware of God's presence is to become aware of the love of Jesus—"to accept Jesus into my heart."

Another of my evangelical friends accuses me of sounding like a Quaker when I talk of God. "When I look inside," he says, "I don't find what you find; I find sin, and I need help." He doesn't like to hear me talk of "the God within." "If I didn't know you," he once said, "I'd think you were talking New Age." He thinks that talk about "God within" is a form of idolatry, a way of making the self feel good, a search for self-esteem. You and I have probably seen this happen. He has a point.

Some of my Catholic friends also hate philosophy and anything that sounds like "proving the existence of God." They think that the centuries of trying to prove the existence of God led to a false conception of Reason and a loss of the biblical emphasis upon conversion in one's way of life. Hardly anybody, they say, "reasons" his way to the existence of God, and by itself reasoning wouldn't lead to a conversion of life anyway.

Others among my Catholic friends don't like images of the bar of judgment and of their own sinfulness—some do, but others don't warm to that approach. They are more likely to use their imaginations to recreate a biblical scene in which they hear Jesus speaking, note the kindness in his gestures and the attentiveness of his manner, feel again the emotion of his listeners. When they make Jesus present to their imaginations in this way, they are drawn toward him and want to follow him. They are moved more by love of him than by consciousness of their own sin.

When I was younger, we used to hear some scary sermons about hell, but I have not heard such a sermon for decades; I wonder if they have entirely disappeared. Usually, these were delivered in alternately loud and hushed voices by visiting missionaries who visited the parish for a week of evening services every year or so, to jar us from our normal habits. Some preachers, even those who seemed kind and had jolly faces and told good jokes, prided themselves on scaring people half to death; but even these took pains to point out that their opening stress on hell was not the real message, just a way to get us to understand the stakes.

The way of guilt and sin has never appealed to me. It is not that I am unconscious of sins; on the contrary, recalling mine I shudder, and do not like to think too much about them. It seems better simply to throw myself upon God's mercy. If the theater of the imagination of my evangelical friend is a courtroom, in which he stands at the bar of judgment, the theater of my imagination is the cosmos, all of creation, and my own tiny consciousness of its vastness, longing to understand more about it. I am led to think of God through my own thirst to understand, my longing to respond accurately.

THE WAY WITHIN

I have always loved the text of St. Augustine which I read as a teenager: "I sought Thee everywhere, my God, but when at last I found Thee, Thou wert within." It is in our minds and wills that God dwells, the New Testament (like the Torah) tells us. It is in my mind and will—in how they actually work—that I come to know at least a little about God. My evangelical friends, I hasten to add, become nervous with this approach. Apart from the Scripture, obviously, I would know pitifully little about the depths of his love, mercy, and patience. But I can learn a little about God from being made in his image.

Oddly, most philosophers in the West think of truth as a characteristic of either reality (as distinct from illusion) or propositions. To think of truth, instead, as the name of a *person*—the Creator and Suffuser of the universe—is not to deny that truth is a characteristic of reality or of propositions. But it is to name what makes them so. The reason that truth is a characteristic of reality and/or of propositions is that there is an intelligent, loving Creator of all things, Who is the origin of all truths—those of reality and those in propositions.

JANA: *Okay, but how do we "reach" truth, that is, God?*

DAD: There are two roads winding over the hills toward God. One road goes by way of a narrative, taking a Bible in hand and telling the story exemplifying who God is, as Fulton Oursler did in *The Greatest Story Ever Told*. This is to imagine God as most Jews and Christians always have.

The other road is philosophical, through thinking about our experiences of life. That means reflecting on human understanding, in which lies our best image of God—the best hint we have of what he is like. This is the path the ancient

Greeks and many outside the circle of Jews and Christians travel.

To begin with, I'm going to take a variation of the first road, the biblical narrative; we will come back to the philosophical way in a moment. I'm going to draw upon some of the images for God that have been cherished in the Jewish and Christian traditions (and, to some extent, in the Islamic tradition) for centuries. I know that you have philosophical interests and a philosophical bent, and may find the philosophical way helpful. People differ on that—also, on what satisfies the mind at any particular moment during life's voyage.

How might we talk about God? To follow the Jewish and Christian narratives, we need to be talking about a God large enough to have conceived and executed all of creation, from distant galaxies still beyond our ken to the horseshoe crabs on Lewes Beach, and not omitting you and me, and your uncle Jim and his daughter Pei, and your little niece and nephew Emily and Stephen James, and your friends Mark and Stephanie, and all other humans down the ages and yet to come. We need to be talking about a God who loves the human beings he first imagined, even with all their weaknesses, flaws, evil and ungrateful ways, indifference to him, rough edges, and woeful failures to fulfill their possibilities: a fairly sorry lot we are, each of us looking inward. This is the God of whom the Bible speaks.

And we need to be talking about a God whose mode of presence with us does not overpower us nor coerce our minds the way blinding evidence does; nor satisfy our longing for security, peace, and certitude; nor bathe our sensibility, emotions, sentiments, and inner longings with unfailing sweetness, comfort, and delight. This, too, is the God of the Bible. The prayer of those who believe in him is "Help me in my unbelief." Since he is not embodied, as we are, there is nothing of him for our senses to lay hold of—not for our eyes to see nor our ears to hear, nothing to reach out and touch, no scent nor taste. For the same reason, our efforts to imagine him (children excepted) must and do come up blank. Since he cannot be reached by our bodies, our emotions, or our imaginations, not even by our feelings, we are pretty much incapacitated in his presence—except for two things.

First, we do have our unlimited hunger to understand, to raise questions, to inquire, and that gives us a lingering sense of restlessness. Whatever is, dissatisfies us; we ask further questions and look toward further horizons. This is our first clue about what it is to be infinite—it is in some dark way *like* having an infinite capacity to ask questions and to understand the answers. A Creator of all might have such a capacity. And a love for what he had created. (What if he had been like a willful child destroying a sand castle on the beach after hours spent building it?)

Second, tradition is "the democracy of the dead" (G. K. Chesterton); it is the community of all those who have inquired into this question; and tradition tells us that forging ahead with such inquiries, accepting all their difficulties, setbacks, and hardships (as Christian does in John Bunyan's *Pilgrim's Progress*) will teach us a great deal. As we force our mind out into this cold empty air, we will learn a great deal about ourselves. This is a voyage of discovery well worth taking for its own sake.

In addition, Judaism and Christianity are religions of

memory—of tradition—as well as of future promise. That is why we need to learn "how to" (how to believe, how to live) in two ways: in part from the past; in part by creating a new future. Traditions live by overcoming new circumstances.

THE WAY OF LOVE

Jana, you want to know what should be going through your mind when you use the name "God." (Is it a name? Is it a term?) Clearly, it is not a name like any other that we know. It's in a league by itself, and it has to become known in a way unlike any other way in which things become known to us. We can't use our senses, or imaginations, or feelings, or (in the ordinary sense) concepts, the way we normally do for things *within* creation. And when you take the sum of all the things within creation, throw a net around it all, you have not caught him.

I love the line of Dante, at the end of *Il Paradiso*:

L'amor che move il sole e l'altre stelle!
The Love that moves the Sun and all the stars!

From that tradition, I also love the Gregorian antiphon that goes like this:

Ubi Caritas et Amor, ibi Deus est.
Where there is Caritas and Love, there God is.

When you hear the crisp, haunting sounds of that chant in a cold and almost empty church at matins or compline (morning prayer or evening prayer, in sung chant), it brings the most penetrating insight, no matter what the state of your feelings, even if you feel like the bottom of a bird cage. For *caritas* and *amor* are two very different kinds of love.

71

What, exactly, do we mean by love? In English we are hampered by having but one word for many different concepts. In Latin, we are luckier. Beyond *amor*, Latin also has four other words for love, each adding a distinctive characteristic: *amor, affectus, dilectio, amicitia, caritas*. (The poor American *love* lumps all five together, and confuses us thoroughly.) Each of these Latin terms requires fuller discussion.

Amor, among loves, is the most general kind of attraction. *Amor* is what Dante names the force that moves the sun and choreographs the stars in their millennial dance across the skies. *Amor* means pull, attraction, being driven together. One can use it of Earth's gravity (*Amor meus, pondus meum*, the ancient metaphor tells us, "My love pulls me like the weight of gravity"); the sudden lightning of attraction between strangers "across a crowded room," as the song puts it; the passions that pull the sexes to cohabit. The ancient poets sang of the stars being pulled by love into their orbits and the eternal order of their dancing; this is the image Dante uses.

Affectus is the movement of sensibilities and affections that even dogs and kittens share with us. Tails wag and hearts purr with pleasure and effusiveness. *Dilectio* is the special love a human being chooses to bestow on another particular person, by choice, beyond mere affection. The term *amicitia* (friendship) adds to *dilectio* the note of mutuality. If (perhaps as a teenager) you have ever loved anyone *(dilectio)* who did not reciprocate that love, you know the pain caused by the lack of mutuality. Mutual love, *amicitia* (friendship), is far more powerful than any other love—save one.

That love is a special form of *amicitia*, but its origin does not lie within us. We would not dream of pretending to it. We would not know how. It exceeds our powers utterly. It is *caritas*. It is God's own love, the love that is the fire of his nature, that in him is so strong it generates another Person, and then their mutual love generates a Third. *Caritas* is the inner life, the unending action, of the Trinity. This love helps explain why *community* is such a crucial idea in traditional concepts of God, even in religions that do not recognize the Trinity. Is it possible to believe that we can participate in God's *caritas*?

When we Christians speak of the Trinity, the inner being of our God, we know not whereof we speak. The point we seize upon, however, is that our God has spoken of himself in such a way that we are to imagine him, not as One in eternal solitude—as Plato, Aristotle, and many of the ancients imagined him—but rather as a community of love and friendship. When we have experienced friendship and love, we have come closest to experiencing what God is like. One God, yet three in one.

No one has *seen* God. Strictly, no one knows what he is like. Yet he himself points our minds in these directions: He is to be thought of as *Communio Divinarum Personarum*, a Communion of Divine Persons. Through acts of human love, he radiates his presence throughout creation, calling unworthy human beings to be his friends, and infusing into them his love so that they might love with it. *Caritas* is our participation in a way of loving not our own, exceeding human love: God's own love. It is our participation—partial, fitful, hesitant, imperfect—in his own loving.

J A N A : *I'm confused. You say* caritas *is "our participation in a way of loving not our own," but I thought you said earlier that* caritas *is simply God's love. So which is it? Is it that we are able to experience* caritas *only when we partici-pate in a "way of loving not our own, exceeding human love"?*

DAD: The Creator's whole point in making the world (Christians hold) was that some of his creatures should share in his love. The Love that moves the sun and all the stars is ours to give to others. So *caritas* has two senses: It names God's own chief activity (the hearty embrace by his will of the good and the true), and it also names our dim participation in that love. When you have experienced love and friendship, don't they often seem like a force greater than you?

To make us able to share in his love, God had to make us capable of reflection, deliberation, choice, and commitment. He had to make us in his image. He had to make us provi-dent of our own destiny, as he is provident. He had to make us free. Responsible, too. Capable of saying no. And capa-ble of evil. And he had to form a universe in which creatures such as we could emerge, an "anthropic" universe (so to speak).

When God thought to create the world, he could not quite show us the fullness of his loving merely by creating the world in its splendor and goodness. He also had to show us the most divine characteristic of his being, his mercy. God willed to make us capable of evil, so that in our wretch-edness he could show us the power of a love that sees sin quite realistically, but wipes it away and lifts us to share in his own power of loving. Divine love is as glorious as a sum-mer day high in the Alps; it is merciful and makes our sins vanish into insignificance, replacing them with his own action in us; it is, finally, self-sacrificial unto death.

In short, love is no simple thing. It is not what we might at first think it is.

In this vast cosmos, such as science knows it, we humans (even as an entire race, from beginning to end) are barely a speck in silent space, unimportant, less enduring than galaxies and stars—less so even than many plants, insects, and viruses. Yet to us in our unimportance God wished to show what he is made of, to let us look behind the veil at the Love that moves the sun and all the stars, and to draw us into acts of *caritas*.

JANA: *Your discussion of the different types of love is illuminating, but I'm still not sure where this path has led us. If I remember correctly, you are trying to explain how we should* think *of God before you go into why we should* believe *in God. But I'm afraid I don't understand what* caritas *has to do with how we should think of God. To be honest, I am still unclear about how to think of God.*

DAD: There are two human experiences that Jews and Christians (and here I may add, Muslims) have always returned to as ways of thinking about God: as love and as insight. We have experience of both activities in our own lives, and can make distinctions about kinds of love and kinds of insight. For now, is that enough? Think of God as love—the highest form of love you have so far experienced. Let that give you some idea of what it is like to say the word "God." But also think of him as insight. These are the two metaphors, signs, I am trying to bring to your consciousness.

THE WAY OF INSIGHT

Let me turn from love to the metaphor of light. In a cartoon, the symbol for an insight is a light that goes on. Think about that experience within your own mind, when you are perplexed and your brow furrows, and you say *"What?"* in a disbelieving tone of voice—and then the sudden, *"Oh, I gotcha!"* when you get it. What is it like, when you pass from one to the other, from the darkness to the light? You have that experience every day, several times a day. That's what it's like to be bright. But even dull people have insights, not so often and not over so large a range of material; it's just human to have this experience sometimes, an ordinary event. If it were not, no one would ever get the point of a joke, or find relief in finally figuring out what she'll serve for dinner, or get the word she's trying to think of for a crossword puzzle, or see what a lawyer's brief is driving at, or figure out a turn in the plot of a movie ("I didn't understand the part where she . . ."). Daily life without insights would mean an extremely low IQ, and a lot of life's enjoyment missed.

I love the term *insight*. It is a good Anglo-Saxon word, without an exact equivalent in the Romance languages, bright with the suggestion of a light in someone's intelligence bursting on. *Insight* doesn't have the smoky, mysterious connotations of *intuition*, or the nonrational, brute suggestion of *hunch* or *instinct*. No, *insight* is perfectly intellectual and clean, although it does hint at vivid imagination and concreteness—the sort of down-to-earthness that the

English language loves. That is because, in fact, insights *always* occur by way of a vivid and exact image or a concrete example. Thus, teachers (good ones) specialize in stories, examples, jokes, images, and diagrams that set the exact focus for the imagination, so that the students can "get the point" through the example, and can build on that insight to gain yet others.

The human mind craves examples as the body craves air—imagination is the medium in which the mind lives and has its being. A teacher can watch students' faces as they struggle to understand a definition, given abstractly, and then see the smiles of satisfaction and the uncrossing of brows when the right example throws a concrete light on abstract words. If some students don't get it, then another example may do the trick—the teacher has to try to identify the roadblock in the student's imagination and find the example that gets around it and unloosens it.

The problem we have with God is that our imagination cannot help us to grasp him; he lives beyond the power of our imagination. That's one reason our minds feel empty when trying to grasp what the term "God" means; no picture is available, only a kind of nothingness. Put another way, we cannot gain insight into God, the way we can into others that we know well and love, or have long experience with.

Even when our imaginations have been fortified by the vivid images of the Bible, in our long hours of prayer we often go inwardly empty. The old feelings of devotion vanish into thin air. He seems to have fled. We approach him as the blind and deaf approach one they love—even worse, we cannot reach out our hands to touch him, as we would a loved one in a hospital. We are left in sensory darkness.

Also in a darkness of the imagination. Also in a darkness of memory. This is pretty grim, really, for those who love God.

You can read the words of the saints and see this, if you don't believe me.

> Thus in your absence and your lack
> How can I in myself abide
> Nor suffer here a death more black
> Than ever was by mortal died.
> For pity of myself I've cried
> Because in such a plight I lie
> Dying because I do not die.

—St. John of the Cross (1542–1591)

What, then, will he do here who finds that for many days he experiences nothing but aridity, dislike, distaste and so little desire to go and draw water that he would give it up entirely if he did not remember that he is pleasing and serving the Lord of the garden; if he were not anxious that all his service should not be lost, to say nothing of the gain which he hopes for from the great labour of lowering the bucket so often into the well and drawing it up without water? It will often happen that, even for that purpose, he is unable to move his arms—unable, that is, to think a single good thought, for working with the understanding is of course the same as drawing water out of the well. What, then, as I say, will the gardener do here? He will be glad and take heart and consider it the greatest of favours to work in the garden of so great an Emperor; and, as he knows that he is pleasing Him by so working (and his purpose must be to please, not himself, but Him), let him render Him great praise for having placed such confidence in him, when He has seen that, without receiving any recompense, he is taking such great care of that which He had entrusted to him; let him help Him to bear the Cross and consider how He lived with it all His life long; let him not wish to have his kingdom on earth or ever cease from prayer; and so let him resolve, even if this aridity should persist his whole life long, never to let Christ fall beneath the Cross.

—St. Teresa of Avila (1515–1582)

It is not easy to be "neutral" in the struggle to be true to one's own identity as a creature of God. Resistance to

God is usually fierce. Moreover, it is usually tangled, almost labyrinthine. In *Surprised by Joy*, C. S. Lewis recounts in vivid, analytic detail the layers of resistance that held him back for years. He needed to plod through it, insight by insight. I recommend that book.

Atheists sometimes like to boast about the darkness that they brave; they compare themselves to Prometheus abandoned on the cold cliffs, cursing the night. Bertrand Russell, Jean-Paul Sartre, even a drunken Dylan Thomas. With all due respect, their boasts are a species of self-pity.

The comfort, peace, and false security that such atheists attribute to believers spring from the unbeliever's ignorance of the darkness in which the true God dwells—Whose Name should not even be written because it is like no other name.

Many people do not believe in God because, perhaps, they are afraid. I resisted saying this when I was young; it seemed like an expression of moral superiority. But wide reading and experience show that there is a kernel of truth in it. Some people really do fear God, as if belief in him will destroy them. I can tell you a story about this.

A short time after the fall of Communism, a large Catholic procession was held in Prague to celebrate the canonization of a Czech woman of many centuries earlier. The streets were full of believers with candles, happy, singing. A Communist university scientist, watching on television, turned off his set with disgust. "For seven hundred years they have been marching for saints," he said bitterly. "For us, they marched only forty years." Even though his daughter and grandchildren were believers, and living in his home, he would not allow anyone to speak of God or religion in his household. He would stomp out of the room. He could not stand it. The justification on which he had built his life, with its compromises, was that the success of Communism in history is the only reliable measure of good and evil. He could not bear, now, to face a higher standard.

So it is with others. If they believe in God, they think, they will lose their autonomy. They will have to become attentive to One beyond themselves, whose Will will matter to them. And, this Will may make demands on them that they would rather not heed.

In order to recognize God's presence in one's mind and soul, one needs to fight through many misconceptions, many fears. If an atheist or agnostic counts up the reasons why she does *not* believe—assuming enough self-knowledge to disentangle them from one another—these would often run into the dozens. Sometimes it is only at the end of the voyage that, looking back, one can see the terrain clearly, and detect where, earlier, things were going wrong.

If I am right about light and love, a mistake about God is a mistake about self-knowledge. It is for one's own sake, then, that insight is important. It is often experienced as a gift. It dawns. There was darkness, then light. Further, being born a believer does not automatically confer on one an adult understanding of God. A voyage through a series of advanced insights is necessary even if one was born a believer. Such insights may seem, on arrival, like gifts, but they usually require the slow ascent of a mountain.

We think of God, then, as light, truth—or, better, the active insight that understands, loves, and sustains all things. The first step in coming to think about God is to learn to think clearly about our own capacity for insight.

Many, many times since you were little I have seen your brow furrowed, trying hard to understand. That is something you really like to do. In fact, you have often frightened me because you understood so quickly and became impatient—a normal Novak flaw—if I continued explaining what you already saw. Well, when your brow was furrowed, I often noted the intense pleasure that enlivened your eyes and changed their intensity when you got the point, and especially if you thought it was a neat point—a little hidden, but in a way obvious once you got around a certain blockage; a way of liberating your mind to gambol down other fields. That's the point I'm trying to make. An insight isn't just a point about something external to yourself, although it is that; it is also a change in your mind and the way it works.

JANA: *I think I understand. An insight provides new connections, sort of like finding a new shortcut between my former house on Capitol Hill and yours in upper Northwest DC. In a more scientific analogy, an insight seems to activate new synapses in the brain that allow the brain to comprehend subsequent ideas, right?*

DAD: Not just new connections, but the empowering, enabling *inner* aspect of those connections. Once you see them, you *know* the new route, you can use it when you want to—and from it learn new routes. An insight adds a dimension to the mind, activates new abilities in it, makes it competent and able in new ways, empowers it, liberates it. An insight changes the intellect itself, not just its relation to the fresh materials it has just encountered.

So there we have a kind of trinity: insight as the point grasped; as the lively and pleasurable act of grasping (a datable event); and as the mind empowered and changed by that pleasant act, and thus liberated for further activities. "She's a person of real insight."

Of the three faces of insight—the point grasped, the pleasurable act, the mind empowered—it is the last two that have most successfully conveyed to Jews, Christians, Muslims, and many others an idea rooted in human experience that, however inadequately, suggests what God must be like. At least, this seems to be the most fruitful direction in which to think of him: God's life is the pleasurable act of insight, in his case instantaneous and total. In God this act is total, his mind is totally empowered, it is an active act of insight, pure and simple.

Also, insights once achieved can then be taught to others. So insights are creative, too. I invent a way to perform heart surgery that no one could do before, then I teach everybody else. My insight has caused a leap forward in knowledge and ability. Therefore, it's a creative insight, and again yields an image of our Creator.

How do I dare to say this? This is the view, roughly drawn, of the deepest writers and sages in the Jewish, Christian, and Muslim traditions (and some others). Here is a Koranic text:

> Allah is the Light
> Of the heavens and the earth.
> The parable of His Light
> Is as if there were a Niche
> And within it a Lamp:
> The Lamp enclosed in Glass;
> The glass as it were

A brilliant star:
Lit from a blessed Tree,
An Olive, neither of the East
Nor of the West,
Whose Oil is well-nigh
Luminous,
Though fire scarce touched it:
Light upon Light!
Allah doth guide whom He will
To His light:
Allah doth set forth Parables
For men: and Allah
Doth know all things.

God is not a physical thing, not like an animal or reptile or any other living body. He is to be worshiped "in spirit and truth," since these alone are akin to his nature. He is thought of as active, an agent, Creator, Providence, Supreme Judge—all terms implying the full activity of insight in the two senses mentioned above: the power and the act of insight.

Thus, Jana, while I have not seen anyone else put it in quite this way, I do not think it is wrong to suggest to you and your friends that the two characteristics of God at which the best human reflection has arrived are insight and love. Jews, Christians, and Muslims have used the following images of him: power, force, energy, actuality, being, person, fire, light, pillar, father, creator, judge, universal governor—all of which imply that he is alive with insight, intelligence, and wisdom and he is moved by love to create and to share. It is practical to think of him this way, since this is the way most human beings in the world who experience his presence in their lives do think of him.

According to the *Encyclopaedia Britannica,* in 1995 there were 5.8 billion persons on this planet. Only a tiny fraction, 259 million, were atheists, almost 2 billion were Christian, and just over 1 billion were Muslim.[1] (Christians and Muslims alone make up more than half the population of the world.) Only a slender fraction of the world's population—13 million—are Jewish; but the power of the Jewish witness has been so strong that it continues in Christianity and Islam.

You should be aware, Jana, that many Christians and Muslims will find it offputting to think that they both have the *same* idea of God. That is not my point, and I do not want to mislead you. The Bible, Jewish and Christian, reveals much about God—in himself and in his relation to humans—that is wholly distinctive. Even Christians and Jews part ways regarding what Jesus reveals of God. My point is not to reach a lowest common denominator. My aim is far humbler than that.

You have probably met philosophers of religion in the university, and in books and magazine articles, who write as if only philosophical ideas about God, rationally grounded, are worthy of consideration. It seems to me wiser to begin with what people who actually try to live in God's will hold about God. Unless you write about *that,* you are missing an empirical basis for your further inquiries.

Furthermore, when you keep encountering "light" and "love" as the human experience that most Jews, Christians, and Muslims (and perhaps others) point to as the di-

---

[1]Approximately 900 million other humans are Hindu and Buddhist, and another 900 million are "non-religious," that is, indifferent, or agnostics, or unaffiliated. The other communities of believers are in smaller numbers.

rection in which they lift up their eyes to God, your soul is fertile ground for the further revelation given Abraham, Isaac, Jacob, and Moses, and even more the revelation brought us in Jesus Christ. If God is light and love, are our hearts not often dark and unlovely? Are we not in need of forgiveness and healing, as we approach his presence?

Jews, Christians, and Muslims—all think of God in terms of *insight* and *love*. Vivid experiences of both of those activities, insight and love, are known to all of us. Through insight and love, we are open to communion with God, to that "conversation" with God (often wordless) that is prayer. Any philosopher or anthropologist who wishes to write sensibly about God, therefore, had better include insight and love in her way of thinking of God, or else write unintelligibly to most of the believers of the world.

What you want to know next, you said, is how we know whether such a God exists. What signs have we? What evidence?

4

WHAT DOES IT DO FOR ME, WHETHER THERE IS A GOD OR NOT?

THE RABBI OF BRATISLAVA

A commentary on the text, "The fear of God is the beginning of wisdom."

—Proverbs 9:10

Someone asked the Rabbi of Bratislava how he knew that God exists.
"Because *I* exist," the Rabbi immediately replied.
"You mean that *you* are the proof that God exists?" said the earnest student, with furrowed brow.
"Not exactly," said the Rabbi. "But if I do not exist, I do not have to worry whether God exists."
The student thought about this slowly. "So worrying is the proof that God exists?" he tried uncertainly.
"No," said the Rabbi. "But it is a good beginning."

—Anonymous

Oh God, we thank you for this universe, our great home; for its vastness and its riches, and for the manifoldness of the life which teems upon it and of which we are part. We praise you for the arching sky and the blessed winds, for the driving clouds and the constellations on high. We praise you for the salt sea and the running water, for the everlasting hills, for the trees, and for the grass under our feet. We thank you for our senses by which we can see the splendor of the morning and hear the jubilant songs of love, and smell the breath of the springtime.

—Walter Rauschenbusch
(1861–1918)

JANA: *I understand your insistence that we have to know what we're looking for before we can begin looking for it—I said so myself—but can you come back to the hard part:* Why *should one believe in God? After all, in the end believing in God seems to be such a matter of faith. While your image of God is very poetic, how do we know? Many pretty ideas don't stand up to reality.*

Besides, so many awful things happen in the world: children die in house fires, young mothers are stricken with cancer, hundreds die in earthquakes. The world seems to be filled with so many horrors (from the Holocaust in the thirties and forties to the Rwandan mass slaughters in the nineties) that it is difficult to believe a supremely good *god exists. How can anyone believe such a god exists if every day, every person—whether rich or poor—is confronted by evil? It is hard enough to see good in one's fellow man; it is impossible to see good behind everything. So why should one believe God exists?*

For example, I remember a friend of mine at my Catholic boarding school: she was probably the most religious of all of us, willingly attending church and actually paying attention and taking it to heart—she even attended Mass on the Holy Days, not just Sundays! But then she spent several weeks in Haiti, helping the poor people in the slums. When she returned, she could no longer believe. She told me that if God existed, he couldn't let people live in such horrible conditions; it was easier to believe he must not exist, because to have him exist and allow this misery was too much to comprehend.

In other words, if God does exist, then he's condoning some terrible actions and deeds on earth—some even done in his name. That sounds like a pretty cruel god. Is it any wonder so many people lose faith?

I must admit, though, it also sounds vaguely similar to the Old Testament God/the God of Judaism. He was a disapproving, vengeful, and wrathful God. But is there such a dissonance between the God of the Old Testament and the New Testament God (a forgiving—and forgetting—and turning-the-other-cheek God)?

But there's also a practical part of my question I really want you to answer. I plan to think some more about how to think about God and whether he exists. But, as I mentioned before, many of my friends already do believe in God, at least vaguely. Their feeling is, though, Why should we care? Just because God exists does not mean we have to believe in him or want to do anything about it.

DAD: Why should you care? Because you want to know the truth about yourself. And, because, if your Maker loves you—as in Judaism and Christianity he says he does—reciprocating his love, and falling in deeper love with him, brings sweetness (and sorrow; and suffering) beyond measure. That is one experiment in truth. Try it and see.

But there is also another. Believe that all the signs of intelligence so manifest in yourself are in vain, and that all is from chance, impersonal and mad, and in the end meaningless, a tale told by an idiot! Believe that if you can. *That* is an act of faith to which your father, who tried—really tried—could not leap.

The problem of evil throws a curve at this point because if there isn't any God, there *isn't* any problem of evil. And if there is no God, then there is a problem of good! (Why is there so much good, if everything is idiotic and, in the end, positively cruel?) So let me deal, first, with why the question about God keeps arising, sometimes quite insistently, even in a secular scientific age. Then we will return to the subject of evil and come to our conclusion.

You mentioned, too, that it's almost impossible to prove the existence of God. People usually get this problem backwards. They somehow put the burden of proof on *God*. The actual problem is with our receptors. God is all around us, and within us, and it is our problem to find the wavelength, so to speak, on which to allow his presence to enter our consciousness. (Quakers will see what I mean here.) This may not be a "saving" awareness of God, but for many it prompts them to listen harder, and to ready themselves for the Word of God. Again, let me warn you. There is no "proof" of God's existence, only a set of arguments that weigh probabilities and follow "signs." There are "ways" to God through intellectual inquiry. To believe in God is an intelligent and realistic thing to do. But it is not like having a mathematical proof in one's pocket.

The second thing, honey, that you must wipe out of your mind is that God is an explanation—I know I'm repeating myself, but this mistake is so common I must. People like to think, now and in past centuries, that some things can't be explained by science, and that to explain those things is what God is for. That is an understandable mistake because we do come to God by way of inquiry. As in other matters, though, it takes time to learn, usually through mistakes, which *sorts* of inquiry are the fruitful ones. (It's almost as if an inquiry into inquiries is the first step.)

In the history of science, there are many examples of hounds barking up an empty tree, when the prey they sought was actually in the underbrush over there. You remember from classes in the history of science how wrongly people thought about blood circulation, until a better way of imagining the role of blood was hit upon—how they thought that "bad" blood had to be bled away, often by what now seem barbarous methods. To rid her of fever, the younger Dashwood sister in *Sense and Sensibility* was bled repeatedly. As one who dreads the sight of blood, the vision of a specially made bowl brimming with blood made me—and I believe you—turn away in horror.

What are the right questions to ask about God? That's the crucial part. Pseudoscientific questions are a waste of time.

In our time, the main reason for not believing in God is that imagination has become hostile to him. People like their comfortable universe, at least people of the middle class and educated people. They can distract themselves with one thing after another. That's what life is, the philosopher Blaise Pascal wrote, "an endless series of distractions."

First, people thought that God is an explanation for how and why the world is, and then when they didn't find a need for God in science—or, indeed, any possible way of reducing God to a testable scientific proposition—they forgot about him. "God is dead," Friedrich Nietzsche wrote a century ago, but "there will perhaps be caves for ages yet, in which his shadow will be shown." Many university graduates, I suspect, have only a shadow of God in their minds, even if they continue to go to church.

If you ask me, pointing to a brown extension cord on the floor, "Is there electricity in that wire? Is it live?" I can think quickly of certain tests. Is it plugged in? Can I plug a radio or a lamp into its receiving end, and get the expected response? But when you ask me "Is God in this room? Is he in me? Is he alive?" we have to turn to tests of a different order. (Besides, you have loaded your question with reasons why you cannot admit that you are in God's presence—the evils you see around you in the world.) Let me begin with the way that the question of God is different from the question about electricity and wires.

Scientific questions are answered by sentences establishing what the facts are and by theorems showing how the facts are related. Questions about God are not scientific questions. But far from not having meaning on that account, they are acts of wonderment that we are creatures able to ask questions in the first place. That we are self-conscious, awakened to a world of poignant consciousness, and unable to deny the many intimations of meaning that bear in upon us from so many of our experiences. We are not just science-machines. We wonder about the fact that we are, and about many other aspects of our peculiar situation. We are able to look up at the stars and to ask them (in my own private version):

How I wonder what *we* are.

That is how we know that God exists: Not by the fact that we wonder, but by *way* of wondering. By way of not being satisfied by a good lunch, an easy chair, a good cigar, and the crinkling of *The New York Times* in our hands—by wondering about ourselves later: How smug and satisfied we seemed after lunch!

In this frame of mind, when wonder is upon us, what is called secular humanism seems as mechanical as a faucet, for our minds are remembering waterfalls we've come upon by surprise in a Venezuelan jungle or around a turn in the Rockies. Secular humanism may be fine when we read the *Times*—that's the frame of mind, the mood, it's written for. When we leave the club, when we baptize our new child or bury our mother, mere humanism seems too thin.

JANA: *I have only a vague idea of what "secular human-ism" means, and I am positive that I'm not alone in my con-fusion.*

DAD: Sorry. About the turn of the century, a number of philosophers and others who were definitely not believers (Christians or Jews), not even theists, began to call them-selves humanists, or just plain naturalists. They believed in reason, science, progress, pragmatic action, common sense. People like John Dewey, Sidney Hook, and others. They even published a "Manifesto," a kind of creed. They re-ferred to themselves as "secular" as opposed to "religious" humanists. Most of them opposed all the forms of modern European disdain for reason, from nihilism to existentialism. They thought existentialism, with all its talk about "the ab-surd," was adolescent—and dangerous; part of the climate that led to Fascism and Communism. Now as yesterday, they tend to be good people, and some have been bravely opposed to political correctness.

Secular humanism, however, is essentially a story of progress and human triumph that is intended to leave humans comfortable without God. The irony is that it has a very low opinion of man and what humans can know; also, a self-contradictory view of history: namely, that history is simultaneously progressive and meaningless.

Back to your question: How can we know that there is a God? We *could* know that, even if we couldn't know by direct knowledge what God is. We often have that type of knowledge about other matters. For example, astronomers have known for decades that certain planets (or other phenomena) must be where they are, even before they obtained confirming observation. In daily life, there are many things that intellects superior to mine might well know directly, about which I am more than agnostic, I am just plain ignorant: how computers actually work; how airplanes can land by computers; what everything is beneath the hood of my car; what IQ *is;* what tiny pills actually *do* to have their effects. But the *existence* of these things I have no trouble knowing, making allowances for, watching out for, and granting a healthy respect for—such existents as electricity, nuclear radiation, the potency of certain innocent-looking little white pills, and many other wonders of modern life.

I once saw a black electric wire down during a rainstorm in a *calle* in Mexico City where we were living, and I wanted to lift it out of the way—but I had no trouble believing that it dare not be touched, especially since an eleven-year-old American boy, a visitor like us, had been electrocuted an hour before by trying to do just that. So far as the eye could see, it did not look dangerous; the temptation to lift it out of the way was powerful. But I knew *that* it was alive with electricity, even though I couldn't see the electricity and don't know precisely what electricity is. We often know the *that* even when the *what* requires more comprehension than we are capable of. It's the same with the black wire in the street in the example above: I don't understand what electricity is exactly, but I know when it's present.

Jana, I want to make a very strong claim now. Many people would be content here with a far weaker claim. Take the weaker route if you want to. But I want to say what I think, knowing you'll find your own way. Many people think that we can know *that* God exists only by faith—in fact, some say, only by faith in Jesus Christ. I have never been satisfied with that. I think we must, and can, *know* something about God apart from faith—at least *that* God exists, if we reflect hard and silently and in an open way about other things we know—including the fact that we know at all, and even the fact that we *inquire*, that *we raise questions*. This is an astonishing fact; no other creature we know asks questions.

My claim is that we can know that God exists with a practical certainty as basic as any other practical knowledge on which we base our lives. We can "know," not take on faith; we can know with "practical certainty." That does not mean: it's practically certain or almost certain. It's *certain*. But the kind of certainty in question is not that of logic or scientific law; it's the kind that we draw upon when we conclude it's practical to *use* logic and/or scientific laws in many aspects of our lives. There's one kind of certainty *within* logic and science; there's another kind when we judge the utility of science and logic to daily life—their application *outside the realms of* logic and science, so to speak.

JANA: *The utility to daily life? Like thermometers or medications?*

DAD: No, not in that sense. I mean useful like the answer to this question: What makes us think that logic and science help us in making key decisions in our lives, such as, Which college should I apply to? What should I major in? Should I marry John (Mary)? Some philosophers have said that such practical questions are not scientific and not simply matters of logic; they are "emotive," i.e., nonrational. But I don't think that's adequate. I thought long and hard about marrying your mother, and I had good reasons for doing so and for judging that our marriage would last. Sometimes, admittedly, especially for her, it was hard. But thirty-four years later, I think I made the best big decision of my life. There is a kind of reason involved in such things—practical reason (*phronesis*, Aristotle called it)—that has its own way of measuring whether a proposed decision is realistic or not realistic, and has its own quite vivid tests (in events to unwind in the future) that determine later how much realism there actually was.

In other words, the *use* of logic and science outside their own proper fields requires a valid but different form of reason. Your mother and I needed to use every bit of learning, psychology, and method of thinking we possessed, while trying to make a good judgment. You know her print, "The Archer"? That's our favorite symbol of what it's like to reach a decision, and let the arrow fly toward the bull's-eye.

You have to allow for the wind and the strength of your bow and the tautness of your string and make a judgment about how true your arrow will fly. A realistic decision thuds home right on the red. There's a lot of intelligence, *practical* intelligence, in daily life, and it's not limited to scientific knowing.

The best path sometimes is a kind of *via negativa*, the way of elimination. Call to mind the practical certainty you have gained over the last few years about some occupations you do *not* want to spend your life in—as, say, a mutual fund investment analyst—and the sort of occupations you still wish to try out. I have tried to persuade you to change your mind on matters of this sort, and you are *certain* with a certainty born of experience, reflection, and self-knowledge, even if not of science or logic, when my suggestions are wrong. You may take time to make up your mind, but you tend to become quite certain and determined, once you do; and I find that admirable and worthy of emulation. It is a sort of precondition of excellence in living a life. Dante has the lukewarm blowing back and forth outside the gates of hell like dry and restless leaves.

Some people do not like to approach the question of whether God exists as a matter of knowledge; they want to talk only of faith, which here is the only thing they value. As if "being saved by faith" means going down on all fours, and not using to the utmost our capacities to know. True enough, in this area our minds thrust us into no more than a kind of darkness, a "darkling knowledge."

But this much we know about what we are: We are free and we can know. The God who made us (if there is such a God) made us free at the same time, and made us to know.

And, yes, we know that we are not completely free—that we cannot free ourselves from our most persistent faults, try as hard as we might. And we know that our knowing is often obstructed by our false loves, hot desires, coldness of heart—our minds are by no means pure, unobstructed, undistracted, untempted by evasiveness. Still, we can know and we are free, even if within limits.

Admittedly, we do not see God. We can know only *that* he is. Nearly all the humans who have ever lived have known this. Atheism is relatively rare. And, as Nietzsche pointed out, atheists who follow through on all the implications of their beliefs are nearly nonexistent.

Most atheists do create an *as if* world. They act as if reason is connected to reality, at least for pragmatic purposes. They act as if, in a rough sort of way, things make sense. They act as if progress is the law of history. They act as if reason, justice, truth, compassion, solidarity, and love were more than mere breath expelled by lying lips. But they do not say how and why they believe that reason, justice, compassion, and the rest are in some way better than irrationality, oppression, the big lie, ruthlessness, and cynicism.

What metaphysical commitments justify these beliefs? Atheistic humanists seem to believe that history is good, progressive, and upward. But why? And how did history come to be so? By irrational accident? That would seem to make accident sovereign, and dice as good as rationality.

What happens in actual living is that as we gain experience with the work of insight and love in the world—and the signs of these are in everything we look upon, if we open our eyes to them—our hearts by a spontaneous movement are lifted up in awe, unless we cut that movement short.

"What a glorious day!" we say. But whose glory is it? Whose radiance is shining through? "Thank God the letter arrived when it did," we say. (In novels at least, even atheists say such things.)

Belief in Providence is not the same as belief in Fate or Fortune, Necessity or Chance. But few persons who have ever lived, it seems, have *not* felt the presence of more than human agency in the unfolding of events, even events that seem most random. Otherwise myths of state planning, and belief in progress and being "on the right side of history" would find no footholds in human experience. As they obviously do.

It is not easy to be an atheist, without stealing the clothes of theists and Christians. What do our atheists lack but churches, Albert Camus asked, to distinguish them from being Christians? Atheism is far more parasitical on theism than it cares to confess. The University of Virginia's Richard Rorty may say that he believes that there is only chance, that contingency (that is, chance) runs "all the way down," so that the world rests on no "foundation" of reasonableness. Yet his operating beliefs—in pragmatic method, solidarity, progress, tolerance, democratic methods, and much else—are not those of someone who believes that madness and chaos rule reality. One could live a very comfortable, ordered, and rational life believing as he does.

It would be *very* odd if concepts such as *progress, tolerance,* and *democratic methods* (based on reasoned, civil argument) would work in a universe truly governed by madness—where everything occurs randomly, by chance, without order or rationality or even intelligibility.

Many people, Jana, don't see this point. They believe that the universe might be ordered in some mechanistic or Darwinian way. They want to hold on to the rationality of things, with one exception. At bottom, they hold that "it just happened"—there is no sense or meaning to it, nothing to wonder about or raise one's heart about. Just shrug, and attribute it to chance. They do this on the ground of "rationality." But what is rational in holding that, wildly improbable as it is, this world just happened to turn out as it did—filled with intelligibility, laws of science, predictable (and explainable) occurrences—by sheer chance? That in our vast galaxy (only one in untold numbers of galaxies) life should appear, and then human life, and then human consciousness and inquiry and science, is a staggering, stunning fact. To assert that this fact has no significance is to deny our rationality at its root. It is to imagine, as I said earlier, a tale told by an idiot, signifying nothing.

Grant me that God usually works through schemes of probabilities, contingencies, unique occurrences, and fields of chaos—as ancient teachings on God as Providence in a world of singulars supposed—rather than through geometric logic and in the ways of eighteenth-century rationalism. Then, if the symbol *God* means a principle that things make sense "all the way down," and if *atheism* means a universe suspended in midair—left there by an ultimate principle of chance, fate, or other expression of unreason—then at its deepest point a commitment to atheism is a commitment against intelligence.

JANA: *Okay, let me make sure I understand you before you go on. It is* because *chaos and madness do not in the end rule reality that we know God exists. In other words, it is the order and rationality of reality—sometimes obvious and other times not—that show that there must be something behind existence; that there was—and is—one design and logic behind our existence. So some proof of God comes in the "predictability" of life and nature (such as the seasons, the scent of freshly mowed grass, and the young child gurgling her first words when the psychology book says she will), while other proof comes from the unpredictability—it is, after all, his creation and plan, not ours.*

DAD: No, I am not reasoning from "the order and rationality of reality." Nor am I reasoning from "design and logic." You are attributing to me an argument both from "predictability" and from "unpredictability." That would be to have it both ways. After all, much that is at present "unpredictable," because of our lack of knowledge, is subject to further investigation, and may well become thoroughly predictable at some later date. I am reasoning less about the nature of reality, as we gradually come to know it, than about our faith in our own powers of inquiry, an often humbled faith but a vital and dogged one. I am saying that our confidence in our own capacities for insight and judgment—insight to get the point, judgment to winnow out which insights can actually be verified—should give us confidence to expect that the origin of our intelligence, and the origin of the world in which it finds itself and does its work, are closely related; indeed, that the source of both is the same. We *act* as if we trust our powers of inquiry. Why not trust these "all the way down"? (See again, Romans 1:18ff.)

Usually, secular persons (including ourselves in a secular frame of mind) think of truth as a property of propositions.

We treat truth as an impersonal property. But make a supposition—think of truth as a person, an intelligent Creator capable of understanding and loving, insight and choice. In other words, match up the image of God that we were discussing last chapter with our trust in our own powers of understanding and choosing. Suppose that God (understood as insight and love) is in fact the Creator and Provident Governor of the universe, as the vast majority of human beings have always held, based upon their experience of things. If that supposition may be countenanced, then all that we discover through science, together with all that we do not yet understand, may be thought to be radiant with intelligence "all the way down" to their Source.

What is to be lost by this move? We seem to make it by our *actions*. (We pursue inquiry unremittingly, for instance.) Why not draw the implication from what we are already doing? We *act* as if the universe is understandable "all the way down." Why not conform our belief to our actions? Is it so important to us to be *willful* in resisting God's bursting in on our awareness?

Even if to plumb those depths fully is far beyond our capacity, to decide the question about God by this route is to place one's trust in insight and judgment "all the way down." It is to hold that the sense one finds in the world is itself sensible because it is the expression of a creative intelligence. Something like that is what we mean when we affirm that the symbol "God" names something real— names, in fact, the source of everything real, the Existence that makes existents *stand out* from the nothingness of the things that do not exist, and breathes *existing* into all the things that come to be.

Like almost all humans everywhere (and most still today) the ancient Mayans—a civilization that, as you know, fascinates me, ever since my trip to the Yucatán in January 1996—told vivid stories about the Creator. The Mayan buildings are so intricate, vast, and heroic in conception and labor that they force a Eurocentric mind like mine to rearrange its sense of time and culture. However rough and brutal was the Mayan sense of how to understand and make use of their religious reflections, there is no doubt that they pushed sustained inquiry as best they could. They had no Moses to focus their sense of the power experienced in the cosmos on a single concentration (as it were) of truth, light, being. They did not rise above large, rough images of God based upon the animal and mineral kingdoms—rain, frog, jaguar, serpent, waterlily, fish. But they were reaching for something vaster and deeper, worth more than life and blood. Err they may have. But they left behind more of beauty and wonder than Mussolini, Hitler, or Stalin.

JANA: *Speaking of Hitler, et al., you've been avoiding the power of evil. How can we believe in or accept a god that allows so many horrors to occur every day? Don't forget my friend's disillusionment after her trip to Haiti. If life ends up being so miserable for so many people, why should we believe in God?*

DAD: Evil is too big a subject for me to comprehend. Here is the best I can do.

The evils and horrors we see make us doubt either that God is omnipotent or that he is good. But it is not as if the Jewish and Christian Bible doesn't confront that doubt head-on. Look at the sufferings of Job and the "suffering servant" of Isaiah (Chapter 53)—look at the Son of God bleeding on the cross, nails in his hands and feet. If God does this to his own Son, what should the rest of us expect?

God as an artist made this cosmos, this history, *as a whole*. Could he have made light without dark, good without evil? Could he have fashioned a type of human being different from us, humans who of necessity, seeing him, were overpowered with love of him, unable to turn away from him, and maybe untemptable? One supposes he could have. Why he did not, I do not know.

Yet even atheists have to be satisfied with this world; it's the only world they—or we—have got. We both, non-believers and believers, have to do the best with it we can.

Both Jewish and Christian traditions have been willing to look it in the eye—rebel against parts of it, hate parts of it, refuse to agree to parts of it, even curse parts of it, and yet, in the end, bow in wonder, awe, fear, gratitude, and love. It is a wondrous thing, this earth, this world, this history, a truly wondrous work of art beyond every other art. It evokes every passion and emotion known to art, and some that art does not yet know. You can see why Islam praises Allah the Great.

Not to wonder at the greatness of the deed—the creation of history and the world, and all that we know and *don't* yet know—is to be half dead. The beauty of creation is so exquisite it should strike us with terror. And, as the Bible teaches us, fear is the beginning of wisdom.

You mentioned a friend, pious and devout, who lost her faith in the Christian God when she went to Haiti, where she encountered a depth of misery and poverty that stunned her. Did she think that Christ on the cross was ignorant of poverty and misery? That life in Haiti in 1990 was more ignorant, poverty-stricken, ravaged with disease, and of briefer average mortality than the desert kingdoms of the Middle East in 29 A.D.? I sympathize deeply with your friend. I have often had the same feelings. Still, I resist them, for several reasons.

First, suppose I gave up my faith; would that make the condition of the poor I care about better?

Second, the faith of the poor does not seem to be shaken by their misery; on the contrary, their faith means more to them the deeper their misery. Isn't it that way with all of us? Abstractly, we can't understand how God permits poverty and misery, war and deprivation. Yet, plunged into suffering from such things, we turn more to God than we did in our comforts.

Curiously, it is middle-class people who, seeing destitution, doubt that God is good. *Destitute* people seem touched that God cares about them, loves them, and, through the Psalms, Exodus, and the passion of Christ, voices for them the realities of suffering and death—and hope.

Third, I have to trust God. When my cousin Margaret lay in pain for months with a consuming stomach cancer—she shriveled down to nothing—I couldn't understand. I could see in her eyes, too, that she didn't understand, and felt utterly abandoned. My mother died in similar inner confusion, or so I thought. Although she suffered (not so much from pain as from fear) only for a week—it was such a *long* week. It was awful to watch. I do not understand why she should have suffered so. I turn back to God, reading Job, and think it must be all right to *accuse* God of these things. Such suffering doesn't seem right. God isn't supposed to be this way. But perhaps our idea of God is too shallow. It is hard not to accuse him, though. (Of course, his response to Job was, "Where were *you*, Job, when I created the heavens and earth? Where were *you*, Job . . . ?")

Many brought up as Christians in our time have drunk deep of a sentimentality about real life that ill prepares us for the world as it is. It is wrong for us to attribute our naivete to God. God is the God of reality, with all its horrors and terrors, as well as its glories and joys. It is wrong to cut him down to the size of a pious holy card. The French novelist Léon Bloy wrote in *The Woman Who Was Poor* that the sermons of bourgeois priests come out of their mouths like air expelled from a hen's ass. Sentimental Christianity makes a mockery of God—it hasn't even begun to cope with what God intended the crucifixion to symbolize about *his* vision of human life. Human life wasn't meant to be pretty.

You yourself have known plenty of suffering. You know very well that life is at times a desperate struggle and by no means a pleasant reverie. It is true that you have been blessed with material comforts and means and relative ease. But these do not always mark their recipients as happier than those born with far less and, on the face of things, under the pain of poverty. The misery of badly governed peoples on this planet even during our lifetimes, let alone the brutal sufferings of millions in the past, is exactly what the Bible is addressed to. The Jewish people labored in cruel and wretched captivity in Babylon for generations, and again for generations in Egypt.

Not without reason has Christianity—New Covenant and Old—appealed far more strongly to the poor and wretched of this earth than to the comfortable and the powerful. The latter can hardly even understand what Christianity (or Judaism) is about. Take up your *cross* . . . ? If Christianity is not flamingly revelatory of the realities of

Haiti, it is less than it claims to be. And it actually *is*, as a matter of fact, attractive today even in Haiti and wherever people suffer and die. Christians *expect* to face suffering in life:

> We bring before you, O Lord, the troubles and perils of people and nations, the sighing of prisoners and captives, the sorrows of the bereaved, the necessities of strangers, the helplessness of the weak, the despondency of the weary, the failing powers of the aged. O Lord, draw near to each . . . Amen.

—St. Anselm (1033–1109)

JANA: *In an interview you did in* The Washingtonian *magazine while we were working on this book, you said something that really helped me with the concept of evil. You said that God is not a "Pollyanna" and he "doesn't promise us any happy endings." Those two ideas—simple though they are, perhaps because of that fact—made me see things in a new way.*

DAD: The God of the Jewish Testament sent trials and afflictions upon everyone he loved: "Whom he loves he makes to suffer." Abraham, Moses, Job, David—all without exception. Consider the New Testament, and what God did to his own Son. *To his own Son.* Will he treat us any more gently? Do we have any right to *think* he will treat us any more gently? As I said in *The Washingtonian,* our God is not a pretty God. It is not too much to say (as Job did) that he is cruel—or, at least, very tough.[1]

---

[1] When we say "cruel" of God, we do not mean "evil" but speak only from the point of view of human suffering. When we learn God's ways better, and dimly grasp his aims, we see that his hardness is softer than the kindest ways of humans, gentle and merciful beyond compare. But it is wrong to deny the pain of those ways.

JANA: *In thinking about pain, I've learned one thing: "To stop complaining and help others." I got this from a story I just read in a book called* Teaching Your Children About God *by David J. Wolpe: "A man once stood before God, his heart breaking from the pain and injustice in the world. 'Dear God,' he cried out, 'look at all the suffering, the anguish, and distress in your world. Why don't you send help?' God responded, 'I did send help. I sent you.' "*

I understand your argument for why God must exist. The probabilities of everything we know of—and don't know of—occurring by utter chance is less than nil.

But what does it really do for me, whether God exists or not? I'm still not so sure why I should care or what I should do about it. You said I should care because I "want to know the truth" about myself. What exactly did you mean by that?

DAD: No one can make anyone else care. Your attitude and that of others your age is so different from what most of my friends and I felt when we were growing up. At that time, not only God but religion seemed to us as common as apple pie, as much a part of life as patriotism, in some ways the deepest and more important thing. For example, vocations to the priesthood were so many that new seminaries were constantly being built, and old ones expanded— convents and women's colleges run by nuns, too, and hospitals, and missionaries galore.

The main thing I want to say now is, give God a chance. In Judaism, Christianity, and Islam, too, God wants each woman he called into being to know that her Creator loves her—knew her before she was born and will rejoice in her forever. God is not a watchmaker, who wound the world up and shook it to get it moving, and then said, "Frankly, my dear, I don't give a damn."

On the contrary, run and jump and hide as we may, God pursues us as a hound pursues a hare. He is always chasing us. He doesn't mind our wrestling with him, our combat against him, as Job wrestled against him. He wants us to come to him as free women and free men, standing erect. It is as free persons he values us and cherishes our love, not as slaves.

If there is a God, Jana, you are a different person from what you thought you were. The center of gravity of your universe suddenly pivots. It goes out from you to Another of far greater Light and Love. Yet this displacement does not annihilate you. On the contrary, it gives you a significance and an importance you didn't have before. It empowers you and emboldens you. You see more clearly the task to be done with your life—to make the circle of Light and Love grow in every direction imagination searches. There is much to be done. And you see, then, why the cause you serve cannot be defeated. No darkness, however protracted, can in the end prevail.

Your conscience is not taken away from you. How could it be? It is your lifeline, your electric cord, so to speak, the source of your Light. Your mind and its personal responsibility are not taken away from you—your autonomy is not lost. How could they be? These are what is most godlike in you, and the vessels of your unity with God. It is only that your autonomy is now seen to be theonomy, that is, your true self has a homing instinct—it seeks God like a heat-seeking projectile, and it is in God that your independence is fulfilled: God's rule (*theo* + *nomos*) is your self-rule (*auto* + *nomos*). What you earlier saw as *mine* you now see as more than that: it is also *his* at the same time as it is yours. The *his* in yourself is a great deal larger, and more penetrating and more luminous than the *mine*.

Yet the Creator has chosen you to be his presence in the midst of your neighbors, and to be to them as he would be. You do not feel as if you have been alienated from yourself, cheated, dwarfed. On the contrary, you feel fulfilled beyond your expectations, your merits, or your former, self-contained possibilities.

But I don't want to suggest that the transition is easy. The pain of turning to God can be very great. Here is how C. S. Lewis described what happened to him at Oxford one night, the night he admitted the reality of God into his life but two full years before he actually became a Christian:

> Remember, I had always wanted, above all things, not to be "interfered with." I had wanted (mad wish) "to call my soul my own." I had been far more anxious to avoid suffering than to achieve delight. I had always aimed at limited liabilities. . . . Doubtless, by definition, God was Reason itself. But would he also be "reasonable" in that other, more comfortable, sense? Not the slightest assurance on that score was offered me. . . . You must picture me alone in that room at Magdalen, night after night, feeling, whenever my mind lifted even for a second from my work, the steady, unrelenting approach of him whom I so earnestly desired not to meet. That which I greatly feared had at last come upon me. In the Trinity Term of 1929 I gave in, and admitted that God was God, and knelt and prayed: perhaps, that night, the most dejected and reluctant convert in all England. I did not then see what is now the most shining and obvious thing; the Divine humility which will accept a convert even on such terms. The Prodigal Son at least walked home on his own feet. But who can duly adore that Love which will open the high gates to a prodigal

who is brought in kicking, struggling, resentful, and darting his eyes in every direction for a chance of escape?

—Surprised by Joy

Some say that a child's very first conscious act is to recognize the tenderness of its mother, and to accept with joy the relief of taking her breast—the infant is needy, flails about, and finds succor. This is what it is like to find God and why we should care about finding God.

I like to think that God is pursuing you. These lines by Francis Thompson meant a lot to me once, in my twenties:

> But with unhurrying chase,
> and unperturbèd pace,
> Deliberate speed, majestic instancy,
> Came on the following Feet,
> And a Voice above their beat—
> 'Naught shelters thee, who wilt not shelter Me.'
>
> I fled Him, down the nights and down the days;
> I fled Him, down the arches of the years;
> I fled Him, down the labyrinthine ways
> Of my own mind; and in the mist of tears
> I hid from Him, and under running laughter.
>
> Up vistaed hopes I sped;
> And shot, precipitated,
> Adown Titanic glooms of chasmèd fears,
> From those strong Feet that followed, followed after.
>
> But with unhurrying chase,
> And unperturbed pace,
> Deliberate speed, majestic instancy,
> They beat—and a Voice beat
> More instant than the Feet—
> 'All things betray thee, who betrayest Me.'

—The Hound of Heaven

II

PARTICULARS

At the heart
of Christianity
is the sinner.

—Charles Péguy
(1873–1914)

The only tragedy
is not to have
been a saint.

—Léon Bloy
(1846–1917)

5

WHY IS OUR FAMILY CATHOLIC?

The difficulty of explaining "why I am a Catholic" is that there are ten thousand reasons all amounting to one reason: that Catholicism is true. I could fill all my space with separate sentences each beginning with the words, "It is the only thing that . . ." As, for instance, (1) It is the only thing that really prevents a sin from being a secret. (2) It is the only thing in which the superior cannot be superior; in the sense of supercilious. (3) It is the only thing that frees a man from the degrading slavery of being a child of his age. (4) It is the only thing that talks as if it were the truth; as if it were a real messenger refusing to tamper with a real message. (5) It is the only type of Christianity that really contains every type of man; even the respectable man. (6) It is the only large attempt to change the world from the inside; working through wills and not laws; and so on.

—G. K. Chesterton
(1874–1936)

Most gracious Father, we humbly beg you for your Holy Catholic Church; that you would be pleased to fill it with all truth, in all peace. Where it is corrupt, purify it; where it is in error, direct it; where in any thing it is amiss, reform it. Where it is right, strengthen and confirm it; where it is in want, provide for it; where it is divided and rent asunder, do make up the breaches in it, O holy one of Israel.

—William Laud
(1573–1645)

JANA: *Now that we've covered why religion is necessary and why God is important, it would be a good idea to ex-*

plain where we are coming from, Dad, where our bias lies. For you—and I in many ways as well—are biased. Our family's tradition is the Catholic Church. A tradition that you followed in a very literal sense by originally studying to be a priest, and almost becoming one (obviously I am very lucky that you felt you could serve God better as a layman!), and that Uncle Richard also followed by becoming a priest. From this tradition within the family (both your side and mom's have a tradition of Catholicism), I have a history that I can return to and explore. Dad, I know that your earlier writings—which I will admit I still have not picked up and read quite yet—had to do with struggling over belief. But once you wrestled your way through that question, how did you come to choose the Catholic Church? While it was (and is) the church of our ancestors, you could have struck out anew, yet I know that you have given a lot of thought to the matter and then stayed. Why do you think—as made obvious by your choice of it—that Catholicism is the best religion?

What exactly is the Catholic Church? Is it considered the first church of Christianity, from which all other religions have branched off? If the Catholic Church has so much to offer, how do you explain the fact that so many other religions broke away from the Church? I know that Catholicism has a sometimes corrupt and shameful past, so how do you get beyond that? Beyond, that is, the Inquisition and the materialistic and evil popes that have checkered the Church's history? If a religion provides tradition and continuity, then how can a member of that religion reconcile the occasions of human evil in that religion's tradition?

And what about the pope? I am very much intrigued by

and attracted to this particular pope we have today—John Paul II is a remarkable, impressive, and inspiring figure: as a human being, as a leader, and as a pope. But I'm not sure if I'm completely clear on exactly what the pope's role is. Are his pronouncements God's will? Are they infallible? (And what exactly does that mean?)

What are the nuts and bolts of Catholicism, its main tenets? In other words, what do you have to believe in to be a Catholic? For example, it seems to me that if one does not embrace the idea of the sanctity of life (at both ends of the human life cycle), then one cannot call oneself a Catholic, let alone a Christian.

I am very curious on this subject because not only have many friends complained to me about certain issues that they strongly disagree with (usually concerning women in the Church and birth control, and usually complaining that "the Church has to get itself into the twentieth century, for goodness sake"), but because of my own feelings. It seems to me, even though I do agree with the Church on many if not most of its teachings, that if there is no freedom for discussion, dissent, and disagreement within the Church, then the pope is no better than a dictator. I am not arguing that the Church has to be a "big tent" and let in people whose views not only contradict the very essence of the Church but would undermine its very existence, but without freedom of opinion, it is no wonder that so many different people broke away from their Catholic roots to create new branches and new religions. While many of these new religions concentrate too much on the wrath of God—the damnation and hellfire and eternal punishment for one's sinful life—and not enough on the joy of God and his love (at *least for me, that kind of religion is not appealing), many others seem to have taken much of what is good in the Catholic Church (or what was good at the time they broke away, leaving behind the corruption) and focused upon those aspects, improving upon them and concentrating on spreading them and God's love to every individual.*

It is difficult to reconcile those two images (although both are Christian religions), but it is easy to see how they are both based on ideas within the Catholic Church—which then makes Catholicism more confusing as it must obviously try to explain this seeming contradiction. (One side of which is the more wrathful God of the Great Flood in the Old Testament and the other the turn-the-other-cheek God who loved humans so much he sent his son to be sacrificed for us in the New Testament.)

In other words, Dad, I am just as unclear on the Catholic Church as I was about religion and God.

DAD: Jana, I think you are approaching the Church in a nonfruitful way. You seem to want to reduce it to something it isn't: a set of tenets that I could describe *bang, bang, bang,* and that you could then weigh *bang, bang, bang.* It isn't like that. Also, I don't think you really mean "biased" ("our family is biased"); any one perspective is necessarily finite and revisable. "Biased" implies distortion, whereas a "perspective" is only human.

The Church is primarily an inner life, a participation in the love that God has for his creation, a communion that rescues the world from its malice and indifference and slowly builds on earth "a city on the hill"—*Thy kingdom come, thy will be done, on earth as it is in heaven.* The

Church is like yeast working in history. Most of its work is invisible.

You must think of the Catholic faith as a life, a way of living in and with others, not as a club held together by a set of rules and tenets. The empirical test for it is in the living. Although others are bound to disagree, let me lay down a dare: Living as a Catholic is the most intellectually satisfying—and endlessly challenging—life there is. Try it and see. That is why persons drawn to truth and beauty (the splendor of being) are drawn to it. Besides, no other religion even presents itself as true—as the comedian Lenny Bruce used to say, "the *only* 'one true church.' " Even if you don't agree with Catholic faith, you must admit it is always supportable, point by point, with reasoned argument, backed up by the centuries and especially by Scripture. Catholics positively *invite* public disputation with others. If you want to know *why* anyone stays Catholic, it is because its faith has the ring of truth, and tests out in the living of it.

Yes, there are "beliefs." But these are more than a set of propositions to be debated—more like ways of seeing things. For instance, "Trinity" means that God wants us to think of him more as a communion of three persons than as a solitary Intelligence. He is like the love among independent friends. In other words, "Where there is love"—that is, independent love, the love of *caritas*—"there God is."

The same with "Incarnation." To become incarnate means to take on human flesh, human substance, human nature. The Greek goddess Venus took on human form from the foam of the ocean crashing on a beach—only *assumed* a human form, rather as a mask or a disguise. By contrast, Jesus of Nazareth was conceived in the womb of his mother Mary from the first moment of his gestation; he was fully human (no mere mask), fully divine. If you don't simply reject it, this is powerful stuff. You don't want to play with it, anymore than with natural gas and matches. This is not just a "tenet." If you grasp its implications, and welcome Christ into your life according to his words, it will shatter what you were before. Be careful with these words—"Jesus Christ, the incarnate Son of God." You are either willing to take them in, or not. *The Light shined into the darkness, and the darkness grasped it not.*

So it is with the rest of the "creed"—the list of the "symbols" through which those who accept the way of seeing reality taught by Jesus Christ understand the drama of human life. Each of the "tenets" of the creed opens up a new way of seeing and acting. That way of seeing has changed the world during the last two millennia. That revolution in "seeing" is what we celebrate at the year 2000.

To study the Catholic faith, study the liturgy. The liturgy is the action of the people at prayer—an expression of the whole of creation groaning in rebirth, acknowledging the beauty of God. You may not realize it, but each year the liturgy of the Church, Sunday by Sunday (and also day by day) relives the birth, preaching, death, and resurrection of Jesus Christ. Each day's readings are almost entirely composed of texts from the Jewish Testament and from the New Testament. The most consistent and constant prayers (in the chanting of the Hours seven times a day and all through the Eucharist) are the Psalms of the people of Israel. Like the movements of the planets and the seasons, the liturgy cycles with slow regularity, saturated with the Scriptures, in a movement from birth to death, and rising again.

There are two sayings I like about the Church, from opposite poles. One is: "At the heart of Christianity is the sinner." The poet Charles Péguy said that; he is thought to have become a Catholic just days before he was called up for the defense of France in 1914, and shot through the head on his first day in battle. Christianity came into being because of the sinner, for the sinner; everything begins there, returns there, works there. The other saying, by a French colleague of Péguy's, a crotchety "prophet of the Absolute" named Léon Bloy (who once opened a novel with the line: "This place stinks of God!"), runs as follows: "The only tragedy in life is not to have been a saint."

Between those two poles, pulled this way and that, each Christian struggles.

JANA: *Okay, but don't forget the details. While this image of the "idea" of the Church is very comforting, I really want to know about the pope, the creed, the whole works. God is in the details!*

DAD: I'll come back in a moment, as you will see, to your particular questions about the pope, infallibility, the main items of the creed, etc.—I'm not avoiding them. The most important thing to grasp is that Christ came to communicate the inner life of God to us, so that we might live by it. "You live, now not you, but Christ lives in you," St. Paul wrote. "Put on the mind of Christ." That is, let Christ—God—think through you, feel through you, act toward others through you, the same Word by Whom and in Whom and with Whom were shaped all the things that were made, the Pattern the Creator used as an image to diffuse through everything that is—the Image of suffering love. "He was a man of sorrows, acquainted with our grief." (Isaiah, 53; cf. Handel's *Messiah*.) It is especially in suffering that we are closest to him.

That's the main thing. The rest is housekeeping. That would take a book, not a chapter. But let me try to hit the highlights. Here are the most important "tenets."

The heart of the Catholic faith lies in the Eucharist—the sacrifice of the Mass, the reliving of Christ's atonement on the cross. At every instant of the day, somewhere around the world, both the Last Supper and Calvary are being celebrated in an eternal and universal *now,* as if time has been defeated, as if in one eternal instant God's Son is always being presented to God from the cross. In this sacrifice, Jesus reveals God's own nature: suffering love, love even to the point of a humiliating death, self-emptying, complete. "Not my will but yours be done," Jesus says to his father on our behalf. Here he echoes the words of his mother at his conception: "Be it done to me according to thy will. *Fiat mihi secundum voluntatem tuam.*" His life begins and ends with this self-giving assent. This communion between human will and God's is the reason for our creation. In the third stanza of Dante's *Paradiso,* T. S. Eliot thought, is the most beautiful line in all of world poetry, for the softness of its vowels and the depth of its insight into the heart of being:

E'n la sua volontade è nostra pace[1]
In his will, our peace. (iii.85)

---

[1]Thirteenth-century Italian differs from contemporary Italian.

Let me turn from this line to its celebration in the *Eucharist,* which means thanksgiving. The Mass (as it is called)[2] is in the form of a sacrificial meal enacted through a slow and stately dance and accompanied by readings and prayers. Its participants relive the suffering and death of Jesus Christ in Jerusalem in the year 30 A.D.; his body and blood are offered at the consecration of bread and wine. These most common foods—bread, wine—are the stuff of life, daily sustenance. These common elements the Lord lifted at his last dinner, in the upper room, in the presence of the twelve, while saying the words repeated at every Mass:

> Take this, all of you, and eat it: this is my body, which will be given up for you.
>
> Take this, all of you, and drink from it: this is the cup of my blood, the blood of the new and everlasting covenant. It will be shed for you and for all men[3] so that sins may be forgiven. Do this in memory of me.

Like Judaism, whose rite of Melchizedek and whose Seder dinner at the Passover the Eucharist imitates, Christianity is a religion of memory, renewing an event that is alive in the present and will be alive in the future, too: God's covenant with humans, the first (with the Jews) and the second (with the Gentiles). These covenants are eternal. Humans might renege on them (humans are free, and irresolute); God, never. His love is unblinking as the sun. In our weakness, we can turn away from him, avert our eyes, turn

---

[2]From its last word in Latin, "sent, completed."

[3]The traditional Latin text says for "many," not "all." This post-1965 change is troublesome.

our feet in another direction. This is the succinct definition of sin given by Aquinas: *aversio a Deo*, a turn away from God, averting one's life from the Light. A preference for darkness. A longing for nothingness.

The Eucharist is the cult that fired the heart of Western civilization, inasmuch as the Catholic cult recapitulated the Jewish cult, translated it into Greek and Latin, and then carried it across the world to the Gentiles, in a culture-forming explosion of energy: more than a thousand years of the building of monasteries and libraries, the inspiring of cities built around schools of music, languages, painting, mosaics, architecture, grammar, and all the arts, and institutes of new sciences such as botany, chemistry, metallurgy, geography, physics, mathematics, horology, and engineering. All these things are offered to God at the Mass, all human work, all of creation. The Mass is all creation at prayer.

After the consecration of the Mass, the entire people rises for a brief summation of the Christian creed, in three parts:

> Christ has died.
> Christ is risen.
> Christ will come again.

A great deal is packed into these words. "Christ" means the long-awaited Messiah of the Jews, the Son of God, at one with the Father and the Holy Spirit. This summation of the faith involves both a backward look—has died, is risen; and an anticipation of the future—*will come again*. The preordained course of time, in other words, has not yet been run; the future has not yet been prepared; before he comes again, much must be done. Herein lies the origin of the modern concept of progress. Time is not circular. It is an arrow.

The essence of the Catholic creed is summarized in these three terse sentences at the most solemn moments of the Eucharist. But understandings about how to interpret the essence of Christian faith are many. How can unity of faith be assured? Christ prayed for the unity of the Church. Unity is a crucial imperative, on the essentials and in spirit and brotherly affections.

JANA: *Excepting the belief in the real presence of Jesus in the Eucharist, most things you have said so far do not seem specific to Catholicism. My question is, What makes the Catholic Church different from the other Christian churches? Why shouldn't I just be a Methodist?*

DAD: Do not, Jana, discount the enormous benefit of the Eucharist—the gift of physical participation in the Lord's supper through union with his own body and blood. This Catholic view may be a scandal to evangelical and other Protestants, but taking Jesus at his literal word, this nourishment is important for our souls as bread and wine for our bodies. You underestimate its power for your inner life at your own loss.

The Eucharist is easy to take casually and without gratitude. Study is indispensable, study and meditation. To take into yourself as bread on your tongue in the Eucharist, as Dante remarked, "the Love that moves the sun and all the stars," the Creator of the Alps and the Rockies and the Andes, and all the oceans and the plains—in this form, in which he makes himself so humble on your behalf—is a gift beyond description.

As for any comparison with other denominations, Jana, I like to stress the unities. There are important differences, and we'll come to those. To understand them, you need to know history. (My father, with his sixth-grade education, loved to read Church history—a fascinating way to learn about the world, he said.)

Sixteen and a half centuries before you were born, two bitterly opposed interpretations of the heart of the faith swirled around throughout the Mediterranean basin, until leading bishops in the Church gathered at Nicea, in present-day Turkey, to winnow through these alternatives to formulate an accurate creed. From the beginning, Christians had understood this basic imperative: *Keep the data pure: Do not tamper with the data*. What God revealed through Jesus and the prophets, as understood always and everywhere in the Church, needs to be handed on exactly from generation to generation, not just word-for-word but understanding-for-understanding. Authority of belief comes from God. The eyewitnesses to Christ's teachings, therefore, those who actually heard his words, were accorded special reverence—not for themselves, but for the authenticity of their reports. Guarding that authenticity has been the imperative of orthodoxy—rightful teaching—ever since.

St. Athanasius (293–373 A.D.) eventually became the hero of Nicea, but in the beginning he was worried about possible abuses that might arise from a formal creed. What if people memorized the agreed-upon formulas while assigning to them different and mutually contradictory interpretations? Even worse, what if people memorized the formulas and began to think that faith means repeating correct formulas, without changing their habits of life? In other words, what if they practiced correct *verbal repetition* but not correct *living?*

Those denying the divinity of Christ had become so bold in the Church, even including many bishops, led by the dynamic preacher Bishop Arius, that Athanasius finally dropped his resistance to a credal formula, and threw his support behind the need for a mandatory rule of faith, tightly expressed in a clear but succinct statement. The final product, approved by a universal council of bishops at Nicea in 325 A.D., and ratified by the successor of Peter in Rome, has been known ever since as the Creed of Nicea or the Nicene Creed. It is the oldest and most commonly used of the canonical creeds. Catholics use it at every high Mass, but so do nearly all the Christian churches of the Protestant Reformation. Within each denomination, there developed a distinctive tradition for interpreting certain key phrases. Nearly all basic divisions in Christianity spring from such differences. Even where there are differences, however, the degree of common faith (and common understanding) is quite impressive.

Even by the time of the Nicene Creed, one observes that a certain abstract precision has been nurtured by the Catholic Church through prolonged combat and fierce argument. Fresh interpretations of doctrine, at first striking and illuminating, were often quite appealing, and would attract many followers before being submitted to rigorous examination. (When creeds are *lived*, it sometimes takes two or three generations for their implications to show up in daily life.) Thus, the widespread third-century view that Jesus was fully human, but not truly divine, only a "representative" of God or a kind of "human imitation" of God, was ultimately rejected, because it did less than full justice to Jesus' claim to be one with his Father. The acceptable formula, Nicea decided, is "true God and true man." Each phrase of the Creed, in other words, was fought over, and hammered out in one intellectual battle after another.

It is probably worth reprinting the Nicene Creed. Here is your list of basic "tenets," the essentials, in the form finally approved in 381 A.D. But it's pretty abstract, I warn you. Take it slowly. It has four main parts: Father, Son, Holy Spirit, and Church.

> We believe in one God,
> the Father, the Almighty,
> maker of heaven and earth,
> of all that is, seen and unseen.
>
> We believe in one Lord, Jesus Christ,
> the only Son of God
> eternally begotten of the Father,
> God from God, Light from Light,
> true God from true God,
> begotten, not made, one in
> Being with the Father.
> Through him all things were made.
> For us men and for our salvation
> he came down from heaven:
> by the power of the Holy Spirit
> he was born of the Virgin Mary,
> and became man.
>
> For our sake he was crucified
> under Pontius Pilate;
> he suffered, died, and was buried.
> On the third day he rose again
> in fulfillment of the Scriptures;
> he ascended into heaven

and is seated at the right
hand of the Father.
He will come again in glory
to judge the living and the dead,
and his kingdom will have no end.

We believe in the Holy Spirit,
the Lord, the giver of life,
who proceeds from the
Father and the Son.
With the Father and the Son
he is worshiped and glorified.
He has spoken through the Prophets.

We believe in one holy
catholic and apostolic Church.
We acknowledge one baptism
for the forgiveness of sins.
We look for the resurrection of the dead,
and the life of the world to come.
Amen.[4]

In each decade of one's life, one reads the Creed a little differently. Life itself teaches us lessons about one part of the Creed, then another. In my fiftieth year, I wrote a line-by-line reflection on this Creed, in the light of my own experiences and perplexities at that time.[5] I see more in it today. It bears a lifetime of growing into.

---

[4] Let me slip in a textual note: the Latin version of the ancient creed began *"I believe"*—*Credo,* first person singular, the *Credo in unum Deum* that you hear in the great Bach Mass—but the modern English translation (above) begins *"We* believe." The prayer is, of course, the prayer of a community (as in the modern translation); but I like the emphasis upon the individual person assenting to it, joining a fresh voice to the communion of the living and the dead. In general, I prefer ancient versions—they are more exact. I prefer Nicea's *"Credo,"* *"I* believe." The new Catholic Catechism has sections on both "I believe" and "We believe."

[5]*Confession of a Catholic* (1983).

JANA: *As I did not know much about them, these details about the Mass and the Creed are fascinating. But I'm still not sure exactly what it means to be Catholic. Why a church, a complicated, heavy institution?*

DAD: Excuse my roundabout ways, but I don't want you to get so lost in the trees that you forget the shape of the forest. We believe in one God, whose nature is not only personal but that of a community of persons: Who reveals his name as Father, Son, and Holy Spirit. God so loved us that he sent his Son to live among us and teach us the meaning of love: to be faithful to the will of his Father, through suffering, mockery, and disgraceful death by crucifixion, because of our sins. By his Spirit, his Son fashioned a primitive community from twelve unlikely men, who became uncommonly strong even though scattered to the winds, becoming martyrs (like their teacher) in teaching his words to all nations. Within two generations, Christianity was rooted in the entire Mediterranean basin and spreading outward in all directions.

I wish you would read Church history, like my father. It recounts an adventure as wild as any on earth. It is filled with suffering, blood, sadness, triumph, passion, tragedy, heroism, betrayal, joy, humbling, discovery.

The Roman Catholic Church, for all its glaring and universally recognized sins, has maintained a stunning continuity down the ages, while changing often from culture to culture, from age to age, something like the caterpillar in the cocoon becoming a butterfly, or the acorn an oak. It is now what it was in the beginning, and yet it is remarkably different. It has learned many lessons from history. It is not a static community; but its principle of change is fidelity to the original deposit of faith entrusted to it. I have always liked the surprising line about the Roman Church by the great nonbelieving historian, Lord Macaulay (1800–1859):

> She may still exist in undiminished vigour when some traveller from New Zealand shall, in the midst of a vast solitude, take his stand on a broken arch of London Bridge to sketch the ruins of St. Paul's.

It is the *inner* life of the Catholic people that is the decisive reality—a part of human life hard for outsiders to see. Despite all the sinfulness and mediocrity of most of us, it is often stunning to see the holiness God brings forth in some members of this messy church. Side by side with the most sinful and corrupt popes of the eleventh and other centuries, there were beautiful and devoted lives being lived and there were many saints, known and unrecognized. (I often wonder what marvels of holiness we will one day discover to have been active all around us in ordinary people whose inner depths we never suspected. They were polite to us, and reserved about themselves, so we never noticed. Sometimes I say a prayer for unknown holy persons, to strengthen them and to be strengthened by them.)

The best way to understand what it is to be Catholic is through the lives of exemplary Catholics—Jesus, first of all; second, the first of those He redeemed, his mother; and all the saints.

JANA: *Say a little more about Jesus Christ. I have trouble thinking about him, not as a man but as god. It's the same problem I have thinking about god, in general. I liked what you said about light and love, and I'm groping toward the step beyond the idea that everything that is, has meaning and can be inquired into. But what does this have to do with Jesus? I have the impression that Protestant churches, like the Baptists, make more out of Jesus than Catholics do. Is that right? They seem to talk more about him.*

DAD: It is customary for unbelieving philosophers and artists (like Goethe) to write of Jesus as one of the great moralists or preachers of all time. Even Thomas Jefferson wrote out in his own hand a personal notebook of all the moral teachings of Jesus, in four columns, one for each of the languages of the New Testament. Jefferson praised Jesus for presenting the most sublime and the most practical moral teaching of all time. As president, Jefferson even had his version of the New Testament distributed at government expense to the Indian tribes of the Louisiana Purchase, so that they could learn the moral code crucial to the prospects of liberty. But there is a real problem with this high praise for the man Jesus.

If this man was only a man, he wasn't a very admirable moralist. This man said God was his Father. He said he himself was one with the Father, and also one with the Holy Spirit. He said he would die, but then on the third day rise up from the dead. He said that the bread that he held in his hands, and the cup of wine, were his body and blood, and that those who ate and drank of these would live with him forever; and he did not back away from those hard words even when people began to leave him because of them. He compared this miraculous body and blood of his (in the bread and the wine) to the miracle of the manna in the desert. He said he would come again to judge the living and the dead. He said that on the last day he would raise up both the living and dead and that, body and soul, the just (those he made to be just by his suffering and death) would live with him forever. He was the only religious leader ever to promise everlasting life to bodies as well as souls. (It is important to repeat this: He said his teaching is not solely about souls; it is about our bodies, too, as temples of God's presence.)

This man Jesus did not merely comment on the Scriptures; he spoke as one who claimed authority to authorize new ones, to revise what had already been written, and to replace it with new formulation. No wonder many who heard him dismissed him as a heretic, pretender, and danger.

The truth is, Jana, you have to meet this man yourself and decide: If he is not who he said he is—the Logos, the Word, the Son of God, one with the Father and Holy Spirit, God among us—he is a megalomaniac, a mad man. He is not a trustworthy teacher. You have to study him and live with him a while, and decide.

A decision by you about your relation to Jesus is a momentous decision. It will affect not only the way you read history but also the way you understand yourself. Christ's life is history's axial point. Before him, everything is preparation. After him, everything changes. Look at him only from the point of view of how his work made Judaism known to the world. Today in this world there are 2 billion Christians, only about 13 million Jews. Still, the God of Abraham, Isaac, and Jacob is known to virtually the whole world, and the idea of one God and one standard of truth is, if not universally clung to, everywhere known. So is the idea of history having a point or a purpose—that is, of progress—and the idea of personal responsibility in conscience. In other words, the idea of liberty. Christ altered history at its core. He is its Lord.

These are some of the reasons why the very early Catholic churches, East and West, have over the central altar huge mosaics of Jesus as Lord of the universe, Lord of history: the Word, in whose image all things were made.

I think that the Catholic people have been fighting a double battle on behalf of Jesus for many centuries. First, they fought to prevent the image of Jesus in the gospels from degenerating into an image of a nice, sentimental man, a kind of cuddly universal hugger. Against this, they sought to focus on his lordship over creation, his role as God and Judge. Second, against those who tried to spiritualize and etherealize Jesus too much, and to treat him as a distant godlike figure remote from everyday life, St. Francis of Assisi created the Christmas creche with its very human setting: God become man in a cowshed, under the warm breath of farm animals. *True God and true man*, as the Nicene Creed formulated it. The role of Mary in showing us the humanity of Jesus in her womb and at her breasts has won heartfelt gratitude from Christians from the beginning.

On your point about the evangelicals, Jana, I too have noted the tenderness toward Jesus in the hymns and expressions of evangelical Protestants, which I wish Catholics would emulate. Evangelicals seem to stress so much more effectively a personal encounter between each of us and Jesus, as if we ourselves stood in the scenes described in Scripture. Nonetheless, the philosophical turn of my own mind requires abstract reflection on the nature of God and the Logos; I need more than tenderness. On this point, the reflections of the Church Fathers—from St. John Chrysostom (the Golden-Tongued) in the East, to St. Augustine in the West—are very rich. To my mind, no inquirer in history is more serene and spacious in thinking about these subjects than St. Thomas Aquinas.

I strongly encourage you to read a good life of Christ soon. Every generation produces its own marvelous studies, reflecting the prevailing temperament and interests of that age. The person of Jesus is rich enough to bear such endless reflection. Also, it is a good discipline for a young writer to follow the practice of Dostoyevsky: to read a little from the New Testament every day, concentrating on the figure of Christ, until it soaks through your imagination. You can't go wrong doing that. You cannot go wrong, even if you are not a Christian; for it will open up your mind to the most fundamental springs of the Western imagination. But you should open up your heart to conversion, as well, not merely seek to be educated. Otherwise, you won't quite experience the seduction that God can perform.

JANA: *Can you give me an example how this helped Dostoyevsky?*

DAD: Humble charity, Dostoyevsky wrote, is the most powerful force in the universe. One act of charity—a smile of kindness given for nothing—takes only seconds to girdle the universe, he said. There is a kind of electromagnetic band of love (of that special kind of love, suffering love, *caritas*) surrounding the world. Such *caritas* is a love for others *as others*, for what they *are*, rather than for what use, pleasure, or utility they provide anyone else. To this wavelength of the spirit, every human spirit is connected. Some persons pump into *caritas* new energy; some draw its energy down. *Caritas* (exemplified in Christ dying for us on the cross) is the life force of the human spirit. All associations draw from it. Even every band of thieves depends upon a minimum degree of community. *Caritas* is the inner life on which the Christian faith by every symbol, act, rite, and liturgy is trying to put us "on line." This vision shaped the movement of many of Dostoyevsky's novels.

JANA: *And the main source of this is in Rome?*

DAD: Not for Dostoyevsky! He hated Rome, with the thousand-year memory of the Eastern church. For Catholics, the papacy is not the source, only the servant, of this love. Each successive papal reign brings forth a flawed and less-than-perfect representative of Christ. If you look at the popes—264 of them including Peter—you will not see Christ in them, not at least with the eyes God gave you.[6] *Faith* may instruct you that in that man—in those gray or green or blue or brown eyes, behind that wide or narrow, smooth or furrowed brow, under those bushy or thin or whitened or black eyebrows—lies the vicar of Christ chosen for his time and place.

The same faith taught the generation of Jesus that what they saw was not solely the young man who met their eyes but the Son of God. It was not so obvious then that he was God-among-us. He seemed to many to be merely the

---

[6]You can find a list of them, by name and date, in the *Catholic Almanac*.

commoner, Jesus of Nazareth. It is not so obvious, either, that Wojtyla or Roncalli or Montini or Pacelli or any of the other 260 incumbents in that office are Christ's vicars. Yet they are.

Their charge is to keep the faith on its foundations and to strengthen their brother bishops in their universal mission: to preach the gospel, the whole gospel, and nothing but the gospel. Their office has traditionally been described thus: to be the servant of the servants of God. Their function is to be the worldwide Church's symbol and living center of unity—to keep the worldwide churches of the many nations together, singing from the same sheet of music. They protect individual bishops isolated in nations in which dictators bully them, imprison them, even slay them (as Thomas of Canterbury was slain by Henry II on December 29, 1170)—they protect such bishops by giving them a reason to speak to dictators truly: "I cannot do as you ask me because I represent the pope, who does not permit me to do as you say—your quarrel is with him." In this way, virtually no Roman Catholic bishop was forced to cave in under Communist oppression from 1917 to 1991; all had the possibility of clinging to the bishop of Rome as to a lifeline, as did Slipji, Mindszenty, Stepinac, Wyszynski, and so many others.

Recently, a front page article in *The Washington Post* described the pope as an old male "dictating" to Catholics a "black-and-white" position on euthanasia that overlooks "the gray" areas. (But just what *is* the middle ground between killing someone—euthanasia by a blunter name—and not killing him?) But the pope does not "dictate." He has no authority of his own. He is *dictated to* by the teaching of

Christ, as worked out in the intellectual tradition of the Church down the ages. This teaching is recognizable independently of his person. He is a faithful reporter of that teaching, not a creator of it. It is not his to alter or to bend to his pleasure. It disciplines *him*.

In fact, if the pope misreads the common faith or misstates it, many voices in the Church—other bishops, priests, theologians, lay persons—will remind him of authentic authorities and earlier witnesses. He is as much a servant of the teaching of Christ as they are. Often enough, popes have been chastised by the faithful for papal infidelities. There have been many saintly popes (a higher proportion than in any other profession), but a brace of very bad ones, too. The appearance of bad popes teaches Catholics that our faith is not in human beings, but in God who has chosen to work with clay.

On some occasions, the college of bishops has been more reliable than a particular pope. More than once, a single saint—St. Catherine of Siena (1347–1380), for example—went over the heads of passive bishops, upbraided the pope, and by the force of the gospels, young woman though she was, shamed the pope to return the papacy from Avignon to Rome. In this sense, the Church is governed by checks and balances. One part of the Church is always in reserve as a check and balance to other parts. (The example of St. Catherine shows that, in the church, holiness trumps legal authority.)

In our time, a strong pope is calling an end to the drift and laxity characteristic of Catholic life in Western Europe and the United States since 1965. Wojtyla has sounded a wake-up call. This has won him the high honor of making many enemies in the church.

JANA: *Your assistant Cathie wrote on an earlier draft that she hated the concept of papal infallibility: "I don't see how you can say that a pope isn't human like the rest of us, a sinner. He isn't superhuman. Why make him into a kind of God?" Good question!*

DAD: She's right about the pope being a sinner. In the tenth and eleventh centuries, there was a string of really bad popes whose behavior would singe your socks off. And even the best of them, as I tried to suggest above, are only human, sinners like you and me. Popes examine their consciences before God and confess their sins to another priest regularly, like you and me. The word for being free of sin is "impeccable." Impeccable the popes are *not*.

Yet Scripture clearly singles out Peter among the twelve, and Jesus himself assigns Peter special offices and gives him special promises. The Church of Jesus needs a Peter, a center, a point of reference and responsibility to "confirm the brethren." "On this rock [the Aramaic name Jesus gave Simon, *Kephas*, means *rock*], I will build my church," Jesus said to Peter, "and the gates of hell will not prevail against it." (Matt. 16:18) The real rock, of course, is by no means the man Peter, but the grace of God working in him and the church. As it says again: "What you bind on earth shall be bound in heaven, and what you loose on earth will be loosed in heaven." (Matt. 16:19) Needless to say, Protestants strongly dispute the meaning of these texts.

Still, down the ages, even before Peter established a Christian community at the heart of the Roman Empire, in Rome, Peter's special ministry served the other apostles and the whole church, not solely his immediate flock; and it has continued to do so afterwards at Nicea and all the other councils, for example. Recognizing that the papacy has been a wedge of division among Christians, John Paul II has urged other Christians, as the new millennium opens, to offer suggestions about how that office can best serve all Christian communities—how should it be reformed?

Down the ages, for instance, the authority of the successor of Peter has been tempered by experience, and channeled and disciplined by checks and balances. The effective authority of the successor of Peter can be no greater than the consent the faithful give it. If all turn their backs upon Peter, he is powerless. If all pay him a due measure of obedience, it is because of the authority Jesus vested in Peter and his successors, not for any other reason. A somewhat misleading aura has grown up around each pope (poor man!) from the prestige of great predecessors. But experienced men and women quickly see through it to the reality of the man beneath the outer garments. It is the office, not the aura, that in the end gains and holds respect.

The bishop of Rome is said to have the charisma (gift) called infallibility, a special protection of the Holy Spirit, the Spirit of Truth, that takes effect only under four strict and narrowly drawn conditions that are seldom fulfilled. Its use is rare. Most popes have never invoked it. A pope is granted the special grace of making such a decision about the authenticity of purported teachings of the Church (in the sense of deciding whether something is of God or not) if and only if he does the following: (a) limits his comment to propositions of faith and morals; (b) self-consciously, formally, and publicly intends to teach the whole Church with this special charism (grace, gift); (c) speaks in accord with the teaching of the universal church—as it has been at all times and all places; and (d) speaks in communion with all the bishops and the whole Church. In other words, "infallibility" is not a gift to the pope. It is a gift to the whole Church, for the sake of the whole Church, held within limits by the witness of the whole Church. The pope is no Lone Ranger.

God did not abandon his Church to the waves of history, without giving her a gyroscope by which to stay true to course, no matter what the buffeting.

Protestant writers, especially evangelicals, find the office of the pope a hateful scandal, and even today some think of the pope as "the whore of Babylon." They recognize only one authority, Sacred Scripture, and hold that the Holy Spirit directs each individual, no one of them in a special way (not even for the sake of the community of faith). Scripture alone, *sola scriptura*, is one of the Reformation's two greatest battle cries. (The other is *sola fide*, salvation by faith—trust—in God's saving power, and that alone.) By contrast, Catholics note that the New Testament, for example, was not put in its current form until 373 A.D. and 397 A.D., in two separate councils of the Church confirmed by the pope. Scripture itself does not invoke the rule *sola scriptura;* in fact, in many passages St. Paul and others speak of protecting the teaching handed down from Jesus through the apostles. Scripture is no doubt the chief fruit of this intergenerational transmission. But Scripture must be understood in the context of the community that preserved it, the community that steadily winnowed out false gospels from true.

I think you have probably encountered, Jana, the visceral antagonism many Protestants still feel toward anything having to do with popes. The papacy is an antisymbol for some. Of course, many Protestants admire this particular pope, John Paul II, for his fearlessness in announcing the gospel even to hostile audiences. "This is a pope who knows how to pope!" one of my Baptist friends says, with an admiration that surprises him.

On such matters, Christians have been divided for centuries. It is not an insignificant matter. Still, on so many other matters, there is a wonderful unity.

JANA: *What about freedom for discussion and dissent? I hear lots of objections about that, too. Even from Catholics.*

DAD: On practical questions, like religious liberty, democracy, and the right to personal economic initiative, Rome was cautious, or even wrong, for many years, while a few thinkers such as the American Jesuit, John Courtney Murray—sometimes under fire from the orthodox—led the Church in new and better directions. In its worldwide structure, the Catholic Church has a set of checks and balances. At some point, when the matters at stake are not official doctrine, but some practice or other, bishops (in one region or several) lead the way; or a group of theologians; or lay people; and, at other times, the pope has been the lonely, heroic and far-seeing figure. In the heat of argument, in the generation that must make a crucial new turn, it is often very hard to see who is right.

Was Pius XII right during World War II (not knowing future events) to avoid dramatic condemnations of Hitler's Holocaust? Hitler's attempt to exterminate Europe's Jews—and millions of others—was an unprecedented evil. Some say the pope should have spoken out fearlessly against him, even if no one else did. The pope's decision was not a matter of doctrine—of course Hitler was doing great evil—but about how best to limit the evil. Some argue that a papal confrontation with Hitler, especially in the years before D-Day (June 6, 1944), would only have inflamed the Führer and led to worse horrors. The Catholic bishops of the Netherlands early condemned the Nazis, for example, and the Nazis replied with great violence. In hindsight, I wish the pope had spoken out (but that's easy to say). Others I greatly respect judge that Pius XII made the best of evil circumstances. The wartime Rabbi Pinchas Lapide, in *Three Popes and the Jews*, estimates that practical Catholic relief efforts, led by the popes, saved 840,000 Jewish lives. Nonetheless, the "scandal" of relative papal "silence" has been great.

Is Pope John Paul II wrong today to speak dramatically and loudly against abortion? Many liberals say so. He probably has learned from the example of Pius XII: Silence never again!

A harder example. Recently, Pope John Paul II called upon the witness of Jesus in choosing his apostles, as well as the witness of the apostolic church, of the fathers, and of the church of all ages and all nations to assert that he has no authority to decide that women can be ordained priests. Cardinal Ratzinger, whose task in the pope's administration is to study fidelity to Christ's teaching, affirmed separately that this papal assertion is an infallible statement, not by virtue of any assertion of John Paul II (which lacked the requisite formality), but by virtue of the unbroken and universal teaching of the Church. We'll come back to this particular question later (Chapters 6 and 10).

This debate will no doubt go on for decades. Nonetheless, we have a firm indication from the successor of Peter that his office lacks authority to alter the practice Christ instituted.

JANA: *Don't forget my question about the two ideas of god—the wrathful and the merciful—and the differences between the Old Testament and the New Testament.*

DAD: Be careful not to accept stereotypes about the God of Judaism, who is in fact exactly the same as the God of Christianity, every bit as tender and merciful and faithful to his promises. The God of wrath hates evil; the God of mercy is tender toward repentant sinners. Jana, I need to explain something about the unusual—and asymmetrical—relation between Christians and Jews. As Jews see it, Judaism does not need Christianity for its self-understanding. But Christians do need Judaism, just to understand ourselves. To be a Jew, a Jew doesn't have to be a Christian. But to be a Christian, a Christian has to be to a remarkable extent a Jew. Never forget that in becoming man, God had his pick of all peoples, and chose to be born of a Jewish mother, to become Jewish, and to root his first community among Jews.

Jesus was an observant and faithful and appreciative Jew, and everything he said and did was aimed to carry Judaism forward. Christianity, so to speak, carries Judaism to the Gentiles: makes the God of Abraham, Isaac, and Jacob known to the four corners of the world. The love of God and neighbor sometimes thought to belong to the Commandment of Love in an exclusively Christian sense is actually the Jewish Commandment of Love. Christ carried it further to love even of enemies, but even this has Jewish precedents. For virtually everything Christian, there are Jewish precedents, and Jesus and the evangelists and later preachers delighted in pointing these out. They thought continuity fortified, rather than weakened, the message.

You can believe everything that Jews believe, learn everything that Jews have to teach, even hope that Judaism lasts forever (God's covenant with His people is forever) so that it may always keep its distinctive lessons fresh for us, in the way that Jews believe them. None of this will prevent you from being a good Christian. "Do not think that I have come to abolish the law and the prophets," Jesus said, "I have come, not to abolish them, but to fulfill them." (Matt. 5:17)

Always have a special reverence for Jews. More than any others they are carriers of the deepest mysteries of the human race, the people whom God chose. In times of perplexity, side with Jews. Do not let them be alone. This is the advice my father gave me, during World War II, and even though not at first understanding it I came to see its point.

To defend Jews is to defend something crucial to yourself: Christians must think of themselves as Jews, as their Savior is. I have two or three friends who have also made this their rule, and they turn out to be among those I most admire in many other things as well. It is also deeper than you may at first imagine. Let it rest in your heart.

Regarding the other Christian religions, I see each one of them as teaching *part* of what the Catholic Church teaches, but not all. And I think that they lack, organizationally, the checks and balances required for a worldwide universal communion. They also—many of them—tend to forget the long traditions of the Catholic people prior to the Reformation; this makes some of them vulnerable to the desert heat of modernity, since their roots are not deep enough. Honestly, Jana, I would prefer *not* to talk about their deficiencies, as I see them. All of them produce holy people. Will you let me just say that most converts do experience becoming Catholic like "coming home."

I want to emphasize in conclusion the fact that we are sinners in the Catholic Church, from top to bottom; ours is a church of exceedingly imperfect people. Looking around at us, no one would ever say, "This is the top of the pack, the cream of the human race." It's a pretty lowly bunch God picked for his people. Sometimes I think your generation expects too much. All young people do. I did.

The Catholic Church is always an unfinished adventure. Much depends upon the response that you and I and other Catholics give to God's call within us. Yet, in the end, even when we are weak and fail him, God has ways of making up for our weaknesses, and bringing the Church through storms and dangers and predictions of doom. We have his promise that, until he comes again, not even the gates of hell will prevail against her. Do not ever bet against the Church. History is strewn with losers of such bets, even when all the evidence seemed to support them.

To vary what my priest-friend in Poland says, God supplies for our deficiencies, the deficiencies of the human church, which are many.

Yet I think no religious community on earth has so large (so "catholic") a vision of beauty, and beauty is the splendor of truth, the splendor of being itself. If beauty is a mark of the true church—because all beauty is of God—where else on earth is a more commodious home, than among this poor and humble flock? As James Joyce said of us: "Here comes everybody!"

6

CAN I PICK AND CHOOSE WHAT I BELIEVE?

Give me, O Lord, a steadfast heart, which no unworthy affection
    may drag downwards;
Give me an unconquered heart, which no tribulation can wear out;
Give me an upright heart, which no unworthy purpose may tempt
    aside.

—St. Thomas Aquinas
(1225–1274)

And so I sometimes think our prayers
    Might well be merged in one:
And nest and perch and hearth and church
    Repeat "Thy will be done!"

—Sir Thomas Browne
(1605–1682)

JANA: *First, I want to say up front that I'm not trying
to "cheat" or be lazy—whether intellectually or physically.
Now, say I've picked a religion and a church to belong to
and I embrace what they stand for and believe in, the problem is, what if I don't want to embrace everything? Do I
need to swallow the whole kit-and-caboodle, lock, stock,
and barrel, or is there room within a religion for disagree-
ments? I'm not saying that someone should be able to
choose a Christian church and decline to believe in Jesus,*

for example, or that someone can remain a member while supporting an idea that completely undermines the religion. Obviously neither of those situations is compatible with belief in that particular religion. I would argue that certain subjects, such as the sanctity of life, are not issues up for discussion. But that is not the sort of issue I'm referring to here.

What I am curious about is whether one can disagree with one's own religion on the slightly more "peripheral"— and I use that word with great hesitation—issues such as married priests, women priests, etc. As most people know, the Catholic Church does not allow either married or women priests. Now, since I disagree with the Church on these issues (I particularly would like to see married priests), does that mean I shouldn't bother belonging to the Catholic Church? Or is there room for discussion, debate, and disagreement? Let's face it, some of the other Christian churches do allow priests (or ministers) to be women or to marry—the Episcopal Church, for example—so wouldn't it make more sense for me to become an Episcopalian?

In other words, should I choose the religion I most agree with on all the issues and embrace it? Or, can I reject certain practices of the church to which I belong, and still remain a "true" member? That is, can one pick and choose the issues of one's religion that one is willing to accept?

Again, it is not that I want to cheat to avoid the amount of effort believing and belonging requires, but there are certain stances with which I don't, or may not, agree. What then?

DAD: Let me start by rephrasing your most practical question: On those days when you think that the Catholic Church should allow the ordination of women, just like the

Episcopal Church, you wonder if it wouldn't be more honest for you just to become an Episcopalian. And the same when you think that Catholic priests should be allowed to marry, just like Episcopal priests and the ministers of most other churches.

So, what ought you to do? And, in general, what should others do, who want to be orthodox and still keep some room for choice?

Let me go right to your practical question directly. Afterwards, I can jump to the more general dilemma faced by any believer who wants to be orthodox (faithful to basics, without cutting corners) in a world whose current orthodoxy is to follow individual preferences.

The *easy* course of action for someone of your beliefs is to note that there are a lot of Catholics who agree with you, and to take comfort from their company. Paul Johnson,[1] a serious Catholic, argues that there *should* be women priests in the Catholic Church and that there undoubtedly will be; and the same for married priests. He doesn't consider these to be central points, and I doubt if he is looking to do serious battle over them. (He is willing to fight many other battles on many other fronts.) Perhaps I am wrong about that; he always defends ably what he holds.

There *are* people who think that the issue of women priests is so central that they are prepared to leave the Catholic Church (unless they hope for some change in the future). But most people who express an opinion on these two points do not consider them central enough for so drastic a break. Thus, to your question: Can you still be a Catholic while holding that there should be women priests and

---

[1] *The Quest for God: A Personal Pilgrimage.*

married priests? (I recognize that your question is more general, for all believers, but this is one example.) My first answer is, yes, many Catholics share such reservations, on these or other matters. These are not the utterly central issues of Christian faith. They do not figure in the Nicene Creed, or any other major creed. You could still hold a tremendous amount in common with other Catholics, including all the essentials, and not be convinced on these and similar matters.

One could even say that most people (alas) do not give serious thought to the large inventory of Christian beliefs and could not honestly tell you, if asked, what exactly they thought about all of them. They "believe" them in a notional sort of way. But they have never really made them part of the living tissue of their mind or imagination, and never really modified any particular action of theirs on account of them. Such items of belief are nonfunctioning keys on their piano. (God is very patient with his people.)

A wonderful Italian archbishop, who had some experience with dissent in America, commented: "Yes, such dissent is too bad—but, then, the church in your country is *alive*! People care about their beliefs, and so they argue. To argue is the sauce on the pasta—you cannot eat only sauce, but you would not want a pasta without a sauce!" It is far better to argue against a doctrine you don't believe in than merely to rush over it and ignore it. How would you ever come to understand it (assuming you ever will) unless you wrestle against it?

Before I leave this "easy" course of action, and turn to the harder, let me rephrase the question. Above, you asked: Can I still be a Catholic (or Baptist, or Presbyterian) and hold *x*? Now turn the question slightly and put it another way: If you hold *x* when the Church teaches non-*x*, are you *fully* Catholic (Baptist or Presbyterian)? The obvious answer is no. But that isn't the end of the story.

By "fully Catholic," I mean that you have completely thought through every item of Catholic faith, and made it part of your working practice. One does in fact meet people like that, including many lay people. But there are many good Catholics who have not advanced that far, and yet are quite admirable in their faith—maybe even willing to give their lives for it. In gymnastics, on the dismount from a vault, "perfect" is a very high score. In matters of faith, the marker is higher than Olympic standards. So it is important not to expect more of ourselves than we can give. God doesn't.

In addition, there is a useful distinction to be made about the *spirit* in which dissent is made. It is one thing to dissent with a closed, stubborn, and hostile mind, hardened by an ill will. It is quite another to dissent with an open mind and an open will. In the latter case, one does not understand, but one would like to, if evidence and argument allowed one.

C. S. Lewis recounts in *Surprised by Joy* a long night of argument with two Oxford colleagues, beginning at dinner and continuing until three A.M. when during a walk outdoors his objections to a particular aspect of the Christian creed— one far more central than those you have brought up— slowly dissolved. Thus, even under the best conditions, humans need time to find their way. Not everyone is lucky enough to have two Oxford guides willing to hear out all their objections and help them identify their blockages. (Incidentally, Lewis wrote a very good essay offering reasons why the Christian tradition requires male priests, and why a change here would change the meaning of the faith at its core.[2])

The *hard* course of action that I would propose to you follows from the last points I was just developing. If the easy course is simply to go along, taking comfort from the company of other dissenters, the harder course is to work at figuring out what is wrong (if anything) in your dissent. Remind yourself of the reasons why you attribute any teaching authority to the Church in the first place. If Christ did not entrust that authority to the Church, and if the Holy Spirit does not protect and guide her in the fulfillment of that task, what would be the point of heeding her teaching even for a moment?

The questions you raise have weight chiefly (but not only) in the Catholic Church. But they also trouble believers in other religions and other branches of Christianity, including those Protestant churches in which the church as church does exercise discipline on individual members. (In some cases, church authority is located in the local church, in others in the district synod, and in still others in a national or international body.)

It may surprise you, but serious Protestant teachers also struggle with the authority of the church, and are dismayed by those in the pews who say that "the Protestant principle" locates final authority in each individual conscience, apart from any authoritative norm. These serious teachers are dismayed that many ordinary Protestants take it as their

---

[2]"Priestesses in the Church," in *God in the Dock: Essays on Theology and Ethics*.

birthright to choose a church for themselves, to change it fairly easily according to their own judgment on how it "fits" them, and to decide within ample limits which doctrines to hold (and how to interpret them) as they see fit. They would like to see greater fidelity to the Reformation tradition.

Orthodoxy means "straight teaching" or "right teaching." It means keeping the data of faith pure, uncorrupted, and honest. In courts of law, the defense often attacks the "chain of custody" of the evidence. How do we know that the evidence brought to court is the same as that recovered at the crime scene, and how do we know that no one has tampered with or "doctored" it?

Those religions that rely upon a revelation from God or upon the teaching of a great teacher have a similar worry about the custody of the data. The chain of custody is an important matter. In religion, the chain of custody is called "the tradition"—the record of what successive generations of believers held to be the data, and of the light in which the data should be interpreted. To worry about orthodoxy is to worry about evidence-tampering.

JANA: *Does what you just said mean that to worry about the basic truths of faith is to worry that the tradition passed down to us has somehow been corrupted? That what we believe in today may not necessarily be what God originally intended? For example, as a child I played the "telephone game," wherein one child whispered a sentence to the next child until it went all the way around the circle. Needless to say, when the last child repeated out loud what she had heard, it was usually far different from what the first child had said. Is that problem similar to what you mean by worrying about "evidence tampering?" I need some concrete examples to help me understand.*

DAD: That's exactly the worry about evidence tampering. That's why "tradition" is embodied mostly in written documents, the recorded decisions of councils of the church, for example, and the recorded teachings of bishops and popes and learned doctors and commentators. In Judaism, too, the recorded teachings of the rabbis offer an authoritative body of commentary and interpretation, and a record of concrete advice and the reasons for it. For centuries, however, before writing and reading were widespread, oral traditions were also guarded with great seriousness. Disputed divergences were submitted to adjudication. Jealousy about evidence tampering is as old as religious tradition.

Let me use the two examples you put forward, women priests and married priests. The tradition has treated these as two very different kinds of question. Take married priests first.

At times, priests (but not bishops) have been allowed to be married, as in the Eastern churches affiliated with Rome, some of whose traditions antedate the years in which Peter took up residence in Rome. Even in the Roman church, there have been periods when celibacy was not universally insisted upon. The present practice—mandatory universal celibacy for priests of the Roman rite—is many centuries old, but does not extend back to antiquity, certainly not in an unbroken line. It is less a *doctrine* than a *practice*, but it does have a doctrinal point: the fuller imitation of the chastity of Christ.

The reasons for this practice are largely practical, springing both from material concerns (such as inheritances and legal complexities) and also spiritual purposes. In antiquity and the Middle Ages, land was the main form of wealth and the first-born son was legally heir to the whole landed estate (to prevent a family-damaging division of properties). Thus, the temptation for ambitious clergymen to secure properties through marriage, and to commingle the personal with the churchly, was immensely corrupting of Christian morals. Moreover, for a priest to be "married" to the whole church, for the sake of God, requires a commitment of a different order from those of most vocations in ordinary life. The kind of commitment demanded is extraordinary, and can be met only with God's grace. Not only Catholics but others, too, honor Catholic priests as they honor no other clergymen. The enemies of the Church have shown a special ferocity against priests.

Your mother and I disagree on this, Jana: She would like to see the clergy married; I am in favor of the tradition of celibacy. I even argue that those periods in which celibacy was most cherished and best practiced became especially dynamic periods in the life of the Church, thrusting missionaries to the antipodes, leading many to face any danger, and sending pulses of optimism, vitality, and evangelical love throughout the world. Young men who have full hearts pour the love that they deny themselves for spouse and children into care for all the people. The most loving among them often make the best priests. Your mother counters that priests would understand so many more things, and develop a rounder psychology of life, if they were married and had to cope with kids. I reply that, yes, they would become more like everybody else; I don't see the comparative advantage.

I think your mother doesn't look at the downside of a married clergy, which after all the Church has some experience of in the past. Questions of financial ambition will have to have greater scope, on her plan, and there will be acute questions of inheritances and property, disputes with heirs, and very serious problems about divorce among the clergy. I would be willing to try her path through a small number of experiments in special situations. Experience gained by this path may lead to larger experiments. But do not be surprised if such changes have less favorable results than expected.

The point is, no fundamental doctrinal matter is really implicated in this discussion. It is mainly a matter of discipline, practice, and practical considerations (not forgetting the practical spiritual implications). Besides, a compromise is ready at hand. We could have *two* orders of priests, one celibate for the kingdom of God's sake, and one married. I am not in favor of this compromise, but could live with it. In this line, some four hundred Episcopal priests have become Roman Catholics during this generation, and some have sought and won permission to carry on their priesthood as already married men. This fact adds weight to my argument that in this matter practice is more involved than doctrine. Your mother would like more such experiments, such as the ordination of at least some ordinary married men; but I think that a mixed discipline would compromise young men already committed, or about to commit, to celibacy.

The question of women priests is harder. Thirty years ago, one heard no demand for it, nor did one hear such an argument in earlier generations. Without question, the impulse behind the movement for women's ordination arises from modern feminism, abetted by the power of mass communications. This does not mean it cannot be a movement incited by the Holy Spirit, to meet new conditions in the world. But very heavy reasons tell against that.

This is not the place to go into that whole discussion; we will come to it in Chapter 10. I just wanted to say enough, Jana, to show that the question of women priests is a BIG question.

For if, as is increasingly charged, the traditional teaching is *unfair* to women, *unjust*, then the Church has not just fallen into a temptation here or there, it has been radically sinful since its founding, and was built upon a foundation of injustice.

What is fundamentally at stake is the rock on which to build a humane culture for the future. It is a battle over the axial choice to be made regarding which is the better theology of human life: one that spells out the differences-cum-complementarity to be assigned to male and female—or, at the other pole, their homogeneity and substitutability. Which theology more greatly honors woman, and better arms her for the future, the teaching of feminism or the teaching of the Catholic tradition? Which, radically, is the true and lasting feminism? Which will wither and pass away?[3]

---

[3]The philosopher Eric Voegelin has several wonderful volumes on the gnostic spirit in modern thought—the spirit that disregards the flesh, and treats humans as homogeneous, uniform, interchangeable units. It seems

The explosive depth of this question has led entire Episcopal and Anglican congregations to break from their communion and to turn to Rome. Perhaps you are pulled, Jana, in the reverse direction. I said above that there are some questions that, if taken deep enough, throw one into a crisis of conscience. This is one of them.

The successor of Peter, the pope, says that he lacks the power to change what Jesus instituted. He is not free to make things up as he goes. He is bound as the rest of us are, but with the awesome responsibility to preserve the data tamper-proof. It is important to try to understand why the tradition is as it is. There is always meaning in such things.

If, in the end, you cannot accept it, you must decide how important the issue is, compared to others. My mother, as devout a Catholic as you will find, once said of one item of Catholic teaching, "I will not accept that until the day I die." She said she intended to bring it up with God himself—and then she broke out into a laugh. But she meant it.

By contrast, for others, the issue of women priests cuts very deep in its implications and is a breaking point—some are leaving the Catholic Church over it, and some are joining because of it.

As a matter of record, converts *to* the Catholic Church, at least in the United States, are running at all-time highs. I think it is because of the example of Pope John Paul II; he is not a cutter or trimmer but forthright, and he is unafraid of

---

evident that certain types of feminism are manifestation of this modern tendency. See, in particular, Voegelin's *Science, Politics, and Gnosticism* and *The New Science of Politics*.

the censors of the press. In general, the orthodox branches of religion almost everywhere are growing, both in numbers and sophistication—and also in confidence. Straight teaching flies like an arrow through mush.

I admit to you, Jana, that the position I am supporting could be wrong, even though it is part of the unbroken and universal teaching of the Church, and originates in Jesus himself. Three generations from now, my view may appear to have been very narrow. No one can be sure how the question of women priests will look three or four generations from now. It is always so in the history of the Church. At moments of crisis—that is, moments when great decisions must be made, down either this fork or that—persons of good will and intelligence are on opposite sides. Tradition is not somebody else; it is us. We must decide; it is our turn.

This is a time for ardent prayer, and profound willingness to be proven wrong—that is, a willingness to be open to signs, even subtle signs, of the will of God. If the Church means anything, it is the carrier of his gracious will. If it is not an expression of God's will, it is useless. If we all pray for guidance, God will instruct us clearly enough, but not without much suffering in the meantime.

JANA: *You have avoided the more general point of orthodoxy, the task of not cutting corners, but being true to all the basic issues. What about that?*

DAD: The more general guidance you requested of me, Jana, about which church tradition to join and how to decide which doctrines to take seriously is needed by persons in virtually every religious tradition today. Practically everywhere, two things have happened more or less at once. Individual liberty has appeared, and knowledge about other religious traditions has broken in upon all but the most remote and sheltered communities. Today, practically all of those who go to universities (and sometimes even secondary schools) are likely to learn more about other world traditions, and especially about atheistic or secular philosophies, than about their own religious tradition. If you meet highly educated Hindus or Buddhists, they are likely to have attended schools rather like your own, and to think in secular and modern ways even more comfortably than they can think in religious ways. It is not uncommon for university students to take not a single course on religion during their academic careers. Their secular education has usually outstripped their theological education.

The result is that the minds of most religious people today, if they are highly educated, are already pluralistic, not to say schizophrenic. Usually, their secular knowledge is highly sophisticated, but their religious knowledge is barely elementary. They have learned to think about things *both* in a secular way (in the world) and in a religious way (at home)—sometimes without having worked through the real differences. Sometimes the inward compromise they reach is that their mind is predominantly secular and their heart is predominantly religious. As you can see, this is not a stable or desirable compromise.

Buddhism, Confucianism, Western science, a smattering of knowledge about Christianity, astrology, and other strains of thought are like contrasting crosscurrents in the broad river of our long and leisurely conversations today. It is the fate of all of us in the modern world, isn't it, to have minds a little like a big muddy river—a broad, slow, multi-current, multitemperature stream-of-consciousness? Religious and secular elements of consciousness intermingle uneasily, and most of us lack training for bringing them to consciousness and inner unity.

"Purity of soul," one of the greatest of modern existentialist philosophers, Søren Kierkegaard, has written, "is to will one thing." Religion is a struggle to will one thing. It is a battle for the integration of the self, to put the self in order—to get it in its rightful place in the cosmos and in history, and to get it right with itself.

In his will, our peace.

When our souls click into their rightful place, the tranquility of order reigns. To *stay* in that place is not so easy. "I have not come to bring peace, but the sword!" Jesus said. (Matt. 10:34) To will one thing in the turbulence of everyday struggles is mortal combat. Still, there is a peace even in fighting one's best, and even after getting knocked down, in getting up and fighting again.

My advice is pretty simple. Judaism and Christianity (and some other religions) are about truth and holiness. In this context, holiness means to love the Lord your God with your whole heart, your whole mind, and your whole soul and to love your neighbor as you would be loved. The motive of such love is awe for the love that the Creator has poured out upon you.

Therefore, choose the communion that is most likely to oblige you and nudge you to be faithful to truth—to inquiry,

insight, and the hunger for evidence and sound argument—
and to become holy. Resist the temptation to join the communion that offers you only comfort, sociality, and nice
company. (Look for that in a good club.) Resist also the appeal of aesthetic pleasures at the services—music, poetry,
visual stunningness (whether splendid or spare).[4]

Finally, understand, as Thomas Jefferson did not, that
religion is *not* primarily about ethics. The "religious" is not
the ethical, any more than it is the aesthetic. Judaism and
Christianity (and to some extent other religions) are mainly
about the mystery of God's wooing of human beings. The
wonder is that he would care. That he would go to such
improbable lengths to preserve a tiny dot in the dark vastness of space, where life such as ours could be enjoyed as
an antechamber. That he made our minds and wills imperishable, to enjoy friendship with him forever. This Christianity promises: life eternal as an individual person, body and
soul. It is a daring promise.

I think I have said enough about the gritty work of thinking through the hard doctrines of Christian faith (and any
religion worth its salt). Usually, beliefs form a whole, each
one related to others and shedding light on, or limiting the
meaning of, others.

In Judaism, the rabbis have delighted for centuries in tak-

---

[4]It is tempting to argue that one of the signs of the truth of the Catholic
faith is the beauty it inspires in its churches, worship, and daily life. But it is
important to get first things first. As it comes from the greatest of all artists
(the First Cause of all beauty), existence shimmers with beauty. "Beauty,"
St. Thomas Aquinas said, "is the splendor of being." Artists aim at the *truth*
of things, knowing that if they express the true being, then the splendor—the
beauty—shines through. Similarly, in seeking God in the way he wants us to
come to him, one is best advised to seek *truth;* the splendor of beauty will
follow. To seek beauty first, and independently of truth, is a certain path to

ing disparate passages from the Torah (the Jewish Bible) that seem to contradict one another, and then showing how each one illuminates and modifies the other, so that both together bring greater insight than one alone. Sometimes, this is a little like those old sayings which at first seem contradictory but in practice cry out for each other, such as: "The wheel that squeaks the loudest is the one that gets the grease!" and "Empty barrels make the most noise!" Christian theologians, too, delight in "paradoxes"—the clash of seeming opposites that are on reflection not opposites.

Faith, like life, is not a seamless garment, but stitched and hemmed to fit the curves and bends of angular reality. A man's suit and a woman's gown may be lovely things, but only an observant tailor and an eagle-eyed seamstress know how to make the parts work together without bunches and pulls. In words that apply to the orthodox of all traditions, St. Paul counsels: "Put ye on the garments of Christ!" Before you reject a doctrine, be sure to see how it goes with the whole outfit, where it fits, and why it's designed as it is. It may be more functional than you at first think.

Christian faith is a long voyage of conversion, of learning to see with new eyes, and think in new ways, and act in a new manner. Assent to a doctrine only becomes a real assent—as distinct from a mere notion—when it is put to use. Merely saying the words, or grasping the grammar of the words, is not really belief. One must *do* the belief to really get it.

In Christianity, at least, there isn't any belief that

---

missing both truth and beauty. To rest in beauty rather than in truth is to sow seed in thin soil. That said, I concur that beauty is a sign of truth.

doesn't have something to say about how to live a Christian life more fully. But, of course, many Christians never get past some of the basics and some of the minimal requirements. I don't think you're likely to be like that, Jana. It's in your nature to be all or nothing. (But you do have to watch that lazy streak.)

In summary, then, can you just pick and choose? Not quite. Not without cheating yourself and God. But it is important not to lose a sense of proportion, and to give yourself time to inquire into things, one by one. Faith must be grown into. It does not come ready-made.

7

BUT I CANNOT TAKE THE
BIBLE LITERALLY!

The Hebrew Bible, in particular the Torah (The Five Books of
Moses), has done more to civilize the world than any other book or
idea in history. It is the Hebrew Bible that gave humanity such ideas
as a universal, moral, loving God; ethical obligations to this God; the
need for history to move forward to moral and spiritual redemption;
the belief that history has meaning; and the notion that human
freedom and social justice are the divinely desired states for all
people. It gave the world the Ten Commandments, ethical
monotheism, and the concept of holiness (the goal of raising human
beings from the animal-like to the God-like).

—Dennis Prager
1993

One must read the Bible continually to prevent the image of truth
being obscured in us.

—Julien Green
1961

No individual, no Caesar or Napoleon, has had such a part in the
world's history as this book. . . . If only shards and broken pieces of
our civilization should remain, among them would still be found the
Bible, whole and uninjured. The book that outlived the Roman
Empire will outlive any destruction that impends.

—E. S. Bates
1937

JANA: *The Bible is a good story, I will give you that, but can it actually be word-for-word true? It's a wonderful read, filled with lessons to learn, knowledge, and all the meat-and-potatoes of a modern novel: sex, violence, revenge, murder, betrayal, and redemption. But I have a hard time believing that we're supposed to take it literally.*

It should be quite clear to everyone, for example, that once a person tries to record an event—whether orally, in writing, or visually—the person automatically creates a bias in his or her version. No matter how neutral one believes oneself to be, a particular perspective is introduced by something as simple as the angle from which a particular scene is shot (what gets focused on and what gets ignored) or the notes jotted down (a person can't follow or remember every little detail or occurrence and probably won't be able to interview every person—otherwise a single ten-second event could require hundreds of pages of notes!).

Obviously, then, the Bible must have the same problems. Readers can see this for themselves by perusing the New Testament for the differences between Matthew, Mark, Luke, and John in each of their accounts of Jesus' life and times. Although the essence is the same, the details and focus vary. It is rather like reading the same story in The Washington Post, The Washington Times, The New York Times, *and* The Wall Street Journal: *while all the journalists are reporting on the same event in what they judge is an ethical, proper, and unbiased manner, it sometimes seems like they have covered several completely different and unconnected events!*

And it is not just the shifts in perspective that trouble me, but the simple details that require such a suspension of

*disbelief. While the issue of miracles and the many stories
and parables of the New Testament do not actually strain
my credulity very much (so many things around me on a
daily basis strike me as miraculous—such as life, a flower
blooming radiantly, or even how a fax machine works—that
loaves and fishes multiplying, the sick being cured, or the
dead arising do not strike me as bizarre), the events in the
Old Testament often do. For example, who Cain married,
people living hundreds of years, or God creating the world
in six days (or, as we used to joke in college, God pulling an
all-nighter on the fifth day). I know that evolution has not
necessarily been proved beyond a shadow of a doubt, but it
is easier for me to accept—more logical to my mind—than
creation. (Although, as you mentioned earlier, I have always
liked the argument in the play* Inherit the Wind *that perhaps
a biblical day is simply a term to describe thousands of years;
therefore, creation just describes evolution in a mythlike
manner.)*

*But it is not just nit-picky points. I simply have a hard
time accepting the idea that I should take a book—any
book—literally. The Bible seems to me to be illustrative, a
teaching tool and a guide book; one by which we should live
our lives, but not necessarily in a literal manner.*

DAD: You are lucky, Jana, that you are not a literal person. Ever since you were little, you loved fantasies, poems,
epics, myths of the Norsemen and Greeks and Romans, science fiction, Tolkien, and the Narnia stories. I would describe you as tough-minded, though, rather than romantic.
It's just that you enjoy the work of the imagination. These

are strengths that will help you as you read the Bible. The Bible will test every strength you have.

For centuries, serious women and men have taken a different biblical text in hand every day to let their minds and imaginations dwell upon it, in order to find light in it for how they should act, in this circumstance or that. When we were kids we used to play a game: Open the big Bible at random; without looking, place our finger on the page; and then accept the text under our finger as a message from Providence for that day.

Let me begin with three principles. Remember, first, that the Bible is a book of the church. Second, it is a book intended for people with intelligence, imagination, common sense, a critical instinct, and an ability to compare one part with another. Third, the books that now comprise the Bible were selected from rivals as the books that reflect the Word of God, distinct from those that do not. So it is right to think that every word, every image, every phrase is worth meditating on, mulling over, trying to probe for all its meanings.

The conclusion to be drawn from these three principles is plain: Take every word of the Bible seriously—it comes from God—although not always literally. The literal meaning should be held on to as a kind of banister; but you should recall that a banister enables you to lift your eyes from the stairs themselves to other things. Sometimes the manner of speaking or the exact situation in the circumstances described warns you to look up from the literal meaning to something else. For example:

If thy right eye scandalize thee, pluck it out.

—Matt. 5:29

These words of Christ are obviously meant to shock and to get your attention. Eyes have brought evil into a lot of lives, but you don't see many Christians running around with eyepatches, disguising their self-mutilation. The statement is a very serious one—there may be things very dear to you, seemingly essential to the way you want to live, that need giving up, if you are to be a wholehearted follower of Christ. The warning is serious, and you should have experiences in your life that tell you exactly how you have had to pluck certain errant inclinations out of your life.

Don't alcoholics have to do this in their cure—simply pluck out any use of alcohol at all, since even "a wee bit" would set them off? Don't athletes do it regularly in the things they force themselves to do in training? "No pain, no gain" is an advertising slogan for athletic goods.

What we do to train ourselves for sports, or war, is a frequent metaphor in the Bible for what is demanded, also, in the training of the soul. All the powers and habits of the soul (powers and habits of insight, concentration, will, and determination, in particular), need constant nourishment and training. We must weed out of our lives many things that initially we love in order to free our souls for other things. Sometimes the ruthlessness we need feels like plucking out one of our eyes. (Young men learn what disciplining of the eyes—making choices about what we allow our eyes to focus on—requires. The joking advice, "Look, but don't touch," suggests the tension. The problem, obviously, is that undisciplined looking builds up impulses to touch.)

Let me elaborate briefly on each of the three principles (a book of the church, to be read with intelligence, as the Word of God), in reverse order. *The Word of God*: Judaism and Christianity hold that God has chosen to work with and through nature and history, hardly ever directly and immediately. Yesterday, I was listening in the car to a tape of a lecture on *The Aeneid*, and it set me to thinking about the way in which Virgil imagines the Roman gods acting in history. Talk about miracles! The gods and goddesses use nature and humans as their playthings. They turn warships magically into seafish. They administer irresistible love potions to inflame unswervable passions. The point of this epic poem is that the gods intend puny Rome, the humblest of rural villages, to become a great Empire, and to bring law to even the remotest outposts of the known world. This whole narrative was further intended to honor the splendor of the peaceful Golden Age of Augustus, the poet's patron. (No adversarial role for artists in those days!)

But notice how different the God of Israel and Jesus is from the gods of Rome. The gods of Rome were many, rivalrous, limited, human in their passions (like *spoiled* children, without the virtues, disciplines, and restraints of the Roman heroes), and they fought their petty quarrels at the expense of humans. The God of Israel and Jesus is One, transcendent, the Creator of all things, to be worshiped in spirit and in truth rather than in passion. Every one of his miracles is in some sense a speeding up of natural processes, a compression of time and space. You mention the six "days" of the Creation story in Genesis. So far as the point of the story goes, is it really very different if the Creator exercises his power instantaneously—in a day—or over millions of years? Either way, the dependence of the intelligibility of nature upon a creative intelligence is made transparent.

You might also have mentioned the manna in the desert—sweet bread suddenly appearing among a hungry people. Is that so different from the ordinary wonder that from a few bushels of seed many multiples of bushels of grain can be grown in a single season? As you yourself note, when one observes the "miracles" that conscious living beings may marvel at every day, the fact that the Creator "miraculously" made sweet food suddenly appear (the manna in the desert) seems not to contradict his general providence, but only to be a special case of it. Our daily prospering depends on many intersecting lines of probabilities, the failure of any one chain of which would make life on this planet unsustainable. It would be odd, given the general improbability of sustained human life in the vastness of inhospitable space, to hold that the Creator could *not* produce instantly what in any case He does produce normally over time, through a multitude of secondary causes such as good soil, favorable climate, and abundant seed.

Jews and Christians do not hold that God plays with dice. Nature is his work of art, not his plaything. Because Jews and Christians have an acute sense of artistry, they look to every part of nature—every event of nature—for clues about God's love for them. His ordinary works are full of wonders. How can it be, for example, that the preposterous act of copulation between male and female generates such a marvel as a squealing infant? It doesn't do so always; barrenness is not unknown; but it does so often. The biological processes—the mechanics of it—took centuries to learn about. But even as the mechanics become better known, the scientific knowledge does not quash our wonder. Little Emily and Stephen, generated from your brother and sister-in-law, are no less marvelous for being born in conditions of scientific understanding far beyond those known to our ancestors.

For those who feel gratitude to their Creator for the wonders with which he abundantly sprinkles his creation, greater scientific knowledge of the elaborate workings of his artistry does not diminish their gratitude. Generation by generation, as more is learned, their sense of wonder grows.

The actual transcript of the famous trial in Tennessee falsely dramatized in the movie version of *Inherit the Wind* (which is much less accurate than the play) reveals that William Jennings Bryan was not the bumpkin portrayed in that movie. Bryan tried to show the difference between two divergent ideologies operative in those presenting the findings of Darwin. One theory was closed to any Creator at all, and the other was open to a Creator who worked during eons of time. It was the first Bryan resisted, not the second. Bryan was willing to admit that the Creator worked over a long period of time, as evolutionary findings showed. Bryan was *not* willing to admit that the mechanics of *how* it was done—through some form of slow evolution, say—dimmed our sense of gratitude to the Creator of those mechanics. So great was the animus against "the Bible Belt" in those days that Bryan's argument could not be presented fairly. (Animosity against "fundamentalists" is still a prejudice the educated permit themselves.)

It may well be that one or more of the theories of evolution now in play at the present stage of scientific knowledge (which itself is constantly evolving) have much to teach believers. One or more of them may hold up over time. The true center of the dispute is the openness or closure of such theories to this question: Is creative intelligence at work in the stuff of matter—or not? That intelligibility is involved, all scientific work shouts aloud.

JANA: *You have gotten away from the Bible. Are you saying that we should read the Bible for the insight it can give us, but not take the miracles too seriously?*

DAD: No, take the miracles seriously. Their main point is that everything in us and around us depends upon the creative activity of God. The same God who gave us the Bible through human authors gave us creation through its own natural workings. Therefore, we are wise to cultivate science along with theology. Always use one against the other—theology pushes science to further questions, and science pushes theology. In any one generation, they may be out of phase. In the long run, they come together.

Thus, even in working miracles, God does not offend against the workmanship he exhibited in fashioning the laws of nature. His respect for his own artistry has two aspects. God ordinarily works through ordinary natural processes, not directly. (Philosophers call these natural processes "secondary causes.") In addition, the Creator of all things never relinquishes his sovereignty; he exercises it all the time, but only rarely by direct intervention, and always in line with his original intentions. Thus, even exceptions are not contrary to the beauty and lawlikeness of the whole.

I can think of three senses of "miracle" or "miraculous." We use the first sense for the miracles of everyday life (as we have seen above)—how one ear of corn yields enough seed for two long rows of corn stalks with many ears on each; how the union of an egg from a woman's womb and a man's semen becomes a living infant.

The second sense is used for contingent, natural circumstances that bring about unusually good fortune. For example, on a crucial day during the American Revolution, an unexpected morning fog extended the hours available for the secret nighttime retreat of Washington's army from Brooklyn Heights, enabling his dramatic escape from the British. Again, in 1942 thick clouds parted over the Japanese aircraft carriers at Midway, just as the party of American dive bombers was ready to turn away at the limit of their fuel supply. A third example: a cancer predicted to cause certain death goes inexplicably into sudden remission. Good fortune often has perfectly natural causes.

The third sense is reserved for the sovereign power of God to intervene, in line with his intentions for the whole, by suspending, or adding to, the normal working of ordinary chains of causation—as in at least some of the miracles reported in the Bible. For the God of life to restore life to the dead Lazarus is not contrary to his general intentions, even if it goes far beyond the ordinary; and the same with his rare but unforgettable interventions during the long history of the people of Israel.

In general, Jana, I believe it is a safe rule to hold, when confronted with a claim that a miracle has occurred, that the explanation for it must belong to senses one or two, unless evidence to the contrary is unimpeachable. In other words, it is safe to assume that only natural, normal causes are involved, even if not immediately evident. This is the procedure the Church follows in weighing the "miracles" put forward during the trial of a holy person before such persons are officially inscribed in the canon of the saints. A "devil's advocate" argues *against* the evidence purporting to show that a true miracle (in the third sense) has occurred, by showing that it can be perfectly, adequately explained in line with senses one or two.

Nature itself manifests abundant marvels, surprises, exceptions, unusual occurrences, once-only events. A huge meteor collides with earth, altering the biosphere dramatically—one may describe this as a wholly natural event, even if it occurs only once and never again. At the same time, such an event—were humans to experience it—may have a shattering impact on habits and preconceptions. Despite the fact that it is a wholly natural event, this crash of a meteor might open humans to an awareness of their dependence upon forces far beyond their power, and might well remind some of the sovereignty of the Creator over his creation.

And this brings into relief that second aspect. While preferring always to find interpretations of events that fall within the scope of secondary causes—the hazards of a small planet subject to barrage from outer space—Jews and Christians recognize at all times that God is sovereign over nature and nature's laws. They do not conceive of God as part of nature, not even as a gigantic field of force and energy, suffused throughout nature. He is nature's *Creator*. They do not see nature as his plaything; they have observed how he respects its integrity. But neither do they pretend to understand his ways, or to limit him to their own categories. They are eager to protect God's transcendence.

The practical effect of these two sides to their understanding of God (and of nature) is to prefer to find a scientific explanation for everything that science can explain, now and in the future. Put another way, their chief working principle is that when there is an apparent conflict between science and theology, they are facing either bad science or bad theology. Therefore, it is wise in such cases, especially, to retain a healthy measure of humility and patience.

By its own rules, science is not designed as an answer to every sort of question. From a purely scientific point of view, some questions are unanswerable. Some are even meaningless—in the sense that they are not amenable to scientific experiment. The best—the most honest—scientists regularly restrain themselves, recognizing the limits of science, its methods, and its purposes.

But a few scientists do try to make of science a total worldview. They believe that they have in science an exhaustive taxonomy of human knowledge. This worldview is fairly called scientism, although ideologically some prefer to call it a rather more flattering name, naturalism. When they choose scientism (or naturalism) as a self-conscious philosophy of life, that is fair enough. But they are then taking a step beyond science. They are establishing a context for science in their own lives and the life of society. Those who disagree with them are free to offer reasons, as I have above, why this philosophy is untenable.

JANA: *Are we allowed, then, to be skeptical of the Bible?*

DAD: Another basic principle held by Christians and Jews is that the Bible is intended for a people of insight and critical judgment. Jews and Christians are known as "peoples of the book." Far from being an adversary of reason, Jewish and Christian religion *depends on* reason. Judaism and Christianity are addressed to reason. As we have seen (Chapter 3), one of the most profound names they give to God is Truth, or Light. God, they say, is to be worshiped "in spirit and truth." It is truth that sets men free. More than any other world religion or philosophy, Judaism and Christianity teach humans to love reason. They teach us that it is a high human vocation to wonder, to inquire, and to study the ways of God and his creation. They hold that the pursuit of knowledge is not only blessed, but a way of participating in God's own acts of understanding. Complete and total insight is God's way of being, they instruct us, and humans who would be like him should pursue learning and understanding.

There is no need to minimize the human pride and weakness that have led leaders of Judaism and Christianity at various times to sin against inquiry, even flagrantly, even scandalously. Not least, Catholic leaders at various junctures of Western history, despite their often heroic efforts in establishing libraries and universities and sponsoring the recovery of ancient works that led to the Renaissance, have won contempt for acts of repression of scientific inquiry, as in the Galileo case. For these John Paul II has tendered an overdue public apology, much as the Catholic historian Lord Acton called for a century ago. For a church committed to the idea of God as truth, these were scarlet sins, and did inestimable damage.

These sins do not change the essential dependence of Jewish and Christian faith on human reason, as the receptor for hearing the word of God, and as the seat of the freedom the Creator gave us for saying either *yea* or *nay*. Without reason, religious faith has no receptor to address. That is why Jews and Christians have shown such historical passion for supporting universities and institutes of learning. That is why they so often offer defenses of the reasonableness of reason, as integral to their defense of the reasonableness of faith.

For Jews, Christians, and Muslims reason and faith are not identical. Rather, they are different habits (or dispositions or dimensions) of understanding.[1] They are, however, ordered to each other. Each has it own proper domain, but they can only contradict each other by accident or for a time. There are not two truths, one truth for reason, another for faith. Conflicts between faith and reason may and do arise, and our understanding both of one and of the other is subject to development over time. Thus, in a given generation developments of faith may be sharply out of phase with developments of reason, or vice versa.

In the end, however, reason and faith cannot be incompatible, for their source and object is the one Creator. Patience and humility before truth are the keys to working toward that convergence. In fact, apparent conflict between them is a wonderful spur to new inquiries in both habits of thought, the habit of reason and the habit of faith.

JANA: *What does that mean, "the habit of faith"?*

DAD: When you think of faith as a habit—a skill, a practiced tendency, a way of looking at everything—you see that it is part of your own being, a part of your own mind,

---

[1]One can find vivid debates on these matters among Jewish, Christian, and Muslim scholars in the thirteenth century, for example.

a way of seeing. It has changed you. You don't think of it as something separate or separable from you. G. K. Chesterton wrote once that when he spoke of orthodoxy, he couldn't exactly call it *his* philosophy of life, although it functioned rather in that way, because *he* hadn't made it: "God and man had made it—and it made me." In other words, faith is a way of seeing, and that way was taught him by the Bible and the people formed by the Bible.

When you believe an item of faith to be true, it is not only that you have seen certain pieces of evidence that eliminate other alternatives and mark this one as true. Rather, everything you see through it confirms it, in every act of seeing. What others see, you also see. But you see it now in more vivid definition, and experience more intensely the connections in things. Putting on faith is like putting on new eyeglasses. Better, it is like experiencing a quantum jump in technology, from analog to digital television pictures, for example. You have to see the difference for yourself.

"Better to rule in hell than serve in heaven!" the village atheist used to boast. Better to limit oneself to one's own unaided reason than submit to a sovereign outside oneself. Yes, faith is a kind of submission, at first. Contemplating it awakens nervousness and foreboding. Will believing mean being caught out among the vulgar ordinary people that believers seem to be?

This fear of being humiliated in one's own eyes is real. Yet in itself the submission of faith is submission to evidence. There is no shame in that, only the satisfaction of a long thirst finally slaked. The human spirit was made for God, and on arriving home feels home's traditional comforts. No matter how hard you have resisted him, or how many wounds your sins have given him, "the hardness of God," C. S. Lewis wrote afterward of his own first conversion "is softer than the kindness of men."

What we call Western civilization is really world civilization. There is hardly a single idea crucial to this current world civilization that does not have its oldest and deepest origin in the Bible: Not conscience nor person nor liberty; not individuality nor compassion nor concern for the poor; not progress nor social justice nor the need for checks and balances against unbridled power. Add to these the ideas that everything that is, is in the end intelligible; that truth matters more than interests or powers; that the vocation to inquire and to know is one of humanity's noblest ways of serving God; and that it is the universal calling of humans to be creative, and to change the world, and to build a shining city on the hill. All these civilizing beliefs sprang from the Bible and (often) from no other source.

The great philosopher of science Alfred North Whitehead wrote that the rise of Western science, apart from five thousand years of tutelage under the one God of Judaism and Christianity, is not conceivable. Only so did humans gather the courage to break primeval taboos against inquiry, and to grasp that research is a creative act, in imitation of God.

For all these reasons, Judaism and Christianity *must* defend the integrity and power of human reason. The fidelity of the Jewish and the Christian people to the Creator, to him who variously describes himself as Way, Light, Truth, Life, and He-who-is, demands this much. So does the respect paid to the inquiring conscience by faith: Faith knocks but, if not welcomed, it will not enter. God desires the worship only of the free.

It is a mistake to think—as many moderns, influenced by the pride of the Enlightenment, do—that "reason" and "faith" are opposites. Rightly understood, they undergird each other, mutually. Each has its proper roles and proper limits; each has its own proper sphere and methods, even when their domains overlap. In one sense, reason and faith are asymmetrical: those committed to reason sometimes fear and strenuously resist faith, but those committed to faith have no cause to fear reason, except in the case in which reason out of pride or the will-to-power becomes a kind of hard-shelled ideology directed against faith.

Reading the Bible in a spirit of faith will convince you that God made reason, too, and intends us to develop our reason to the full.

JANA: *Are you saying that it is* through *faith that we should read the Bible? That only through faith can we understand the Bible's meaning?*

DAD: Through reason, too. Intelligent inquiry is important and must be defended. Jewish and Christian faith nourish reason (as a mother nourishes a child). Faith should neither treat its child as an orphan nor try foolishly to halt its passage through adolescent questioning and rebellion. In due course, mother and child learn how vulnerable each is without the other. There are many things we do not need faith to understand—truths of science and common sense. Atheists and unbelievers can understand a great deal about the

Bible. Those with faith should also push their reason as hard as they can, exercise it, make it work.

True faith has great respect for reason. Reason is a crucial tool in exploring much that is at first hidden, both in the Bible and in the world. That is one side of the coin. The other is that, since the author of the Bible is the Creator, one may properly and most fruitfully read it prayerfully. Reading it is part of a conversation with God—sitting for a half hour, say, reading, reflecting, and silently lifting one's attention to God, is the most fruitful way to read it. Meanings that you have never opened before will open up to you, to jolt you into changing your life.

JANA: *The thing that bothers me is not your first two principles: that the Bible is intended for intelligent people; and that, coming from God, it can be read critically. What bothers me is church, tradition, authority. Why can't I just read the Bible by myself?*

DAD: You can, of course. But remember that the Church, the tradition, the whole people of God, organized as God would have them organized, is the believing community that formed and accepted the canon of Scriptures in the first place, rejecting as deformed some extant books, and welcoming others as bearing the signs of God's authorship. Like virtually everything else that comes from God, this authorship was indirect, through the mind, heart, and hand of human authors struggling to speak as God wanted them to speak.

God did not "dictate" the text of the Bible, but inspired it, and the believing community has so accepted its authority. For this reason, the biblical text is owed a reverence and an intensity of study owed no other.

But even the whole career of the Bible itself is a kind of story. Some Protestant churches reject everything in the Catholic Church that does not have explicit biblical grounding. *Sola scriptura,* some say, "Only the Bible and nothing but the Bible." This is how they think they differ from the Catholic Church.

But where did the Bible come from? Who wrote it, and when? And who chose which books to include with the Bible (the canonical texts, as it is said) and which to reject? Answer: The Church did this, by reflecting on its communal memories of the preaching of the first apostles and *their* first converts. As we saw in Chapter 5, even the Bible depends on the tradition and authority of the church community. That the present books of the Bible are the ones so included, and not others, is not commanded in the Bible itself. Although some parts of the Bible refer explicitly to other essential parts, the choice of the canon is for the most part extrabiblical.

Experience shows that reading the Bible is endlessly fecund. Reading it, one kens God speaking directly to one's heart. Every year when one goes back to it, fresh meanings appear. No other book is half so rich. Those who do not read it are much impoverished.

The biblical text has emboldened hundreds of millions down the centuries. It has led slaves in chains to know that their Creator regards them as free women and men, equal in dignity to any others. It has flung into the hearts of the poor and the sick and the dying burning rays of hope and peace.

In the light of the biblical text, the ignorant fieldhand without shoes is the equal of the lawyers and bankers of the country club and the courthouse; to his heart God speaks as directly as to theirs.

The contrary is also true, St. Augustine reminds us in his reflections on the Psalms: Do not think that the rich man at your side in the church is hard of heart and proud—in God's eyes he may pray with more purity of heart, humility, and detachment than the embittered poor man on your other side.

To the Bible, wealth and power and position are outer garments, mere show, a distraction from the inner theater of the soul, wherein principalities and powers wage war. In that theater, the name of every player is cherished in the heart of God. To all alike the script of Scripture holds out lines to listen to—and to speak.

Read the Bible daily, Jana. Read it for yourself. Think about its words slowly. Savor them.

8

What Do We Mean by Hell? And Heaven?

When Moses heard his doom, he urged every argument to secure a remission of his sentence. Amongst other things he said, "Sovereign of the universe, arise from the judgment seat, and sit on the throne of mercy, so that I die not. Let my sins be forgiven by reason of bodily sufferings which may come upon me. But put me not in the power of the angel of death. If thou wilt do this, then will I proclaim thy praise before all the inhabitants of the world, as David said, I shall not die, but live, and declare the works of the Lord." Then God said to Moses, "Hear the rest of the verse, 'This is the gate of the Lord, through which the righteous shall enter.' " For all creatures death has been prepared from the beginning.

—*A Rabbinic Anthology*

Through me one enters the sorrowful city; through me one enters into eternal pain; through me one enters among the lost race. Justice moved my high Maker; divine power made me . . . I endure eternally. All hope abandon, ye who enter here.

—Inscription over the gate of Hell in Dante's *Inferno*
c. 1310

Heaven at present is out of sight, but in due time, as snow melts and discovers what it lay upon, so will this visible creation fade away before those greater splendors which are behind it.

—John Henry Newman
(1801–1890)

MICHAEL NOVAK • JANA NOVAK

Heaven is the presence of God.

—Christina Rossetti
1879

JANA: *I never did make it more than part way into Dante's* Paradiso *although I eagerly finished his* Inferno— *the good life is never as interesting as the bad. It is Dante's trilogy (we can't forget* Purgatorio*) that forms my vision of heaven and hell. But that is not much, and it leaves many gaps to be filled. Like many people, I'm sure, I have no more than a grainy, out-of-focus, black-and-white picture in my mind. Especially of heaven.*

Somehow, though not surprisingly, it is not hard to imagine and accept popular images of hell fires burning, torturous eternal punishments, and smirking devils guarding their brood. Yet the idea that this scene of my imagination is what is truly meant by hell seems oddly wrong. It is hard to believe that a god usually portrayed as forgiving and caring would sanction eternal torture with no hope of redemption. Now purgatory, that makes sense: Forgiveness. Redemption. God lets those who have sinned work their way into heaven.

So what is meant by hell? Is it just an image to strike fear into people's hearts? A bribery technique to encourage people to be on their best behavior by acting moral and good? A metaphorical tale that adds weight to one's conscience? Or does hell truly exist? Is there a physical location called hell, where fallen angels inflict pain upon evil people? Exactly how bad does one have to be to end up there? One can logically assume Hitler is in hell, but what about a thief or a rapist? Where's the cutoff? If it's something fixed, say ten or more murders, does that mean that everyone else ends up in purgatory? Or do only certain religions believe in purgatory? For those that do, what is it all about? Is it sort of like serving prison time for bad deeds? Like multiple uses of swear words equal six months and cheating on your spouse equals one hundred years? So that basically everyone ends up in purgatory for at least some time? But isn't the basis of Christianity forgiveness? If we recognize we do wrong and ask for forgiveness, isn't god supposed to forgive us (so that we should still be able to get into heaven)?

What happens in the religions that don't believe in purgatory? Does that mean that some infractions become marked as "not bad enough to keep you out of heaven," while other seemingly minor infractions send you to hell? Does it end up being all-or-nothing?

What happens to people who don't "believe," but still lead very good lives? For example, Socrates, who lived before Christianity existed, or people who believe in a different religion (which comes back to the issue of many different religions and which one is "right")? In the case of Catholicism, where one must be baptized to be "saved," what happens to newborns who die before baptism? Previously, they went to limbo (from my understanding a peaceful place like heaven, but without the presence of God), but the Church dropped the concept of limbo a while back, so now what happens?

If one does "qualify" for heaven, what does that mean? Is heaven a real place that our souls go to? I'm sure it's probably not at all like the movies portray, with people wandering around the clouds with wings and halos. But then, what is it? Is it another world of peaceful coexistence—a

Utopia where we can meet all of our dead loved ones, ancestors, and famous forebears? Or is it simply nothingness and our thinking capabilities will cease so that I, who I am, "Jana," no longer exists? (Although this sounds more hellish than nice.)

If it is our souls that make the journey to either heaven or hell, then do only beings with souls exist in either place? If so, which creatures have souls? Will there be animals in heaven? Will I get to see Peppie, our family cat that was recently hit by a car, again? Or does Christianity consider animals to be without souls? I know that many Christian religions have a Sunday set aside to honor animals—my roommate told me that in her Presbyterian church, members tell stories about pets on this day. Besides, doesn't the Bible say all creatures are important and loved by god? How lonely it would be if there are no animals in heaven—it doesn't sound much like heaven to me.

Most importantly, what will daily life be like in heaven? In hell? For example, in heaven, without worldly worries, will people be free to simply indulge their earthly likes and passions? In other words, writers will be free to write (no writer's block or money worries!), scholars to study, scientists to experiment, etc.

But I must admit, putting "earthly" images on "beyond earth" places like heaven and hell seems wrong. It doesn't necessarily make sense that either place would seem anything like an "earthly" place, just more peaceful or hotter. Perhaps humans are too limited to grasp what heaven and hell are like, which is why we try to tame them and concretize them by imagining heaven and hell as physical places. It could also just be that hell means one's soul ceases to

*exist—it experiences the nothingness mentioned earlier.
Therefore, heaven may mean the soul is finally and completely embraced by god and becomes a permanent part of
that universal unconscious.*

DAD: I'm glad you asked me about hell first, Jana, and
heaven second, because I have clearer ideas about hell than
about heaven and purgatory. This is at least in part because
Scripture is much clearer on hell. Mostly, though, it's because it is easier to reason our way to the nature of hell than
to the nature of heaven or purgatory.

Scripture is unambiguous about eternal punishment.
The Jewish Testament has vivid intimations of "Gehenna,"
but the New Testament—supposedly (in modern liberal
consciousness) so much softer, warmer, and more forgiving—is especially insistent and emphatic in its descriptions:
Those who are resolute in evil will suffer eternal torment
under three different sentences: banishment, punishment,
and ruin. The words of Christ himself—the words of divine
mercy incarnate, who was beaten, mocked, flogged, and
nailed to the cross in order to redeem all, including the crim-
inals who died with him—are unyielding. It is a mistake, and
false to Scripture, to sentimentalize Christ. Or human destiny. Here are the three terrifying images that Jesus uses:

THREE IMAGES OF HELL

Banishment
Go far from me, you that are accursed, into that eternal fire
which has been prepared for the devil and his angels. (Matt.
25:41)

Punishment
Whereupon they, in their turn, will answer, Lord, when was it
that we saw thee hungry or thirsty, or a stranger naked, or sick,

or in prison, and did not minister to thee? And he will answer them, Believe me, when you refused it to one of the least of my brethren here, you refused it to me. And these shall pass on to eternal punishment, and the just to eternal life. (Matt. 25:44–46) (Knox transl.)

Ruin
And there is no need to fear those who kill the body, but have no means of killing the soul; fear him more, who has the power to ruin body and soul in hell. (Matt. 10:28)

Many Christian writers back away from this teaching on hell, and even sometimes the teaching on purgatory. Hans Urs von Balthasar, perhaps the greatest theologian of our century, speculated that by God's universal salvific will every human being is in the end saved; no one is in hell forever. Another brilliant writer on this subject, C. S. Lewis, wished with all his heart that there were no such place—or that none were in it—but he could not get around the unequivocal words of Christ. Nonetheless, Lewis ventured that among the dead the damned get a second chance—a chance to reverse or to reconfirm their will. Obviously, the whole idea of hell sits badly with those who love God—and one another.

You ask, Jana, a series of questions: Is hell just an image intended to awaken fear? A form of intimidation? A merely metaphorical tale to dramatize the significance of morality? A physical place? And what is the cutoff point for going there? Is Hitler there? If not, why not? My quick answer to the first three questions—is it intimidation, metaphor, physical place?—is, in all three cases, no.

You also ask about the cutoff point—what counts as worthy of hell? The cutoff point is a resolute and deliberate and determined choice of the pleasures and desires of the self, and a rejection of the love of God. Such a deliberate turning away from God is usually continued through a series of acts, in an habitual way. (It is quite another thing to *will* to love God, but then out of weakness to fall, even again and again, and then to seek forgiveness and self-reform. Willfulness and weakness are worlds apart in the life of the Spirit.)

The eternal fate of Adolf Hitler is often used as a twentieth-century shorthand for the immemorial human sense of the terrible justice owed to determined evildoers. Humans *do* have such a moral sense. There are some evils for which saying you're sorry is not enough; if no punishment is forthcoming, no restitution, no amending of your ways, then the universe itself seems askew. The cry of justice is especially loud when the evildoer is pleased with the evil he is doing. C. S. Lewis in *The Problem of Pain:*

> Picture to yourself a man who has risen to wealth or power by a continued course of treachery and cruelty, by exploiting for purely selfish ends the noble emotions of his victims, laughing the while at their simplicity; who, having thus attained success, uses it for the gratification of lust and hatred and finally parts with the last rag of honour among thieves by betraying his own accomplices and jeering at their last moments of bewildered disillusionment. Suppose further, that he does all this, not (as we like to imagine) tormented by remorse or even misgiving, but eating like a schoolboy and sleeping like a healthy infant—a jolly, ruddy-cheeked man, without a care in the world, unshakably confident to the very end that he alone has found the answer to the riddle of life, that God and man are fools whom he has got the better of, that his way of life is utterly successful, satisfactory, unassailable.
>
> Can you really desire that such a man, remaining what he is (and he must be able to do that if he has free will) should be confirmed forever in his present happiness—should continue, for all eternity, to be perfectly convinced that the laugh is on his side?

What is an omnipotent God to do with such an evil person? Once he has limited his omnipotence by giving human beings responsibility for their own destiny, he cannot force them to mend their ways. He cannot forcibly place a new will within them. He has already sent his only Son to die for them. He has had his truth preached, his sacraments administered, his warnings given. He has shown them every mercy. Still, some laugh. Some mock. Some ignore. If he sticks to the rules of the game as he established it—then human beings must have their will.

And that's what I think hell is. Hell is having what you want: that is, *not God*. You have banished God from your life, and that is what you get. You get what you have without God: all that is due to your precious, stinking self. And you get it forever. Hell, Scripture tells us, is banishment. Just so. Hell is self-annihilation. That's what life is when God's light—being, truth, beauty, understanding, love—goes out. Hell is darkness, and weeping and gnashing of teeth, and the torment of isolation from all but self-love (and its alternative face, self-loathing). "Hell," wrote the atheist Jean-Paul Sartre in one of his most gloating, triumphant moments, "is other people." Yes, it is that, for the egotist. But an even worse hell is *oneself*, isolated from other people, from hope, from being—and from one's Creator. T. S. Eliot in *The Cocktail Party:*

> Hell is oneself. Hell is alone, and the other figures in it merely projections. There is nothing to escape from and nothing to escape to. One is always alone.

Out of self-respect, I do not see how the Creator can change his rules, even when the abuse of personal freedom is so wholly self-mutilating. The only way he could do so would be to abrogate the liberty of evildoers. And to walk away from justice.

JANA: *I don't understand, though, why God can't, in the end, give the damned a second chance. Why can't he, at the last second, as C. S. Lewis proposed, give evildoers one more chance to repent—or else to reconfirm their original choices?*

DAD: I sympathize with you—and C. S. Lewis—in thinking that God should give the damned a second chance. But what, then, if they scorn this second chance as extortion? What if they prefer defiance, like (they think) Prometheus? What if they would rather "reign" in hell than "serve" in heaven? At some point, final is final. It can never be pleasant to see a life go horribly wrong. Freedom is more terrifying than we imagine.

In truth, maybe God does give each soul, at judgment, one last chance. Maybe many avail themselves of it, especially those who sinned only out of weakness, not out of malice. In those cases, though, surely an omniscient and merciful Judge would already have swept them into his arms, at the slightest hint of sorrow. A parent would do that, gladly. We all know, and God knows, how weak we are.

But you must also force your mind to confront (a) true evil and (b) a fixed and stubborn, defiant will. Don't you believe humans are free to enact evil and to maintain a defiant will? Such persons make their own choice for hell. No one has condemned them but they themselves.

Besides, Jana, the real question isn't Hitler. The real question is you and me. Where do our minds and hearts and wills deliberately aim?

JANA: *After death, will I, "Jana," no longer exist? Is it only beings with souls who go to heaven or hell? Is it only our souls?*

DAD: Here again I plead ignorance. I don't understand. Alone among the religions Christianity says that salvation is not just about our souls but includes our bodies, too. Not, obviously, in the physical form that they now have, yet in some adapted form. The emphasis is unmistakable: bodies, too. Our bodies are holy, not merely "prisons" for our souls; they are an essential part of ourselves, not just the outer casing of the mind. What God has in mind by this, I cannot decipher. We did not make ourselves; he did. Yet Scripture's emphasis on the human person as body-and-soul together has so great a ring of truth that I take God at his word.

JANA: *Does this mean our soul is intrinsically and inescapably linked to our bodies? So that one should not make a division between our bodies and our soul (like, "the flesh is evil, but the soul is good")? So that the ideas of heaven and hell really mean that I, who am Jana as I know myself now, will actually live forever?*

DAD: Yes. Hardly anything that Jesus says is more clear. It rings true. Take away disease and infirmities, and our natural instinct cries out for eternal life and dreads dying. Dying is nearly always treated as unnatural, a kind of punishment, and not only in Judaism and Christianity.

Still, this is a hard saying. As soon as you try to imagine it in concrete terms, you run into obvious difficulties. At which age will I be? If a "body" takes up no space, what kind of "body" is it?

We know from science that material things are not what they seem to our senses. Analyzed into atoms and smaller particles and forms of energy, what appear solid objects to the eyes appear to the scientific mind quite other—almost, by comparison, immaterial.

Yet it is clear from the way you posed your question that you are thinking of sharp sensory knowledge. But this, too, we know we can recreate through memory. Sometimes the scent of jasmine or honeysuckle will transport us across years to a sensory impression as vivid in memory as it once was in the flesh—so vivid that our whole body trembles. In using this example, C. S. Lewis does not assert that in eternity we shall only "remember" the vivid life of our bodies. Rather, his point is that we already experience more than one mode of sense knowledge.

When we speak of the human body-and-soul "in glory," as the phrase goes, or of the "glorified" body, we mean that it will be transformed, not as it is now. We do not know what this will mean. Of course, we are still rather ignorant about what our bodies mean here—both our science and our common sense tell us remarkably different things. Both suggest that the boundaries of mind and matter remain mysterious even to conceptual specialists, let alone to mere amateurs like us.

We take God at his word, and leave the method of realization to him. You must take Christ either as a lunatic/megalomaniac or as who he said he is. There is no third choice.

JANA: *What about "eternity"?*

DAD: Let me begin with a child's story:

ALBERT TALKS TO GOD
ALBERT: Lord, what does a million years seem like to you?
GOD: Like a second.
ALBERT: What does a million dollars seem like to you?
GOD: Like a penny.
ALBERT: Can I have a penny?
GOD: Just a second.

The problem for us is that we are so habituated to time that we want to think of eternity as a very long time. The two best images that we have for time is as a line, one point after another, or as an arrow in flight. But eternity isn't like that. Eternity is "outside" time, as if the long line of time, beginning to end, is, from eternity's point of view, one simultaneous moment.

It is natural for us to imagine that God has "foreknown" things in time; that he sees them "before" they happen, and that he also knows "the future," which for us is not known. It is more accurate to imagine that he sees all of this in one simultaneous grasp. For him all time is "present." There is no "fore-" to his knowledge. Eternity is like all-cupped-up-at-once simultaneity. Sometimes we experience intimations of what this might be like.

Let me mention two examples from my own life, as illustrations.

When I first went to Europe at the age of twenty-three,

it was without formal introduction to painting of any kind. The museums of Venice and Florence bowled me over, took my breath away. When I walked in upon Botticelli's "Spring" in the Uffizi Gallery in Florence, I couldn't move. I sat down and gazed. I lost all track of time.

In front of the painting, I felt a simultaneity and over-abundance of pure and perfect concentration. Not brow-furrowing concentration, but that intense, relaxed, restful pleasure that the medievals called "contemplation"—*con* (with) + *templum* (temple), to be in the temple with, the temple of one's own mind and heart, in the presence of su-perabundant *being*. It was the first great painting I discov-ered on my own. It was a kind of first love.

A more trivial example, maybe, but one that is the old-est in my memory: I must have been about nine or ten. I was playing football on a hot day in September, on a large football field in a corner of the field. You need to understand how much I loved playing football, how intently I loved to concentrate—for I felt I wasn't as good as the others, not as big as some, not as fast as others, but that I could make up for that by being smarter and paying more intense atten-tion, anticipating sudden turns in the game. I specialized in trying to surprise. On that September day, faraway I heard shouting, as if coming from some other planet. Gradually— while I was intent on the boys on the other side breaking from the huddle with the play (one of them looked furtively at me, so I made myself doubly ready)—it was clear that the sound from afar was my name being called. But it *couldn't* be. We had only just started playing. It couldn't be more than ten—at most twenty—minutes ago since we began. After the play ended, and I had knocked down a pass thrown in my direction, my mother was shouting *It's six o'clock, dinner is ready, your father is waiting, come!* Somewhere, three hours had disappeared. I was shaking my head about it, walking across the grass as the game was breaking up. The air *was* cooler, evening was coming on, and every muscle in my body ached. But it had felt like one eternity, one rapturous moment, all-wrapped-up-in-one. I never felt the time passing. I had been outside of time. My idea of heaven!

JANA: *What is "heaven"? A place?*

DAD: Is heaven a place? I think you know that wherever I travel in the world, however wonderful and beautiful the place, if your mother is not with me I am not entirely there. I see, I appreciate, but without her the experience is always half-full. I will tell you something stranger. I even felt this way before I was married, while I was alone as a seminarian. Climbing in the Alps or whatever, I always felt the experience was incomplete because I had no one to share it with, no one who would see it with me as I saw it. To experience something alone can be poignant beyond expressing. But part of the poignancy (for me at least) is that the circuit is not complete; another person whom I love has to be there with me, for my satisfaction.

Heaven is not like being in a place, but it is like being in a presence. It is like seeing and experiencing at highest intensity together, wordlessly, outside of time. It is like one of those long, lingering kisses of youth, the first of the most dear, that one then wishes could go on forever. If you read

The Song of Songs, you will gain an idea of heaven, through the eyes of a young love.

I know it is hard for those who barely know whether they believe in God, and who have not conversed with him for more than a few hours in their lives, here and there, and who have not learned how to draw near him wordlessly for long stretches, to imagine that "being with God" is worth very much. The very thought leaves them cold.

Try talking with God—simply opening your heart to him, without having to say any particular words (or any words at all)—and reminding yourself that you are always in his presence, that nothing about you is hidden from him, that you don't have to try to make any impression, there's no need to flirt, all you have to do is *be, quietly, resting in his presence, alert and willing.* This is the way you come to the experience of "being with God." The greatest prayer in the world is a simple "yes" to his presence. He is there *before* you make yourself aware of and ready for him.

The greatest prayer known to the church is Mary's response to the words of the Archangel Gabriel, telling her that she would conceive a child of God, and that the Lord is with her. She was already betrothed to Joseph. All sorts of problems loomed. She said: *"Be it done to me according to thy word."* Be x done to me, when I do not fully know or understand the x or what will follow from it. *Yes.* The first moment of human liberation is receptivity.

Ivan Karamazov, in Dostoyevsky's great novel, said that he could never say *yes* to God as long as one innocent child cried, abandoned in the night. And yet to assume that God, the Creator of love, loves the abandoned child as much as Ivan Karamazov, seems not so large a leap. Still, Karamazov says *no*. His will to say *no* blocks the grace of God's love from entering his own heart.

JANA: *I don't understand what one is supposed to say "yes" to. Is it to accept what life—God—has thrown in our path? Is it to accept God's will for our life as a whole? Is it to accept the world as it is?*

DAD: It is to trust God. To trust God in all respects. It is not unlike the covenant of marriage. Do you freely entrust your future life to this man? Yes or no? Our "yes" to God is also a kind of covenant, "for better or worse, for richer or poorer."

We do not know what the future will bring, what the *x* will be, in "Be *x* done to me according to thy will." Not knowing, we align our wills with God's will. A young married woman I read of learned this prayer from her father, a Presbyterian minister in Cincinnati: "Lord, I will what you will for me today and for the future; I want to go where you want me to go; I want to be what you want me to be. My will is to be at one with your will in all that I am and do and hope." For fear of where it might lead her during a difficult period of her life, she was afraid to say this prayer during several months; she couldn't do it.

So her father told her to say another: "Lord, help me to be willing to say that prayer again." This she did, until the strength was given her to go back to her childhood prayer. It again transformed her life, by opening her to the darkness she was afraid of until light at last reappeared. Even in the dark, she once again was at peace, in tune with her Divine Lover.

Accepting reality as it is, however, also means accepting our responsibility to change the world, "to build up the Kingdom of God on earth," to nudge "the City of Man" until it more closely resembles "the City of God." To say "yes" is not a recipe for passivity, but a response to a challenge.

What I love about *The Brothers Karamazov*—I used to read a different Dostoyevsky novel every Easter week (a wonderful way to get in the spirit of the passion, death, and resurrection of Jesus)—is the radical clarity that Dostoyevsky brings (in Ivan and Alyosha Karamazov and Father Zossima) to the fundamental human question: To the presence of God, do I say *no* or *yes?* That is the substance of hell and heaven. An eternity of *no* or *yes*. To be fixed in inescapable isolation and self-enclosure, apart from insight and love, confined within oneself; or to be open to "the Love that moves the sun and all the stars." That is the choice we make.

There is much about God I would like to know. And there are many inquiries I have never reached the end of, and that I would like to push to the end. I always loved painting; I always loved poetry—and theater. There are a great many persons whose friendship I would like to try out. Insight I don't think is ever bereft of energy. I don't anticipate being bored, in the infinite Light and Friendship of our Creator. I like being with your mother, and our interests never lead us to boredom but only to frustration for want of time. To me it is amazing just to learn about people in all their endless variety, strange angles, and odd turns. The wonders of God solely on this earth are beyond lifetimes of absorption, and we are unable even to imagine those he has held in reserve, for after this brief preview. I don't try to imagine. I am content to be surprised, in his time, in his way.

That is why I didn't like the word "bribery" that you used in your question. I don't think that heaven and hell are offered to us as bribes—or extortion. As C. S. Lewis points out, we get what we choose, in either case. No more and no less. We get what we love. If I love poetry it is no "bribe" if I get to read poetry; it is just the exercise of what I love. If I love your mother, it is no "bribe" that I get to marry her; it is just the relation we choose. And hell, as I have conceived it (which I think is in accord with the Scriptures and with tradition), is no threat, but only the full expression of an egotist's choice of his own will, in place of the love of God.

In sinning, no doubt, most people most of the time know not what they do. They have such a vague idea of God that they know not Who it is that they are turning away from. I myself have been once or twice rudely treated on the telephone by strangers, who mistook me for a receptionist or secretary. Their voices changed remarkably when they learned that I was the one they were seeking—and from whom they wished some favor. I imagine that the Creator is more kindly to such persons than I have managed to be. The Creator is never surprised by our behavior. He knows what is in us.

Looking at the bleeding Christ on the cross, I cannot say that our behavior does not sadden him. He must greatly will that it would not occur, since the load upon him is already unendurable. Since he died to take away our sins, I am certain that the least signs of sorrow on our part, whose genuineness is vouched for by plain efforts of amendment, are sufficient for him.

But among those who, far from showing sorrow, glory in what they do, what can the God of liberty do? He is bound to respect personal liberty.

JANA: *But what sins count as serious? What is the cutoff point? Eternity seems like such an unfair punishment.*

DAD: Humans may be excused when they fail God, for they—we—are weak. But how can we be excused when we choose to love ourselves, whose miseries we have no excuse not to know? To put self before God is a delicious folly. We do it all the time. We cannot break from bad habits. We are like statues, struggling to emerge from the stone from which we cannot break free. ("Self-love," St. Bernard wrote, "dies fifteen minutes after the self.")

We have to trust in the mercy of God.

This is how I would reply to the question about *how many* sins it takes to be condemned to hell. It is not a matter of legalisms. It is not the number, but the will. It is not the weakness, but the choice of who you are: with God or for self. Not, of course, the general *wish*, but the tangible deeds that actually reveal what our will loves.

The irony (hard to get through our heads) is that the only way to be for ourselves—for the insight and love in ourselves—is to be for God, and to die to self. When christophobic persons oppose faith because (they say) faith means loss of autonomy, that "loss" is the "death" they fear. But it is not a death at all. It is the casting off of a shell, the death of a chrysalis, in order to emerge in the real life whose germ was locked up in the shell all along. Seeds are meant to become flowers and trees, but to become so must fall into the moist ground and die. Selves are meant to be godlike, and to live and move and breathe in God, but to become so must turn away from the lesser shells of the self. Pain is required.

JANA: *But what about purgatory? As I said at the beginning, purgatory makes the most sense to me because it offers all of us a chance to redeem ourselves. Let's face it, none of us are perfect. We've all stumbled and sinned at some points in our life.*

DAD: I'm not sure if purgatory is a Christian doctrine in and of itself. It is certainly a deduction from other doctrines, firmly supported by the opinion of weighty theologians, and confirmed in the practice of the church over a long period of time. C. S. Lewis thought the concept apt. Like you, I think it makes sense. I would be embarrassed to go before God as I am, knowing what is in me—some of the unresolved appetites. Since God sees right through us, I know I'd flinch. I know it's true that I love him, and earnestly hope that I do not deceive myself in this. (Self-deception is easy.) Yet so often in my life I have come to see that what I thought were virtues were hollow—I had one false image of myself, then another. (Children and spouse are good at puncturing these images.) In any case, while I hope by his mercy to be called to his friendship forever, I could not object if in some unimaginable way I had to bear the pain of being purged from those self-loves and disordered areas of my life that I have not been able to master (and that I have secretly loved). That would seem only fitting. And just. And necessary.

The alternative is to imagine that I am ready for the presence of God. I do not think that I could stand so much light all-at-once. Much there is that has to go: Burn it away!

I know that evangelical Christians hate the concept of purgatory, believing that it detracts from the full and perfect redemption won for us by Christ. Won for us by Christ, period. There is no need for us to flinch before God, they say, because the righteousness of Jesus on the cross washes us clean. This is true.

Still, I can't help feeling a difference between being totally forgiven and needing to be put through a fiery furnace before coming into God's presence. I don't doubt for an instant the efficacy of Christ's love for me, or the Father's forgiveness and love. But I still feel an acute need to have the habitual vices in myself that led to my sins burned out at the roots. Already redeemed, I need to be purified, retrofitted, made ready. This may be an errant, anthropomorphic way of thinking, but I cannot entirely repress it. It is too psychologically true.

Purgatory in this sense may be similar to the radiation treatments and chemotherapy they give you for cancer. No one would seek such unpleasant, awful, sickening treatments casually. But when life hangs in the balance, they seem altogether worth it, however terrible—and in your mother's case they were terrible; they almost cost her her life. I was terrified beyond words.

Why should the soul be different from the body? The stakes for the body-and-soul of the immortal self are far greater than for the mortal body. If chemotherapy and radiation are prescribed by learned specialists to save us from the deadliness of cancer, I find it hard to believe that purgatory as an anteroom to the eternal presence of God is contrary to reason. It will not be long now before I will know.

"Your purgatory, Michael," one priest-critic has joked to me, "will be to read everything you have ever written. That is guaranteed to be both long and painful." Not so funny.

JANA: *Wait, is purgatory more like hell, like punishment? I imagined it to be neither hellish nor heavenly; to be more like nothingness, where what makes it so awful is simply being forced to wait for God's presence. In other words, I imagined it to be like some huge waiting room—take a number and sit. Am I wrong?*

DAD: Pain is the tradition: a kind of punishment, restitution, getting ready. Evening up the scales of justice. It seems wrong that real evildoers should escape all punishment by dint of a last-minute conversion—escape hell, yes, but not *everything*. No doubt, that's an almost childlike sense of justice. But something like it is called for. See Dante's *Purgatorio*.

Yet you may be right, in a way. Perhaps souls in purgatory have so keen a sense of God's loveliness—being so close—that the pain in the soul caused by prolonged separation is itself the punishment. Still, there are those texts in the Bible about how even the saints endure terrible pain from the fires of God's love as they approach his presence. The angels nearest God are called *Seraphim*, that is, Burning Ones.

JANA: *There are some parts of my original question that you have not answered, and about which I am still curious:*

Will there be animals in heaven? When I am in heaven, will I be aware of and able to meet others who died before me—in other words, is heaven just "me" and God or many of us and God? How does one "qualify" for heaven? (I assume the answer to that one has to do with why one ends up in hell; it all depends on the person's intent and will.)

DAD: The best speculations I have seen are in C. S. Lewis, in the chapter on animals in *The Problem of Pain*. Like you, he loved pets and believed that, through interaction with humans, at least a few animals achieve at least a dim shadow of ego and personality. They do not have a soul through which to be in union with God but through their union with humans, he speculated, perhaps in some way God grants them life in eternity with humans. There is nothing in the Bible or in tradition, I think, to take our inquiries further than speculation.

The God who made the beauty and friendliness of animals, though, will in himself convey such pleasures as favored pets afforded us in this life. All creation sings of him, Psalm 50 recounts. Surely, this must mean that the animals, too, express something of him.

> For mine are all the animals of the forests, beasts by the thousand on my mountains. I know all the birds of the air, and whatever stirs in the plains, belongs to me. If I were hungry, I should not tell you, for mine are the world and its fullness.

—Psalm 50:10–12 (The New American Bible)

If the firmament, the day, and the night speak of God (Psalm 19), don't you think that the barking of dogs and the twittering of birds also sings of him? And so with all the animals? In eternity, all those facets of the Creator of which the creatures of this earth are images will summon our exploration.

JANA: *I apologize for belaboring the point, but it used to be that at least the Catholic Church held that only the baptized get into heaven. If that's still true (and if so, why?), what happens to good people who aren't baptized? Such as: babies who die before baptism, people in religions besides Christianity, like Buddhists, and people from before the advent of Christianity or ignorant of it, like Socrates?*

DAD: On this, too, Jana, we can only speculate. What seems reasonable to you? God is far more reasonable than we are. It is legitimate to push our minds as far as we can, while reminding ourselves that we are only guessing.

We do know that there is such a thing as "baptism by desire." Those who love God with their whole hearts, their whole minds, and their whole wills, belong to him, whether the actual baptism by water has reached them or not. A single-minded will to serve the truth enjoys rightfully that "peace on earth" that is promised to "all men of good will"—but, of course, that peace is not peace as the world means peace. Devotion to truth may bring persecution, hatred, and the violence of enemies. The peace it gives is the unity the arrow has with the bull's-eye of its love.

In my experience, there are *plenty* of people in this world—non-Christians of every sort, agnostics, atheists—who are prevented from coming to baptism by obstacles not of their own making, and whose singleness of heart suggests to me that God's grace lives in them. Many such persons are happy where they are; it is the best that they know. God can be the judge, infinitely better than I.

Evangelical Christians argue that, for all of us, love for our own sins leads us to force down in ourselves, to repress, the instincts of nature and grace that would lead us to Christ; and thus that we are all in some ways guilty of our own darkness of mind. This feeling is so strong among evangelicals, I believe, because their own most vivid experience consists of seeing their own personal pattern of sins, and turning from this in revulsion. Then to Jesus, alone in this world, for release and redemption. This experience is for them so vivid that no other way to God seems even faintly comparable. In the light of this experience, they interpret biblical texts in a way that heightens and intensifies it. When fierce winds blow, they cling ever more tightly to Jesus. I find this admirable, without being inclined to see Jesus only in that perspective. The opening words of St. John's Gospel seem to me to invite a more capacious view of Jesus as the eternal Word:

> In the beginning was the Word, and the Word was with God, and he was the same as God, and through him was made all the things that were made; nothing was made without him . . .

—John 1:1–5 (Knox translation)

As the Catholic tradition reads these verses, the image of the Word is in all things; Jesus the Word appears in many guises, and in the most surprising places; his grace cannot be narrowly confined, nor his powers of redemption strictly boarded in.

Even infants, I speculate, can be secure in God's love through the love, aspirations, and concern of their parents—or even strangers. Many cloistered nuns and monks pray incessantly night and day that God's grace will not be frustrated by human inabilities and failures. This is what *ecclesia supplet* means—"grace makes up for our deficiencies."

I am sorry to be so vague, but there is little to be gained by saying more than is known. I think we concentrate on heaven and hell so much—our future surroundings, as it were—because we have hardly penetrated the loveliness of God. Imagine all the beauties of nature and human life that you have ever encountered or still hope to encounter—your Lover imagined them "before" you were born. He is more beautiful than the sum of all the beauties of earth—all the canyons and forests and oceans and mountain peaks, flowers and foliage, poems and plays and ballets, symphonies and arias.

Heaven is to be enveloped in his beauty. Hell is a recognition that to such beauty one preferred solitary confinement in oneself.

That God loves us so much that he invites us into his friendship is unspeakably beyond our dreams and fumbling words of gratitude.

PRACTICALITIES

When Judaism demanded that all sexual activity be channeled into marriage, it changed the world. The Torah's prohibition of non-marital sex quite simply made the creation of Western civilization possible. Societies that did not place boundaries around sexuality were stymied in their development. The subsequent dominance of the Western world can largely be attributed to the sexual revolution initiated by Judaism and later carried forward by Christianity. . . . This revolution consisted of forcing the sexual genie into the marital bottle. It ensured that sex no longer dominated society, heightened male-female love and sexuality (and thereby almost alone created the possibility of love and eroticism within marriage), and began the arduous task of elevating the status of women.

—Dennis Prager
1993

9

WHAT IS CHRISTIAN SEXUAL LOVE?

Human sexuality, especially male sexuality, is polymorphous, or utterly wild (far more so than animal sexuality). Men have had sex with women and with men; with little girls and young boys; with a single partner and in large groups; with total strangers and immediate family members; and with a variety of domesticated animals. They have achieved orgasm with inanimate objects such as leather, shoes, and other pieces of clothing; through urinating and defecating on each other (interested readers can see a photograph of the former at select art museums exhibiting the works of the photographer Robert Mapplethorpe); by dressing in women's garments; by watching other human beings being tortured; by fondling children of either sex; by listening to a woman's disembodied voice (e.g., "phone sex"); and, of course, by looking at pictures of bodies or parts of bodies. There is little, animate or inanimate, that has not excited some men to orgasm.

Unless the sex drive is appropriately harnessed (not squelched—which leads to its own destructive consequences), higher religion could not have developed. Thus, the first thing Judaism did was to de-sexualize God: "In the beginning God created the heavens and the earth" by his will, not through any sexual behavior. This was an utterly radical break with all other religions, and it alone changed human history.

—Dennis Prager
1993

JANA: *The time has come to ask you about premarital sex. Premarital sex is an issue because it is being engaged in by many people—and particularly by many young people. Unfortunately, people don't even think twice before engaging in premarital sex, nor do they consider it a sin that requires a change of behavior.*

For example, in college most of my peers automatically assumed a couple had to be having sex if they had dated for longer than two months. If a couple had dated seriously for a long period (such as a year or more), it was assumed that they were "putting rabbits to shame." Even worse, I remember sitting in a student lounge when I was in the seventh grade and listening to the eighth-grade girls discuss who had sex with whom the past weekend and whether they had been smart enough to use contraception to avoid pregnancy.

Too often, the concept of "love" is nowhere close to the idea of "sexual." On the issue of sex, it's pretty ugly out there.

I know what religion says, or at least what the Catholic Church says: premarital sex is a sin. Intercourse is supposed to be the ultimate expression not only of love between a man and a woman but of god's love for his creatures; it is the moment when a couple physically expresses their union through marriage, and when god replays the miracle of creation through birth. That's somewhat close, right? But what does it all mean? Are all who break this rule doomed?

It's wonderful to witness the rising "Virginity movement," but we still have to deal with reality, that is, the fact that many young people are still having sex. While I think the vast majority of people would argue that teenagers shouldn't be having sex because they're too young (they don't truly understand love and can't truly comprehend the consequences), a good portion of these same people could never imagine telling an "adult" to cease and desist. I even remember arguing with Mom once that I didn't think an older single person should be forced to die a virgin.

I know sex is not just supposed to be physical pleasure, but understood in its deeper meaning of love, union, and procreation—with the added bonus of being enjoyable. But what do you say to the people who honestly believe that they are fulfilling these requirements, yet aren't married? And what about homosexuality? Finally, how do we reconcile society's very sexual reality—where premarital sex is embraced, accepted, and even honored—with religious mores? Religious conventions may be good and valuable reminders, but so few people seem to practice them nowadays.

The ironic thing is—if this is true—that other cultures don't have the same problems the United States does. Someone once told me that in some more "overtly" sexual cultures, such as Brazil, the rates of premarital sex are lower. As if their open embrace of, and appreciation for, sexuality allows them not to feel the need to act upon their urges. But here, with our Puritan-like strictures, we condemn sexual images while furtively indulging our urges.

So without taking the easy route—just saying it's wrong and after all, we'd all be much happier and have better experiences if we reserved our sexual activity to a committed, trustworthy, and loving relationship, i.e., marriage—please explain sexual love in the context of religion, and reality.

DAD: Back in 1966 or so in a course I was teaching at Stanford I was supposed to be giving a lecture on this same subject, and had a carefully worked out lecture plan. I would spend the first part of the lecture on the good things about premarital sex, then point out the deficiencies (as people actually experience these). Then I would end up on the ideal form of sexual love, in marriage—the form that fulfills all the aspirations of the other forms. I had collected some great texts from literature that allowed me to make all these points in terms of human experience, without even bringing in religious judgments.

Trouble was, the first part of the lecture went so well that I got a little carried away, and just as I was finishing it up the bell rang for the end of class. I had never quite gotten to the things that are wrong with premarital sex, only the parts that made it seem good and right. Worse still, the next scheduled class fell on a holiday, so our class would not meet for the crucial part of the lecture for an entire week.

"Oh-oh," I told the class as they were rustling their books and chairs to leave, "don't do anything until you hear the last part of the lecture. See you in a week." The laughter was loud.

Jana, you've already made one important point about this subject: the horse is out of the barn. We are living in an age of very corrupt morals; it's a little like living through the excesses of Rome in Christianity's earliest days. Then and now, Christian teachings arrive as a sort of culture shock: "You *have* to be kidding!" (A friend of mine jokes, "If God doesn't do something about America, he's going to owe an apology to Sodom and Gomorrah.")

Two other observations right up front. First, in Christian teaching, of all the sins, those of the flesh are the least serious. Dante, for instance, depicted nine circles of hell, and placed those who sinned sexually in the least severe. He judged (and so did all the Christian ages) the sins of the soul to be far more deadly: arrogance, pride, despair, closure of heart. Sins of the flesh flow mostly from weakness of the will. One wants to resist, but the attraction is too great.

In a way, sexual sins are attempts to be like god, to be desired, to forget our finiteness, to shed (for a blind moment) our insecurity. Sexual sins are, in several senses, lies we tell ourselves.

Anyone who knows how weak human beings are—even otherwise good human beings—understands how powerfully sweet sexual temptation can be. It is especially so when "everyone is doing it." It even seems unfair to be asked to resist. (I remember vividly the hot summers of adolescence, and how unfair I thought it was of God to give Catholics so hard a moral code—more exactly, how unfair it was to have me be born Catholic. Why couldn't I just have been an unbeliever, and done what desire impelled me to do?)

The second point is that *not* everybody *is* doing it. When you look at the polls, always look at the substantial minority of young men and women—one quarter to one third—who are *not* having sex outside of marriage. Given the way sexual activity is lavishly discussed, advertised, and promoted by popular culture, that number always seems to me astonishingly high. Suppose the true number were only 10 percent? Or 5? There are many groups of 5 percent or less to which one would like to belong. Even fewer than that would show that a commitment to chastity can be carried out.

Chastity is different from abstinence. The latter is

merely negative, a kind of avoidance. Chastity is a habit of heart and mind to be cultivated, a way of looking at things, a wisdom about context and order, a part of the practice of self-government. It is a way of sharing God's life.

Jana, can I talk with you a little about the background of this question? There is an essential insecurity about human life, for humans at any age. We are not infinitely lovable; we are going to die; we are not God. There are a great many things about ourselves we do not like.

In heeding the commandment, "Love your neighbor as yourself," the curveball is "yourself." Most people find themselves very hard to love—easy enough to pamper, but not so easy to forgive, and not so easy to love. When you learn to love yourself in the right way, love of others is much easier. But so is everything else, including self-restraint—and chastity.

Yet as teenagers and twenty-somethings, this essential insecurity is especially acute.

Most sexual sins, I think, spring less from actual sexual passion than from a burning need to find comfort against the normal loneliness and insecurity of being human. If I am right, this helps to explain why, immediately after illicit sex, one often feels no better at all. The means is not proportionate to the end. Besides, one feels a little cheap about using another person as a means.

We can lie to our conscience—cover it with lies, smother it—but our consciences finally do not lie. The truth about ourselves moils around inside us waiting for air.

I hate to see the innate truthfulness of young people become corrupted. When a woman allows a man to penetrate her, he and she are joining their bodies as one. In the normal run of things, unless they take precautions, with significant probability this union engenders a child—a union of their gene streams, the living sign and fruit of their commitment and their oneness. The upbringing of a child is a long and painful task, and nowadays it lasts for more than twenty years. So this sign of their long-term union—their copulation—is a magnificent sign, indeed. It is very important to the future of the race. It is important to their family, to their community, and to their own future. A child is not exactly what they are thinking about, of course, only the assuagement of their feelings and the slaking of their thirst for sweet pleasure. This is exactly where the falsehood lies. They lie together.

Condoms, contraceptives, diaphragms, and the pill, some may say, have done away with all that "nonsense." Making love nowadays has become a little like shaking hands, a gesture of companionship, not much more than a kiss used to be. (Kissing used to be so wild a pleasure!) So much the worse. When the most sacred sign of union for the lifelong friendship of a man and a woman—the most godlike, noblest, and most satisfying of all friendships—is shared casually, the sign can never mean again what it says: that two have become one flesh for all time (and all eternity). Will lovers ever again be able to swear eternal love? Will anyone ever know who is using whom? Will any woman, or any person, ever be more than a useful *thing*?

In the Christian view, sexual acts are inherently good—a great and blessed gift of God, sweet, pleasurable, unitive, noble, sometimes fruitful of the most marvelous of miracles: new, throbbing life. In addition, sexual sins in illicit unions are in many ways the least of sins and the most understandable. (Of these, adultery is the worst because it is a betrayal of another, a flagrant lie, and the breaking of a vow made before God and family.) Alas, however, the misuse of human sexuality compromises the whole meaning of human personality, and undercuts the human ability to be the most self-governing of the animals and the most like God.

JANA: *What exactly do you mean by "compromises the whole meaning of human personality"? Do you mean that sex without love and not in the context of marriage reduces humans to no more than objects? That to be self-governing humans we must always view each other and treat each other as equals and as humans—not as means to an end?*

DAD: That's about it. The battle with our own sexuality is tremendously difficult. It is an arena of almost daily combat from the time of adolescence onward. It has spawned probably the best and funniest of "war stories"—really good jokes of many kinds, from the rollicking to the scabrous. The entire human situation, especially with regard to sex, is comic. To approach sex with a measure of levity enhances it. That is the best protection of its beauty.

Add to this the other dimension you mention in your question, the alleged puritanism of the United States, compared to the more "overtly sexual cultures"—Catholic nations such as Brazil or Italy. The most vivid dramatization your mother and I have ever seen of this difference occurred in a presentation of the Ballet Folklorico of Mexico that we saw about 1968 in Mexico City. The entire evening's program was full of sexual symbolism, flirtation, and innuendo. Yet every gesture was somehow performed in the context of family and community. It was sexy, sensuous, flirtatious, suggestive, but not—how can I say?—"dirty." It was not disordered.

Sex in its rightful place seems very clean, good fun, true, ennobling. I think European and Latin women have a striking way of being both sexy and self-governing. A certain approachability combined with maturity, even at a young age; a sense of themselves as persons having spiritual weight, quite *female* persons. Such sexuality is something to emulate.

I think you are wrong, Jana, about the numbers for illegitimacy in Brazil and elsewhere in Latin America.[1] I had the same idea—that illegitimacy is lower there—but when I inquired there I learned that their numbers (although not officially tabulated) are probably higher than ours (and ours now stand at 30 percent of all children born). This is partly because the custom has grown up among married men, even those who are poor, of having girlfriends on the side who bear them other children, for whom many men cannot or do not provide. The streets are full of such unattached children, as one can see. Disordered sexuality is an international problem. And the U.S. is no longer puritan.

In popular psychology, the sheer power of sex to disrupt human lives is vastly underestimated. Popular magazines insist that we should treat sexuality just like any other human drive—and then proceed to idealize it more than any other.

---

[1] Although official figures on illegitimacy in Brazil are not kept, 8 percent of all Brazilian teenagers give birth each year, 2 percentage points higher than in the United States. Most of these teenagers, of course, are unmarried, yet in Brazil (where early marriages are common) a full 14 percent are in fact married.

The covers of magazines at the supermarket checkout counters in our neighborhood, and now elsewhere around the world, are wonders of self-delusion. If one compares what women's magazines say about men, and men's magazines about women, one wonders how the opposite sexes in this modern world ever find each other.

I have no illusions, Jana, about a Christian view of sex making much headway against the forces of American popular culture, or against modern culture in other sectors of the world. I hear much that is good "blowing in the wind" these days—a new seriousness about the family, a wake-up call regarding the sufferings and disabilities that thrive among the millions born out of wedlock, the return of teaching about abstinence and chastity, a new approach to their own sexuality among significant numbers of young women. Essentially, however, we will have to endure the present age, as Christians have had to endure many others like it in the past. Our best hope is that there are cycles of decadence and rebirth, rotating slowly from principled standards to rebellion to permissiveness, and then again from decadence to a renewal of conviction. For us too, one day, cultural renewal will return.

Meanwhile, the best strategy is to burrow in and to endure. Whatever others do, one retains one's liberty to seek a different way, and to hope for better times.

Three thousand years ago, Judaism was distinctive in the Middle East for its rigorous teaching about monogamy, and above all about the seal of divine approval on the union of male and female. "Man and woman he made them," the Torah announces right at the top of Genesis. *This* is the image of God: man and woman joined as one.

JANA: *Isn't the disapproval of homosexuality due to that image? Is homosexual coupling considered wrong because it is an act of sex just for pure pleasure with no higher meaning? But even so, wouldn't Christ say we must still love and support the individuals and not discriminate against them (as he took care to accept outcasts in his time)? What if it is more than just sex, and the gay couple professes to truly love each other? Why, exactly, is homosexuality considered wrong? Are those who are gay merely feeling natural desires that they are supposed to control and not act on?*

DAD: Why is homosexuality wrong? Christianity learned this point from Judaism, and placed it in a new context. Unlike the other religions of the Near East (and many of the Mediterranean cultures), Judaism held that a man lying down with a man is a misuse of the Creator-given gift of sexuality. It may be understandable as a temptation and an attraction for some—all sins are understandable as temptations and attractions, or else humans would be sinless—but it is wrong. In Scripture, it is worse than wrong. It is "an abomination." What is so wrong about it? Even those who think Judaism and Christianity are wrong about homosexuality may benefit from understanding the reasons for such a strong and unbroken tradition.

An especially precious image of God is given the world in the union between man and woman; in their joining, human nature becomes complete. It is as man and woman that human beings are images of God, not as man alone or woman alone. Homosexual acts are, in effect, a mockery of God's image. This teaching made Judaism quite distinctive in the ancient world.

As a pro-homosexual philosopher from the University of Chicago recently wrote, the ancient peoples of the Mediterranean (except for the Jews) were not concerned about people's gender preferences:

> Ancient categories of sexual experience differed considerably from our own. . . . The central distinction in sexual morality was the distinction between active and passive roles. The gender of the object . . . is not in itself morally problematic. Boys and women are very often treated interchangeably as objects of [male] desire. What is socially important is to penetrate rather than to be penetrated. Sex is understood fundamentally not as interaction, but as a doing of something to someone.

Dennis Prager, a prominent Jewish writer, points out that "Judaism changed all this," by denying that human beings are sexually "interchangeable." For Judaism, sex is about love and fidelity, and a man and a woman joined together are a privileged image of God. Judaism ensured that for human beings sex would become "fundamentally interaction," and not simply "a doing of something to someone." Judaism threw out ancient Near Eastern customs of cultic sex and temple prostitutes. It demanded that males discipline their sexuality by confining it to the marriage bond between man and woman in mutual fidelity.

The biological inadequacies of homosexuality are obvious. Even in cultures in which homosexuality flourished, at least in some sectors of society, its psychological and moral deficiencies were apparent. Homosexual acts were regarded even in some pagan societies, even in some that saw in them some utilities, as acts that cut counter to what makes the human race and human individuals thrive, as acts that frustrate nature. Judaism added the reflection that the Creator intended human sexuality to express the union of man and woman in the permanent relationship of matrimony. Judaism taught that matrimony mirrors something about God and is best suited to the long-term rearing required by human offspring. A man and a woman belong to each other in matrimony through a covenant that is a replica of the covenant between the Creator and his people. That is why both adultery and fornication are forbidden in the Ten Commandments. Sexual love is perfected in a covenant—a covenant, not a mere contract, a permanent person-transforming communion—that signals a love made fruitful for future generations. Other uses of sexuality (noncovenantal) are deemed sterile, illicit, and offenses against the Creator.

Outside the marital framework, sexual acts sow disorder and destruction. They eat away at the honesty and dignity of those who give way to them. They harden the soul. They signify a union that does not exist. They distort both the image of God and God's covenant with his people.

Nowadays, moreover, there is a hidden premise in the air that a desire implies a right. If you have the desire, you have the right—maybe the duty—to satisfy it, and it would be cruel to be self-denying.

I have seen in writing the claim that an enlightened person today has a fundamental moral right to do anything sexually with any part of her (or his) body, and with anyone or anything she (or he) pleases. In this view, there is no created order to respect, no commandment of God, and no religious teaching about the right ordering of freedom in sexual love. One inevitable consequence of this view, of course, is that sexual acts are emptied of significance. They are like twitches or tics, amoral and inconsequential, and detached from any reality beyond desire. Given this widespread view, one can see why in a survey of sexual satisfaction many years ago, *Redbook* learned to its editors' surprise that religious women enjoy sex far more than secular women, and the more strictly orthodox, the most. It figures.

Anyway, on the basis of the hidden premise mentioned above, homosexual advocates say that it would be cruel to deny them the fulfillment of their sexual desires. They further argue that marriage is a universal right, which is being unfairly denied them. They argue that on both counts they are aggrieved and victimized.

From a Jewish and Christian point of view, however, these claims are weak. First, the same morality that applies to single heterosexuals outside of marriage applies to homosexuals: no fornication, no adultery. Not that such acts are not pleasant, alluring, at times almost irresistible—only that they fall short of the measure of human dignity.

Second, matrimony is a Jewish and Christian institution (a sacrament, Catholics say) designed and privileged for a specific purpose: to sanctify the union of man and woman as, together, an image of God and the God-given framework for the rearing of children. (Children are not hamsters; they cannot be machine-fed by bottles—they tried that in Rumanian orphanages, and raised children with grave affective disorders. Children must be held and talked to as persons over many years.) Gabriel Marcel, the Christian existentialist, wrote in "The Mystery of the Family" that it is not an institution merely for friends, even long-term friends, or roommates, or chums.

In our society, of course, there is a significant (and highly successful) body of homosexuals, including some of the most talented people around us. Many of them live chastely and, like other people, the vast majority are honorable and in many ways virtuous. It is right for Jews and Christians not merely to show tolerance toward them, but to show respect. They too are made in the image of God, and are children of God. Better than we, they know to what an extent their sexuality is both burden and gift—as ours is. Some are quite saintly. The full range of God's love is open to them, if they do his will. That standard is the same for them and for us. No one escapes, no one of us, without carrying a heavy cross.

In order to love your mother and father, Jana, you do not have to approve of all that we do, or to say that what you think is wrong in our behavior is right. It is not only *possible* to love a person, and yet not approve of some of their actions; in a universe of sinners, that is the necessary condition for brotherly love. If a member of our family were gay, we would want such a one to love us as we love her or him. Family members of great spiritual need are not unknown in our family; at various times, each of us has leaned heavily on the others.

JANA: *So the idea is that we should accept homosexuals, but not their acts of sex, which corrupt the image of God. We shouldn't discriminate against gay people (particularly, one can't justify violence), but support them. In other words, love the sinner but hate the sin.*

DAD: Yes. The fact that our society has become more open and tolerant about homosexuals represents a good step. Tolerance and respect, however, do not require a commitment to moral equivalence or even to moral approval. In a free society, ample space must be allowed for private life. But Jews and Christians and others must not be coerced into stating things we do not believe, approving of acts we do not approve of, or acting contrary to our own convictions. In the first blush of a new freedom, some gay and lesbian activists want more than privacy or even public space to make their case. They want public moral approval.

Moreover, at some point it will be time for an end to the vast public dishonesty in today's propaganda about homosexuality. In the effort to win public support, much is being suppressed—about AIDS and the methods of its transmission, about the practices of gays and lesbians, about the relative frequency of stable, long-term relationships among gays, and many other matters of moral and humanitarian significance. But the spirit of unrelenting inquiry will not forever be held back.

Much of today's discussion, alas, is couched in pieties that are far from reality; but there are some signs of growing public candor. For instance, one serious scholar, who is in favor of permitting marriages among gays, estimates that only a tiny percentage of gay relationships would qualify as long-term and marked by fidelity.[2] His honesty is unusual, but it does make his argument the most powerful I have encountered on that side of the question. As such honesty spreads in wider and wider circles, our society has a chance to reach some sort of legal and moral equilibrium on this vexed question, rather different from the present agitated and dishonest imbalance.

---

[2]Stephen Macedo, "Homosexuality and the Conservative Mind," 84 *Georgetown Law Journal*, 1995, pp. 285–291.

JANA: *Speaking of AIDS, many extreme religious people think AIDS is a plague from God to punish gay people. I can't believe God would do that—isn't that what the covenant after the flood promised and the rainbow to this day symbolizes? What are Christian churches doing to respond to AIDS? (I know the Catholic Church, particularly, is often bitterly attacked by gays.)*

DAD: The Catholic Church in the United States runs the largest single system of medical care and treatment for AIDS patients in the entire country. Some nuns, lay persons, and priests have dedicated their whole lives to this work. They see the image of Christ in those who need both medical care and love. AIDS should not be thought of as caused by God, or even as a "punishment," for God often sends sun and rain on just and unjust alike; the evil prosper, and the good endure afflictions. Of course, as in all other matters, God is not unjust to let us suffer from the consequences of our own acts. But he also asks of those of us who are not afflicted that we open our hearts to those who are, and bring them help. Judgment belongs only to God, not to us. Our job is to extend a hand.

We are lucky to live in a society in which the public laws, while engaging the support of a large consensus, do not have to coincide fully with the moral views of any one party. We can get through even bitter "culture wars" over how to order our public life together, with some realistic hope of reaching a solution that all can live with, and all can support with loyalty and even gratitude. One condition of that happy outcome, of course, is respect for one another even in our deepest and most bitter differences.

The other condition is great honesty in admitting where the other fellow is right and I am wrong. It is not easy to get moral matters right, and that is why we need to be respectful of one another when we disagree. Tomorrow, any one of us could learn to see matters differently. Moral conversions happen daily. Even when convictions are very deep, it is surprising how often a new and unexpected light can make everything look different.

In a way, in fact, a meditation on homosexuality serves to highlight certain essentials of the married love between man and woman that might otherwise escape our attention and thus fail to awaken our gratitude. Among gays and lesbians, the effort to argue that homosexual love should also qualify for legal support as a form of civic marriage has brought to light the benefits of long-term fidelity, mutual sacrifice, self-giving, and other necessary parts of a fully human love. Perhaps some gays and lesbians are in effect admitting that faithful married love between man and woman, in the context of rearing children, is the most perfect form of human love, while a faithful and long-term union between two gays or two lesbians is for them its best available approximation. That may be shading the statement too close to my side of the issue. But something like that cannot be too far from the mark, for that is the structure of some of the current argument.

JANA: *So now we're back to marriage.*

DAD: Yes, the whole culture is. And now I am getting back to my main point: For the God of Judaism and Christianity, the *union between man and woman* is a privileged sharing of the life of God. Neither man alone nor woman alone mirrors God's life as fully as their union. This is the union blessed with children and the hope of the future. It endures every adversity except death, and even then I believe that in some sense this union lasts forever, in the friendship of God.

This is the reason that for Christians marriage between man and woman is a sacrament, that is, an outward sign ratified by Jesus of his own infused life and love. In marriage, men and women are caught up in the love that drives the universe in all its parts. All other sexual loves, attractive though they be, fall short.

I have told you over the years that the two most important books to me in my youth were *The Allegory of Love,* a difficult scholarly book by C. S. Lewis, and *Love in the Western World,* by the Swiss philosopher Denis de Rougemont. Independently, both concur that all the love literature of the world springs from Jewish and Christian teachings about male and female and about monogamy. Only in this religious context is human destiny deeply embedded in the fate of love between one man and one woman. Moreover, the teaching is so hard, and so often thwarted by war and journeying and sickness and death (not to say by unhappy marriages), that very early in the Christian era the literature of the troubadours arose—the literature of adultery and, finally, the literature of falling in love with love. Thus arose, as a parody of Christian love, the ethos of romantic love.

Apart from Christian and Jewish fidelity, this parody has no springboard, no lift. The Western love story depends on the Jewish and Christian view of woman and man. That is why a secular view of human sexuality, further and further removed from Judaism and Christianity, flattens human love. At first, modern (uninhibited) sex seems liberating. Yet rip the meaning from sex and in the end it bores. In a shattering book on sex at our century's end, the young feminist Katie Roiphe writes:

> What could be wrong with freedom? It's not the absence of rules exactly, the dizzying sense that we can do whatever we want, but the sudden realization that nothing we do matters . . .
>
> Gone are the days when illicit couples had to register in hotel rooms under the name "Mr. and Mrs. John Smith." As they ride up the elevator to the sinful anonymity of their double suite with minibar and color TV, "Mr. and Mrs. John Smith" are now left with the naked solitude of their real names: the unsettling knowledge that they are not playing a role in any larger social drama. And along with the freedom this new tolerance allows comes a certain sense of pointlessness.
>
> —*Last Night in Paradise*, 1997

Recently, I was asked in a panel discussion at a conference of Catholics what I would say, if I were a priest, and a couple came to me for marriage preparations and admitted that they were already living together; in fact, had been living together for two years. I fumbled the question a bit—marriage counseling is not my métier—and said, "Two years? It's probably too late to say much, except maybe, to point out the difference between the significance that lovemaking will have for them when it is conducted within the grace of the sacrament, in union with God, and the significance it has for them now." Some such thing, not so smooth as it sounds here. I wasn't happy with what I said. I wished I had had a chance to try again.

Later an older man, a priest, said in a small group that recently a couple like that had come to him. In this case, the couple were in their fifties, widow and widower. They volunteered that they had been living together for several months. "I looked them calmly in the eye," he said with a twinkle, "and told them that if they wanted me to prepare them for a sacrament, they had better go back to living apart again for a few more months, until they got married. This shocked them, of course. But later, I think they were glad. The sacrament meant more to them then. It wasn't just 'an automatic.' They got themselves good and ready." The priest wasn't at all sure what the more progressive people in our group would think, and allowed as how some of the priests he'd told this to didn't much like it. But he made clear he'd do it again. To him, it was a matter of integrity. People have to come to the gospels; he did not want to cut the gospels to them. I liked that.

Dante called his great trilogy *The Divine Comedy*, and truly God's great gift of sex is a comic gift, a helping gift, and a risky gift. Sex is not, perhaps, the keenest of pleasures but it is exceedingly pleasurable, as well as the proximate cause of the miracle of new life. Our longing for sexual pleasure is so great that it wounds many lives, and troubles us all with passions and desires that could capsize us if we are not careful. A good sense of humor helps. Pleasure itself is not to be despised; it is a good and lovely thing. The task is to keep it ordered to a good and full life. Well-ordered, it brings laughter to the lips. Disordered, it brings much sadness, emptiness, and a sense of loss.

I like Chesterton's thought that a human, after all, is a quadruped. It takes two sexes and four legs to make the image of God whole in us. Matrimony is the Creator's best (and most comedic) expression of himself.

And how about this thought? Aristotle held that men and women are unequal, so that men could have real friendships only with men (their equals). A world away, fifteen centuries later, St. Thomas Aquinas looked at friendship very differently. In his usual calm, understated way he wrote:

> The greatest friendship is that between man and wife.

These words are true. Exactly what God's covenant with Jews and Christians intends. God's kingdom in this world begins in such friendships.

10

ON WOMANHOOD: MARRIAGE, FRIENDSHIP, CHILDREN

The Church would just as soon canonize a woman as a man, and I suppose has done more than any other force in history to free women.

—Flannery O'Connor
(1925–1964)

Perhaps not since the first century A.D. have women been so actively and visibly involved in the life of the people called together by Jesus Christ. . . . the Church's health care system, the second largest in the world, is managed almost entirely by Catholic women executives. Catholic women, religious and lay, are superintendents, principals and trustees in the world's largest provider of private elementary and secondary education. (The Catholic Church long ago pioneered in women's education, opening up opportunities for young women in countries where others paid little or no attention to girls' intellectual development.)

—Mary Ann Glendon

JANA: *One of the strongest accusations leveled against religion—especially the Catholic Church—by the nonreligious people I know has to do with women, the family, and patriarchy. Because of the structure of many religions as traditional, patriarchal hierarchies, many people perceive a corresponding pressure to behave in a traditional, patriarchal manner. Women especially, but males as well, often have complained to me that they feel pressured to be nothing more than family units and baby-making machines. Whether it is an internal pressure from religion or a personal misreading by an individual or several individuals, in today's society the issue of "traditional" behavior has particular resonance.*

Many women want either to choose not to have children, whether or not they get married, or to have children and still work. Yet, friends have confessed to me that they get the feeling this is at odds with their church.

This is the crux of some people's problems with religion: a pressure—whether real or imagined—that insists everyone's main goal in life should be to get married, have kids, and raise a family. Yet what about everything else? What about people who choose not to get married and/or have kids, or who, due to circumstances beyond their control, don't get married or have kids?

Are women really supposed to find their true and total fulfillment in raising children and being a wife? Is that Christianity's definition of womanhood? Diapers and boxer shorts? (Mind you, I personally am looking forward to being married and having kids. I am the one, after all, who used to say I wanted to be a bus driver when I grew up so I could drive my eighteen kids around. Needless to say, I've become a bit more realistic about family size and costs.)

Basically, what I want to know is how does the Judeo-Christian tradition define us as man and woman and how does it define relationships? What is the family? What about

*friendship? Is it just doing unto your neighbor as you would
have done unto you? Or, is it deeper and more meaningful?
I mean, look at some of the relationships—familial and
friendly—portrayed in the Bible: Cain and Abel, Esau and
Jacob, Lot's daughters, and Judas' and Peter's betrayals of
Jesus. It is not a pretty picture. (But the nice thing about
the Bible is that it does present some strong female charac-
ters, even if they always seem to be mothers or wives.)*

*So, should I be making a desperate, last-ditch attempt
to pull together a hope chest and a dowry to market myself
to potential suitors—or is there more to life, and Christianity's view of women and life, than that?*

DAD: Since most of the arguments against "patriarchy" in
Judaism and Christianity are addressed against the Catholic
Church, the shortest way to reply to your questions is to
address the role of women in Catholicism.

Very briefly: No, you do not have to have children. The
single life (whether freely chosen or given as one's destiny)
is highly honored, and it is as noble for a woman to have a
career—to do great things or humble things—as for a man.
Yes, marriage is considered the highest and most morally
stretching form of human friendship, the one most blessed
by God, most godlike, and nearest to the life of God himself.
And children are a great gift, a sweet responsibility, a source
of both joy and sorrow, great teachers of one's own soul,
and (alas for the children) an abiding worry—one wants so
much more for them, more than one would allow oneself to
wish for oneself.

Naturally, Jana, since feminists have made a tragic error
in building a fictive right to do evil—to kill an innocent

human life in its mother's womb—into the foundation of the current feminist agenda, they are bound to picture the institutions most deeply set against this error—evangelical Christians, Catholics, and Orthodox Jews—as their enemies. (Abortion is not really a necessary plank of feminism; it is an unnecessary commitment and within a generation, let us hope, will be quietly abandoned.) Your mother and I have probably heard all the charges made against the Catholic Church under the heading of "patriarchy," and for more years than you have. As a woman and public figure (through her exhibitions and lectures), your mother often took the brunt of them in the early days. As an old and traditional institution, the Catholic Church could no doubt improve its behavior on some of these accounts. But some of the heaviest shot misses.

Before Judaism and Christianity, most cultures of the world practiced polygamy, and the male warrior took his wives, or parents negotiated the giving of their daughters in marriage, without the women's consent. Here again is the Jewish philosopher Dennis Prager on the context in which Judaism launched its sexual revolution:

> The gods of virtually all civilizations engaged in sexual relations. In the Near East, the Babylonian god Ishtar seduced a man, Gilgamesh, the Babylonian hero. In Egyptian religion, the god Osiris has sexual relations with his sister, the goddess Isis, and she conceived the god Horus. In Canaan, El, the chief god, had sex with Asherah. In Hindu belief, the god Krishna was sexually active, having had many wives and pursuing Radha; the god Samba, son of Krishna, seduced mortal women and men. In Greek beliefs, Zeus married Hera, chased women, abducted the beautiful young male, Ganymede, and masturbated at other times; Poseidon married Amphitrite, pursued Demeter, and raped Tantalus. In Rome, the gods sexually pursued both men and women.

In the ancient Near East and elsewhere, virgins were deflowered by priests prior to engaging in relations with their husbands, and sacred or ritual prostitution was almost universal.

The idea that each woman is made in the image of God just as every man is, with the same destiny and independent dignity, is a Jewish principle, inherited by Christians.

So is the idea of a fundamental equality between man and woman before the Creator. Neither has dominion over the conscience of the other. Conscience is rooted in the depths of the soul of each.

For his time and place, furthermore, the number of key conversations revealing his mission that Jesus had with women—women of every kind and station—was both extraordinary and revolutionary. From the first, as Rodney Stark confirms in *The Rise of Christianity*, Christianity has had powerful appeal to women, sometimes more so than to men. Among the most faithful and heroic and celebrated of Christians, women have been from the first highly conspicuous. It may well be that there are more women saints than men in the canon of the saints, and to be designated as a saint is to be singled out by the community as a model who represents what the gospels mean in practice, in a real life lived. The canonized saints are those who have been thought to be the most Christ-like, in whom God most visibly dwells. There is no higher role in the Christian universe.

You have already mentioned the great women of the Jewish Testament, truly towering personalities. But there is no institution in the historical record that has placed as many women at the head of great institutions and communities as the Catholic Church has. Thousands of monasteries and religious houses, and hundreds of farflung services that they organized, have for centuries been headed by women. In his profound reflections on the masculine and the feminine in the West, Henry Adams notes that from the eleventh through the thirteenth centuries virtually every throne in Europe was occupied or administered by women. More profoundly, he writes in *Mont-Saint-Michel and Chartres*, in its aspirations the Christian West was thoroughly woman-centered.[1]

> The superiority of the woman [during the time of the Crusades] was not a fancy, but a fact. Man's business was to fight or hunt or feast or make love. The man was also the travelling partner in commerce, commonly absent from home for months together, while the woman carried on the business. The woman ruled the household and the workshop; cared for the economy; supplied the intelligence, and dictated the taste. Her ascendancy was secured by her alliance with the Church, into which she sent her most intelligent children; and a priest or clerk, for the most part, counted socially as a woman. Both physically and mentally the woman was robust, as the men often complained, and she did not greatly resent being treated as a man.

You can imagine, Jana, the comfort that such women took—among them queens and noblewomen managing large estates employing hundreds of men and women—from such passages as these ABCs of the Bible (note the first letter of each line):

A man who has found a vigorous wife has found a rare treasure,
    brought from distant shores.
Bound to her in loving confidence, he will have no need of spoil.
Content, not sorrow, she will bring him as long as life lasts.
Does she not busy herself with wool and thread, plying her hands
    with ready skill?
Ever she steers her course like some merchant ship, bringing
    provision from far away.

---

[1]Chapter XI.

From early dawn she is up, assigning food to the household, so that
   each waiting-woman has her share.
Ground must be examined, and bought, and planted out as a
   vineyard, with the earnings of her toil.
How briskly she girds herself to the task, how tireless are her arms!
Industry she knows, is well rewarded, and all night long her lamp
   does not go out.
Jealously she sets her hands to work, her fingers clutch the spindle.
Kindly is her welcome to the poor, her purse ever open to those in
   need.
Let the snow lie cold if it will, she has no fears for her household;
   no servant of hers but is warmly clad.
Made by her own hands was the coverlet on her bed, the clothes of
   lawn and purple that she wears.
None so honoured at the city gate as that husband of hers, when he
   sits in council with the elders of the land.
Often she will sell linen of her own weaving, or make a girdle for the
   travelling merchant to buy.
Protected by her own industry and good repute, she greets the
   morrow with a smile.
Ripe wisdom governs her speech, but it is kindly instruction she
   gives.
She keeps watch over all that goes on in her house, not content to
   go through life eating and sleeping.
That is why her children are the first to call praise:
Unrivalled art thou among all the women that have enriched their
   homes.
Vain are the winning ways, beauty is a snare; it is the woman who
   fears the Lord that will achieve renown.
Work such as hers claims its reward; let her life be spoken of with
   praise at the city gates.

—Proverbs 31:10–31, The Holy Bible (Knox translation)

Still today, the greatest hospital network on the
planet—the hospitals of the Catholic Church, serving millions around the world—is run predominantly by women,
who manage larger investments in health care than those of
any one nation on earth. This is true, as well, of thousands

of colleges and universities and scores of thousands of secondary and primary schools, of orphanages, and homes for the elderly. Valiant women indeed! They are the backbone and often the practical brains of the Catholic people.

Ignorance of history may distort the vision of some critics. A calm and objective view of the reality of Catholic institutions is not, alas, an inheritance passed on by higher education today.

In the way you put your question, Jana, you are dramatically understating the role of women in the civilizing of the human race through the nurturing and educating of children in the home. This is not the only task women perform but it may be the most satisfying, personally ennobling, and socially crucial work that any of us do. Do not underestimate—I know you do not—the centrality of family life in God's plan for male and female. The oaklike covenant between wife and husband, under whose shade children are raised, is the fleshly embodiment of God's covenant with the human race. God dwells in this covenant, and thus in every family household. The family household is God's dearest shrine, the ordinary daily shrine of his active presence. Husband and wife share in his love—that fiery *caritas* of which the poets and the mystics speak—and it is through their bodily and spirited love that the miracle of childbirth occurs. Out of this love, new *persons*—little centers of insight and choice—come into life, and reflect (as in a glittering prism) a new aspect of God's love. (Since God is infinite, each person adds a new fragment to our knowledge of the divine.)

Jana, as I hinted earlier, I would be the happiest of fathers if it turned out to be your vocation to launch a new religious community and to head an institution dedicated to serving the poor or needy, or some other noble task. Many young women before you, led by God and trusting in his will, have done so. The most crucial element for you, how-ever, is to find your own vocation, whatever it is that God intends you to do with the abundant gifts he gave you. If you attend to his will closely, you will clearly enough learn what his intentions for you are, and he will lead you step by step even when you cannot see the full road ahead. You should read the lives of those who have preceded you on this quest. There are many great biographies of such women, some of whom—Rose Hawthorne, Ann Seton—lived and worked in Washington.

Wouldn't you say that the best-known Christian during our lifetime was Mother Teresa? Pope John Paul II might have been her only "rival," but much of his fame springs from his position.

JANA: *Yes, but what about the fact that no woman can be a priest, let alone pope?*

DAD: As I mentioned in an earlier chapter, our friend Paul Johnson, your mother, and many other serious Catholics who are in no other way "dissidents" hold that women ought to be admitted into the priesthood. I think they are wrong about that. For one thing, the tradition is so clear, so explicit, and so surprising. Judaism aside, priestesses were common among the religions of the Middle East. Judaism and Christianity were distinctive in the religious importance they attached to matrimony, to monogamy, to the act of sexual love, to the personhood of woman as well as man, to the difference between the sexes, to their union as one in marriage and childbearing and child rearing, and to their differential roles in worship and religious life. The idea of family is inherent in the Jewish and Christian covenants.

Secondly, the images for God in the Jewish Testament are almost always male, only rarely female, even though God is without sex; and is spirit, not body.

In Christianity, thirdly, it seems important, since the Son of God was born of a human woman, the Virgin Mary, that One Person in the Trinity is spoken of as Father (a masculine image). It is also important that another came as Son (again a masculine image); i.e., that the Messiah, so long awaited, came not as a female but as a male. This last point is significant. The Eight Beatitudes of the Sermon on the Mount, spoken by a woman, would not have effected the "transvaluation of values" that Nietzsche deplored in Western culture. Christianity, he said, urged upon the fearless pagan male warrior the course of gentleness and meekness that turned that warrior into a gentleman. Nietzsche accused Christianity of feminizing the male. Nietzsche scorned the following injunctions—the Sermon on the Mount—as unfit for warriors:

How blest are the poor in spirit: the reign of God is theirs.
Blest too are the sorrowing; they shall be consoled.
Blest are the lowly; they shall inherit the land.
Blest are they who hunger and thirst for holiness; they shall have their fill.
Blest are they who show mercy; mercy shall be theirs.
Blest are the single-hearted for they shall see God.
Blest too are the peacemakers; they shall be called sons of God.
Blest are those persecuted for holiness' sake; the reign of God is theirs.

Blest are you when they insult you and persecute you and utter
    every kind of slander against you because of me.
Be glad and rejoice, for your reward is great in heaven; they
    persecuted the prophets before you in the very same way.

—Matt. 5:3–12, The New American Bible

Try putting these words of the Sermon on the Mount
on the lips of a woman. A woman preaching what Jesus
preached would necessarily have been understood in a
wholly unchallenging way. Her words would have sounded
the way women of that time were supposed to talk: about
being poor in spirit, meek, humble, kind, ministering to the
sick and dying and prisoners, and the like. For the warrior
male, these words demanded a thorough transformation,
more so than for the female in her traditional role.

You can see from the Beatitudes why it was crucially
instructive that when God became flesh, he chose to come
as a male. Otherwise, the desired transformation in human
consciousness could scarcely have been effected. Had the
Messiah come as a woman, the effects upon human imagination would have been altogether different.

Perhaps for the same reason, when almost all religions
at the time of the founding of Christianity had women
priestesses, Jesus chose only men. Among Catholics, the
priest plays a distinctively *priestly* role, a liturgical and representative role, over and beyond the role of minister. This
helps to explain why those Christian communities that hold
that the priestly, liturgical role is a misinterpretation of
Christ's will, ordain *ministers*, but not priests, and have far
less hesitance in ordaining women in that role.

I have no doubt that your mother, you, your sister, and
many other women that I know could serve in virtually all

the *ministerial* roles of the priesthood—preaching, teaching, baptizing, counseling, hearing confessions, comforting, managing finances, carrying on administration, organizing people, helping the poor—as well as, or better than, males. If the priestly role were merely ministerial, no argument. I agree that women should take over much more of the administrative, managerial work of the church. Already in seminaries and divinity schools, Catholic women constitute about 85 percent of all those in training for ministerial roles.

In the Catholic tradition, however, the priest has, in addition to the ministerial roles, a *representative* role, a liturgical role, a symbolic role. And here female cannot be substituted for male without a great change in significance. Male and female are not always substitutable. To secure the crucial transvaluation of values that Nietzsche despised, a male must play the role of Christ the man. That is, symbolically, what a priest in the liturgy does.

A change in the teaching of the Church to permit women priests, and the shift in its symbolic weight, is bound in any case to be dramatic.

To go yet a little deeper: Christianity does not hold that men and women are identical, and that their roles are perfectly interchangeable. In the Body of Christ, different members play different roles.

> Just as a human body, though it is made up of many parts, is a single unit because all these parts, though many, make one body, so it is with Christ. In the one Spirit we were all baptized, Jews as well as Greeks, slaves as well as citizens, and one Spirit was given to us all to drink. Nor is the body to be identified with any one of its many parts. If the foot were to say, "I am not a hand and so I do not belong to the body," would that mean that it stopped being part of

the body? If the ear were to say, "I am not an eye, and so I do not belong to the body," would that mean that it was not a part of the body? If your whole body was just one eye, how would you hear anything? If it was just one ear, how would you smell anything? Instead of that, God put all the separate parts into the body on purpose. If all the parts were the same, how could it be a body? As it is, the parts are many but the body is one. The eye cannot say to the hand, "I do not need you," nor can the head say to the feet, "I do not need you."

—1 Cor.12:12–21, The Jerusalem Bible

Such differences are no sin against radical equality. In the Body of Christ, all are taught to serve, not to seek power or pride. The will of Christ is that each of us serve others. But the ways in which we serve are not the same for all. The vocation of each is particular.

The understanding of priesthood, as a service to the community, is not the same in the Catholic tradition as in the Protestant tradition. Since in recent years the Anglican Catholic Church has largely abandoned the Catholic understanding on this point, and joined the Protestant, a new fissure has appeared in Catholic ranks. Today the Roman Catholic Church and the Eastern Orthodox Church alone uphold the ancient and unbroken Catholic tradition. Are they wrong? I doubt it.

But we shall all follow the will of God as it is made clear to us. Being in opposition to the rest of the world is not sufficient indication of that will, and never has been—else there would be no Christianity at all.

Catholicism empowered women as individuals in their own right and destiny and dignity, even in the ways in which traditional roles as wives and mothers were to be lived. But in a certain sense, the transformative impact of Catholicism on men was more demanding: to set aside the rough and commandeering ways of the warrior, and to be gentle, meek, and humble. It set before males, especially, the revolutionary ideal of chastity—not solely the ideal of fidelity to one woman for life, but also the positive seeking of chastity in thought and word and deed; and even, for the most devoted few, including some knights, the role of celibacy for God's sake, as a way of giving undistracted service to the community. (Celibacy has always been thought of as a way of imitating Christ.)

The influence of this model upon the following Christian centuries was immense, especially in the development of the model Christian knight and the code of chivalry. Christ introduced the male to the three C's, as Professor Brassil Fitzgerald at Stonehill College used to tell us (with a lisp): "Charity, Compassion, and Chivalry."

The historians moved by Protestant and Enlightenment prejudices have not often done this great story justice. It remains unknown even among well-educated people. Most have been taught to regard the Catholic centuries, before the Renaissance and the Reformation, with contemptuous neglect. These prejudices, thank God, have in our day been abating. The actual record is being slowly and carefully illuminated.

Two practical points: If God wants the ordination of women in the Catholic Church, it will come, sooner rather than later. I do not think this is likely or consistent with God's express will in the past. But God is not deterred by the limits of human understanding in any given generation—or in all generations together.

Contrariwise, if it is not God's will, current passions will abate, and also sooner rather than later. There are many reasons to believe that the feminism of the present is ill-conceived at two or three points. If that is true, time will demonstrate it. A generation or two is not a long era in the history of the people of God.

Second, a question: Don't you think that if women can become priests, women will soon outnumber men in the seminaries and in the priesthood by very large proportions? That males will increasingly avoid the priesthood? (In Latin countries, priests are already accused of wearing petticoats, and the church is sometimes jeered at as a female preserve.) Already, the vast majority of those studying for other ministries in the church—more than three quarters—are women. The effect of that upon the ability of Catholicism to transform male behavior might be immense, and for the worse. Perhaps it is wrong to worry about that, but I do.

Further, I think it is theologically important that God the Father be conceived of in male images, even though no gendered image is truly correct for God. For the Son of God to have had both human and divine parentage, the mother had to be human. A human father and a divine mother would have assaulted the imagination. If the full divinity and full humanity of the Christ are to be imaginatively grasped, the mother must be human and God must be imagined as male. The image of Mary as Mother of the Son of God has from the first profoundly touched the orthodox imagination, as the guarantee of the humanity of her divine Son: *Emmanuel, God-among-us.*

Change the teaching on male priests, and the whole structure of Christian belief changes. Ideas about the Trinity and the Incarnation will have to be adjusted. The humanity of Christ will be called into question. Obviously, so also will the tradition and authority of the Church. Was the Church wrong about this for so long? Then her authority is a sham.

JANA: *Your discussion of why women can't be priests is fairly convincing, especially concerning the conceptual idea of a male and a female engendering son, Jesus, and of the stronger influence caused by a male preaching compassion, charity, and chastity. Yet I still can't see why this gender difference is given such importance. To me it seems a bit overdone.*

DAD: "Man and woman he made them." The differentiation by gender in created human nature reveals something basic to the whole of human history, culture, and imagination; and also to the inner nature of God, whose image is revealed in this complementarity. The liturgy of the Church ought to keep these differentiations intact. The role of male priests is important, but it should not be blown out of proportion. Priesthood is a service, not a privilege. Most of the work of the Church is ministering.

More likely of success than efforts to ordain women priests, I think, is a large increase in the number of women who act as counselors, advisers of conscience, spiritual directors in the daily practice of the Church. These might well be religious women or lay helpers of the poor, an ancient office in the Church. One might imagine every parish having one or two women officially sent by bishops for the cure of souls. They would not act as confessors, but as pastors of the soul in other respects. Similarly, in some dioceses, and also in Rome, women are moving higher and higher in administrative positions. It has always seemed to me that many administrative roles are not properly priestly roles, and could better be filled by specially trained laypersons, women as well as men; and this is increasingly happening, as chancellors of dioceses and the like. The leadership given by Mary Ann Glendon of the Harvard Law School in heading the Vatican delegation to Beijing in 1995 might easily be imitated in other delegations and in other functions, much to the benefit of the church. Professor Glendon is a brilliant thinker and a great Catholic Christian, and served with high distinction and general acclaim.

JANA: *I'm not entirely satisfied by that answer. Another thing: You haven't addressed my question about the pressure on young women to get married and have children.*

DAD: Once I was on a panel with two eligible bachelors in their thirties, in front of an older Jewish audience. These two young fellows were embarrassed by direct questions from older ladies in the room: "When are you two going to get married?" One of them had a quick answer: "I'm still interviewing."

You have to remember: Marriage and having children are important not just to the individuals involved but to the whole community. Generation is crucial to the future of the entire human race, and to every nation and every people. Nowadays, young people have overlearned the importance of the individual—compared to a time hardly five generations ago in Europe (*Fiddler on the Roof*) when marriages were normally arranged by parents or aunts. The young today are often oblivious to the social role they play, which they resent when they learn of it.

"Pressure" is a small price to pay for freedom. Besides, some young people need a little social pressure if they are going to leave their parents' home and make a nest of their own. I used to tease your mother that, in the eyes of some in her home town, I rescued her just at the right time. (Actually, she was being pursued by three other suitors, all lawyers, each eager to become the apple of her father's lawyerly eye.) Ladies used to stop her in the street, gossip, and then inevitably ask if she hadn't found somebody special yet, and if not now, when? For the older generation, youngsters in their late twenties are vessels of anxiety. Sorry about that.

JANA: *I still remember how, after Richard's wedding, I was suddenly the last child left to be married off. I had to resort to telling pestering friends and relatives that, as a Republican, I refused to get married under a Democratic administration! Anyway, the final subject you have yet to touch on is friendship.*

DAD: About friendship: I once began to write a book on friendship, having taught some seminars on that theme for several years. My premise was that in many modern lives, moving away from our families, we often depend more on our friends than on our families for emotional sustenance. New forms of friendship have displaced the old emotional density of family life.

But what *is* friendship?

Aristotle pointed out that friendship is a fully conscious, deliberate love for another person, made mutual by that other person's reciprocating love; and a love, in both cases, based not upon utilitarian calculation, or the use of one as the instrument of the other, but on a shared love for the good and the true. Cicero stressed the good habits—virtues—necessary for such love, and nourished by such love. Friendship is not a matter, so to speak, of gazing into each other's eyes—it is not focused on "the other"—but of jointly looking outward toward a shared vision of the good. It is a lifetime voyage undertaken together, toward becoming better persons, singly and together. (You will recall a taste of this discussion, Jana, when we spoke of love as an image of God. This is one origin of that image.)

The ancient Greeks and Romans placed a very high value on such friendships. But while we can learn much from Aristotle and Cicero, modern friendships are somewhat different. For one thing, the ancients held that a man could have a friendship with a man, but not a woman; friendship requires equality of a sort that men and women did not then share. Two texts of Thomas Aquinas illustrate some important cultural differences between a Christian and a pagan age. He wrote these passages in Naples toward the end of his short life, engaged in argument with Islamic scholars.

> Friendship demands a certain equality. While a child's right to a father rules out one woman having many husbands at the same time, it is in the name of liberal friendship that one man is not allowed to have many wives. The relationship would otherwise be servile. This is borne out by experience, for when custom allows polygamy wives are treated like servants.

The greater the friendship the more permanent it should be.
The greatest friendship is that between man and wife.[2]

I also cherish *The Four Loves,* by C. S. Lewis (one of the first books I ever reviewed in print when I was still unmarried), although in later years I found it more applicable to an unmarried British don than to love in the round, especially married love. I gather that Lewis, too, changed his mind, after his short, poignant marriage to Joy Davidman, as many will have seen in the wonderful movie *Shadowlands.* (In my view, it is, with *Chariots of Fire,* one of the best religious films ever made. For Lewis, the "four loves" are *affection* (even such as one feels for a comfortable chair and old slippers); *friendship* (in his treatment, a little like that between two gentlemen in the same club); *eros;* and *charity.* None of these, in that book, quite reach to marriage.

Marriage is the highest and most searing of all forms of friendship. Friendship between a man and a man—or between a woman and a woman—is very precious. Still, nothing compares to the friendship that brings together the mysteries of the two sexes. Such a friendship is inexhaustibly challenging, especially when both partners are struggling to become better persons, of deeper character, and more rounded virtue—trying to correct their faults, and to be closer to God through each other.

The quirky instinct of G. K. Chesterton for the paradox captures one truth of marriage quite nicely:

> The State has no tool delicate enough to deracinate the rooted habits and tangled affections of the family; the two sexes, whether happy or unhappy, are glued together too tightly for us to get the

---

[2]*Contra Gentes,* 123.

blade of a legal penknife in between them. The man and the woman are one flesh—yes, even when they are not one spirit. Man is a quadruped. . . .

The principle is this: that in everything worth having, even in every pleasure, there is a point of pain or tedium that must be survived, so that the pleasure may revive and endure. The joy of battle comes after the first fear of death; the joy of reading Virgil comes after the bore of learning him; the glow of the sea-bather comes after the icy shock of the sea bath; and the success of the marriage comes after the failure of the honeymoon. All human vows, laws, and contracts are so many ways of surviving with success this breaking point, this instant of potential surrender. . . .

If Americans can be divorced for "incompatibility of temper" I cannot conceive why they are not all divorced. I have known many happy marriages, but never a compatible one. The whole aim of marriage is to fight through and survive the instant when incompatibility becomes unquestionable. For a man and a woman, as such, are incompatible.

—*What's Wrong With the World*

I have no notion of denying that mankind suffers much from the maintenance of the standard of marriage; as it suffers much from the necessity of criminal law or the recurrence of crusades and revolutions. The only question here is whether marriage is indeed, as I maintain, an ideal and an institution making for popular freedom; I do not need to be told that anything making for popular freedom has to be paid for in vigilance and pain, and a whole army of martyrs.

—*The Superstition of Divorce*

Marriage is a great teacher of realism. It is so hard on our favorite faults, and cuts so painfully across some of our deepest illusions about ourselves. Our spouse can hardly help resisting our illusions about ourselves more passionately than we do. If you do not like to hear painful truths about yourself, don't marry! (Faults your spouse kindly overlooks, your children will detect.) Those who love each other want the other to be perfect, and want to think that the self already is. Alas.

Because family life makes us care so much about others, it is a great threat to totalitarian regimes. One by one, we are each more vulnerable to propaganda and manipulation. But when those we love are threatened, we cannot help wanting to resist, even at supreme cost. If a woman risks her life for a stranger, that is heroic. But if she risks her life for her child, well, that is just the sort of thing that mothers do. In families, heroism is ordinary.

Truth, honesty, a longing for perfection, mutual forgiveness, patience with the faults of others, self-acceptance, heroic love—of these, families are the best, most ordinary teachers. That is why they are cradles of faith, hope, and *caritas*.

Build your own family on faith, Jana. It is a rock. Gabriel Marcel once wrote:

> A family is founded, it is erected like a monument whose hewn stone is neither the satisfaction of an instinct, nor the yielding to an impulse, nor the indulgence of a caprice.
>
> —"The Mystery of the Family"

Building a marriage is like building a cathedral, Jana. It is slow work, and often takes more than half a century. In the end, it represents a glorious victory.

11

%

WHAT ABOUT ABORTION?

Letter, dated April 19, 1997:

Mr. Novak:
Another reason to oppose abortion: the haunting feeling of guilt some women carry with them—in my case for 30 years. The following expression rings so true:

Abortion: One dead, one wounded.

Sincerely,
Anonymous

JANA: *I should preface this question by saying that I am pro-life. Therefore, the abortion argument does not need to be made to me. Of course, though, most people my age (especially most women my age) are pro-choice.*

To some of them, it is a very important question of control and male domination. To others, it is simply a matter of protecting women: they worry about the time when women died because they would have "back-alley" abortions. (Although, to the best of my knowledge, the number of women who died due to botched abortions because abortion wasn't legal is less than the number of women who die today from abortion—even though it's now legal—and is dwarfed by the number of children aborted yearly.)

I, of course, believe abortion is a "slippery slope." If we stop respecting and protecting children before they are able to exist outside the womb (that is, survive on their own) then the next step will be to stop protecting all humans who cannot survive on their own: the boy in the bubble, humans on life support, and the elderly. And that doesn't even count the number of abortions that occur in the third trimester, when a baby can survive on its own.

But I do think it is important to address the concerns of those who are pro-choice. For example, many people who are pro-life do not follow through on their beliefs by supporting centers that help women who choose to have the child, or they don't adopt. Nobody says you have to adopt an abused child to be against child abuse. But at least some abortions would not occur if a pregnant woman felt she could provide for her child, or at least ensure that the child gets provided for.

Another problem is posed by those who bomb abortion centers or harass or kill doctors who perform abortions. St. Augustine would say that such actions are wrong—the slippery slope again. If I remember correctly, Augustine said that one cannot/should not kill anyone, even if that act would later save the lives of others. For instance, if you knew the young Hitler, and knew the future, you still could not justify taking his life, as if playing God. Therefore, people who bomb and kill those associated with abortions are wrong, are murderers, are committing a sin. Right?

What happens, though, if the mother's life is in danger? If it were certain that bearing the child would kill the mother, then what? (I would assume that no other exceptions, such as rape or incest are allowable: two wrongs don't make a right.)

Where does the morning-after pill fit in? (Not the RU-486 abortion pill currently available in Europe and undergo-

ing limited testing here, but a high dose of estrogen—several birth control pills—given within seventy-two hours of intercourse. If the woman is pregnant, it prevents the egg from latching on to the uterine lining—a process that often occurs naturally—and if the woman is not pregnant, then it makes no difference.) Is this just as bad as abortion, or slightly less so? On the one hand, using the morning-after pill is not a conscious decision; unlike abortion, where the woman knows she is pregnant and knows that without her interference a child would be born, the morning-after pill is taken before the woman can know whether she is pregnant or not. On the other hand, even though the woman may not know if she is pregnant, she is still consciously deciding to end a child's life, if there is one there to end. As a friend of mine said: The morning-after pill is like walking into a darkened room and dropping a vial of cyanide. You may have no idea if there was a person in the room or not, but if there was, it's still murder, not premeditated, like abortion, but murder nonetheless.

I realize that most religions don't approve of premarital sex, but let's face it: a vast majority of people are still doing it. If, for example, the Catholic Church doesn't approve of contraception, how can one prevent accidental pregnancies? How do you reconcile religion's laws with reality? Or, what about if one's spouse has some sexually transmitted disease, such as having received AIDS from a blood transfusion? Is the uninfected spouse allowed to use a condom or something else for protection?

In reference to contraception, once you're married, are you allowed to practice "planned parenthood"? For example, I have heard a little bit about the Catholic Church's "natural family planning" method. What is it? How does a couple practice it? Where can couples get more information about it?

DAD: Dear Jana, one of the things I most admire about you is your feeling for life. It is more than a feeling; it is a part of your way of being. I remember when you worked with severely retarded children for two summers, turning your back on prestigious Washington internships that would have looked good on your resume. You saw that the children needed love, attention even, and needed to be held and helped to learn how to do even simple things. You delighted in their victories. I visited once and saw that I could never have worked there; the disfigurements got to me, and the patience required was beyond me by far. You have always had an eye for the underdog and the vulnerable and conveyed a sense of optimism about their chances. I love this in you.

True religion, the Bible tells us, is to care for widows and orphans. In other words, the vulnerable. This is what distinguishes Judaism and Christianity from the noble civilizations of the Greeks and Romans; it is the "added value" of biblical religions. Greeks and Romans, like the American Indians, were taught a certain contempt for weakness and the weak. Jews and Christians were taught a preference for the weakest—this is one of the most visible meanings of the birth of the Messiah in a cowshed among the earth's desert poor. It is not among the strongest and wealthiest that the greatest treasures of humanity are to be found, but among the weakest and the most vulnerable.

In the same vein, Jews and Christians were also taught: "Therefore, choose life!" In a vast and cold and otherwise apparently empty universe, precious life has been given as a gift by the Author of life, a Creator moved by goodness and love, a gentle Providence who promises to care for those who trust him. Life is a gift to be loved and cherished. In doubt and turmoil, choose life! Trust life.

The main thing to keep in view is the suddenness of the current regime. As late as the nineteenth century, the safest haven in the world was thought to be in a mother's womb, sheltered by her love. No more powerful image of security and comfort came to mind. That a mother would turn against her child, and that a doctor or midwife would take advantage of her necessity to practice clandestine abortion, seemed like a world turned upside down. *Abortionist* was the worst term of opprobrium in the lexicon. Of course, abortions happened, always and everywhere, but they were almost everywhere thought to be wrong. Even Margaret Sanger of Planned Parenthood was a foe of abortion; birth control was her way of *preventing* it.

The year after you were born, *Roe* v. *Wade* abruptly changed all that. Since then, some 34 million infants have been ejected dead from the womb. I doubt if there has ever been so rapid a fundamental moral change in the laws and practices of a country, outside of wartime and foreign occupation. It did not come about by popular demand. I remember a special vote in Michigan in 1972 in which a referendum on abortion was soundly defeated—mostly by women's votes, and especially strongly in the more Protestant areas of the state. I regret to say that the Catholic vote against was notably weaker.

JANA: *I watch polls very closely, and my understanding is that the majority of the pro-choice/pro-abortion movement are young women from the generation of the sixties and recent college graduates, and also men more generally (who have nothing to lose). But the good news is, I read in* The Washington Post *that a recent survey of college freshmen found an increase in the number of those willing to identify themselves as pro-life.*

DAD: You're right about the men: women much more strongly *oppose* abortion than men. Men, especially young men, tend to be *for* it. The surgery is done on women, not men. Men, alas, are all too willing to have sex without responsibility or commitment, even though that in time destroys men as men, makes them far less than men ought to be, makes them learn contempt for themselves as well as for women. Human sex is supposed to entail accountability, children, permanence, responsibility for one another—in short, love. In the simplicity of our appetites, men can hardly help wishing, Why couldn't sex be just like shaking hands? This attitude provides the perfect context for abortions. Ironically, this regime comes in the name of women's *liberation.*

Is it really a better world—for women, as well as men—when those formerly regarded by the law as human persons, protected by the community, were suddenly after 1973 treated as objects to be discarded? Once this attitude is given the aura of solemnity by the law, who will be the next persons to become for others mere objects? Men are certainly more likely to regard themselves as less than responsible persons, and to continue unchecked in treating women as objects of desire. Moreover, violence to newborn infants a few hours or weeks out of the womb is likely to seem to young people under pressure as lawlike as violence to the preborn only a few days earlier. (Such a case dominated Delaware newspapers shortly before Thanksgiving, 1996: a teenage coed gave birth to a child in a seedy motel, and her panicky teenage boyfriend allegedly threw it in a dumpster in the cold night air, where the next morning it was found dead of a crushed skull. Such stories are multiplying.) Some are likely to treat infants as objects, just as they treat the unborn. Child abuse is likely to become more frequent.

As you suggest, Jana, once the circle of persons protected by law is broken, and one class is stripped of its rights, the same logic, fed by self-interest, will soon enough strip others. According to federal courts in the Northwest, the logic of *Roe* v. *Wade* now applies as well to the terminally ill. The elderly, whose care is socially expensive and whose illnesses demand long-term compassion, are being categorized as potential cases for legal killing. Will their lives, too, now be legally aborted?

According to the social contract explained by John Locke in his *Two Treatises of Government,* if individuals are to abandon the jungle and to enter into civil society, they must give up the practice of individual violence upon others, whatever their own self-interest or convenience, and surrender all such practice to the state. Only the state, under institutions of due process, may use violence. Only such a surrender of individual violence can bring social peace. Such peace is clearly in the larger self-interest of every individual, and without it no one is safe. For one key class of formerly protected persons, *Roe* v. *Wade* has repealed the social contract. Once that contract has been ruptured, we must expect it to hemorrhage.

I can think of no other generation in the history of liberalism that *narrowed* the circle of persons whose rights are protected by the law. Since at least the Magna Carta, the history of liberalism has heretofore been marked by an enlargement of that circle: from the nobility to property holders, from males to females, from former slaves to universal suffrage. In our time, that circle is once again getting smaller.

JANA: *And the ironic thing is, I wonder how those who are "pro-choice" will feel when that tide recedes to abandon them or one of their loved ones.*

DAD: You mention, Jana, the need to "address the concerns" of those who are "pro-choice." I can see the good effect that that effort has had on your own thinking. But their concerns really do get a full airing in the press. Practically all national journalists—in the big dailies, the newsmagazines, and on television—make the pro-choice case; many admit they don't even *know* anybody who is pro-life. It's partly a matter of social class. While Democrats since 1972 have deliberately become the party of abortion, and under Reagan and Bush the Republican Party became the party of life, what most still separates pro-life Democrats (such as former Pennsylvania governor Robert Casey) from pro-choice Republicans (such as New Jersey governor Christine Todd Whitman) is the bright line of social class.

I have often had the pro-choice case presented to me, in public and in private. Often passionately. Sometimes cogently and almost convincingly. I can see how intelligent and good people can make that case. To do so, though, it is necessary to treat what is aborted as less than a human individual.

During the presidential campaign of 1972, when I worked for George McGovern, the argument I used to hear was that the aborted child was "just a part of the woman's body"; as one woman journalist told me, a "glob." New genetic knowledge now makes plain that the aborted child has her own individual genetic code, different from that of her mother. About 1970, the argument from doctors was that abortion is a "purely scientific" question, and that religion and faith were being introduced improperly. (I was so rebuked by a famous surgeon from New York at a conference on medical ethics.) Today, science has established that the aborted child is not only human, but also an individual with its own unique genetic code, and doctors have reversed field. Whether to accord this individual legal status as a "person," some doctors now tell me, is a purely religious or ethical question—by which *they* mean "subjective," not based on reason. Reason says the aborted one is *not* "part of a woman's body" but an unmistakably separate human individual.

JANA: *Science has also made it possible for children born as many as three months prematurely to survive—yet it is still legal to abort them up until the last moment before delivery at nine months.*

DAD: In 1997, the Democratic leader in the Senate proposed a ban on late-term abortions (the last three months), a ban every other civilized society enforces. So politics is also moving. But I'm concerned with the philosophical discourse, in advance of the underlying argument. Here, at last, the emphasis is shifting from the mother's "choice" to the one aborted. And that's a huge change. Science has paved the way for that.

Still, in the public arena, many on the pro-choice side are still trying to disenfranchise people of faith. They imperialistically declare that only their reasons have standing before the law, while convictions allied to religious faith are illegitimate. They do not entertain the possibility that their reasoning, even as reasoning, is weakened even to the point of tottering by evasions, half-truths, and sleight of hand—subterfuges which, if they did not want to approve of abortions at any cost, they would not allow themselves.

One major subterfuge is to call their position pro-choice. But the biblical injunction itself can be summed up: *Therefore, choose life! Both* sides are in favor of choice. The excruciating moral question is not *whether* there should be choice, but *which* choice. Only one choice respects the other *as other*.

Of course, the latent message in the slogan is that the one to be aborted should no longer be treated as a person endowed by her or his Creator with inalienable rights, including the right to life, but rather as an *object* of the individual mother's choice. But this is to repeal the Lockean social contract in a crucial area, of great consequence in other areas linked to it by logic and principle. If the courts change the definition of life and person at the beginning of the human journey, consistency will eventually force them to change it also at the end of life—and also in many of life's boundary situations (persons unconscious from car wrecks, or tumors, etc.).

Such changes of definition must be made by the body politic as a whole, not by random individuals nor by courts alone. For the lives and deaths of every citizen, and of their loved ones, are at stake. No one can abrogate from all citizens this power to choose the regime under which they will live, or the content of the social contract to which they swear allegiance. Such a redefinition is a public, not a private, matter. It can only be settled fairly and civilly by a public—that is, openly political—contest. Let the people as a whole decide, either in a national referendum, or—more in accord with our federalist structure—in individual jurisdictions.

Since ours is a pluralistic culture, and sincere consciences differ, I do not imagine that we all have to live under one national law; sound law must be based upon public consensus. If the matter were put to a public vote in individual jurisdictions, I can imagine at least two or three states voting for the abortion "license." (Abortion cannot, for various reasons, be a "right," except by improper usage.) Most states would almost certainly vote for either a strict or a less strict pro-life regimen; the preborn would be guaranteed the normal protections of law, except in cases of rape and incest. The "health of the mother" exception is subject to vast and unscrupulous abuse; but in some states, I imagine, a tightened version of it might express consensus. Some cities, such as New York City and Los Angeles, might be permitted to count as separate jurisdictions for the purpose of such laws; they might well vote pro-abortion, and the rest of the state vote pro-life. But a uniform code throughout each single state might be socially healthier, and each of the states could live under the consent of the governed in each.

I would not find such local patchwork ideal, and would in every case make public arguments to persuade people what a wrong abortion is. Yet that way, surely, lies greater social peace—and a more just civil pluralism—than we have at present. That way, above all, lies a just constitutional order, distinct from the present rule by privileged elites.

Moreover, after a generation or two, the differences in state cultures might be quite surprising. Pro-abortion states, I predict, will experience greater violence in other areas, such as violence against children and women. The habit of treating individuals as objects spreads. Such experiences might help to persuade still more people that abortion brings abundant evil fruits in its train.

JANA: *But, Dad, what you have just described sounds to me like what was attempted in the nineteenth century to deal with the problem of slavery—that is, the Missouri Compromise. Needless to say, that idea was an absolute failure, mostly because* on principle *the abolitionists were right and could not accept such a compromise. A black could not rationally be a slave—less than a human—here and three blocks away be a human. Everywhere and always blacks deserved to be considered the humans that they are. So how can you sanction repeating the same unprincipled compromise—mistake—again?*

DAD: It is a compromise, and it might be a mistake. Here, as in the case of Lincoln, prudence has to rule. Lincoln never fought the War "to free the slaves"; he temporized about that principle, and fought "to save the Union"—precisely so that the slaves could be freed. If Stephen Douglas had won on the issue of choice—he called it "popular sovereignty," which Lincoln abbreviated as "pop sov"—Texas might have been divided into as many as five new states, giving the cause of slavery ten fresh Senate seats. Still other states might then have entered the Union, embracing slavery by popular choice. In the Union, Lincoln knew that slavery was "on the road to extinction," and he meant to keep the Union together to make sure that, in due course, slavery disappeared. By clever argument, he showed that Douglas must, logically, support "pop sov" even if it led to the repeal of the Fugitive Slave Act (which returned runaway slaves to their masters). In this neat way, he turned the South decisively against Douglas.

We are again in an era when prudence is required—prudence and patience. Abortion is on the road to extinction. Its principles cannot be sustained. "Pro-choice" is a brilliant ploy, but just as empty of substance as Douglas's "pop sov." *Everybody* is pro-choice. ("Therefore, choose life.") Life is a difficult choice. But it is the only choice one can make consistently both for a child in the womb and for oneself. No one can have a right to own a slave or to become a slave. No one can have a right to take a life. "Choice" is a tinny symbol.

Every year that passes brings new evidence and new arguments to the pro-life side. The problem is to convince people to pay attention—especially mothers, especially "pro-choice" feminists. For many, abortion has come to mean independence from pregnancy and independence from men. It has gotten all mixed up with feminist ideology. Actually, being pro-woman and being pro-life go very well together. The "contradiction" is an ideological accident, and is not sustainable across generations. The crucial issue now is one of persuasion, not law. *Leges sine moribus vanae,* I saw on a truck at the University of Pennsylvania recently—an apposite motto for William Penn's University—"Laws apart from moral habits are empty."

But you make a good point. Prudence is only prudence, a judgment of probabilities, not certainties. So my approach could be a mistake. Civil rights laws were *laws* before they became accepted mores; sometimes the law is a teacher of moral habits, not a follower.

Another point you mention, Jana, confirms my argument—the fear among some of your friends about the infamous back-alley abortions of the past. You remember Hadley Arkes, the Amherst Professor you probably met when you worked at *Crisis,* where he does a monthly column. I remember him writing that there are far more deaths and serious injuries from abortion today than there ever were prior to 1971. I once telephoned him about this, and he said it is because there are today vastly more abortions—twenty-eight thousand per week, ten or more every minute of every working day—vastly more abortions, even though abortions are available in only 16 percent of American counties. (In vast stretches of this country, no one will perform abortions. Almost two thirds of all abortions are performed in specialized abortion clinics, mostly in big cities.)

No medical school today, the papers recently reported, teaches this ugly specialty to new doctors. Many doctors and nurses who have assisted at abortions have expressed their repugnance, especially since they are often in one room for the abortion, then in the neighboring room trying to save the life of an infant of similar age. The passional dissonance is excruciating.

The result is that huge abortion mills are kept busy in relatively few places, and reputable and duly monitored professional care is stretched thin, while unscrupulous providers take advantage of the widespread breakdown in journalistic oversight. I have never seen television cameras at an abortion table, have you? They have shown live births and heart transplants on television, though. Journalists can hardly be expected, perhaps, to show zeal in exposing abuses or problems in causes to which they are deeply committed, especially if these causes are already largely unpopular. If the truth were told, these causes would be even more unpopular. In the culture wars, truth is the first casualty.

Again, Jana, you are holding pro-life people to a *very* high standard—that they should, without public support, finance local centers in which pregnant young women might choose life rather than abortion; and adopt children on their own. Of course, many pro-life people are doing exactly these things, even at great cost to themselves, and even though many of them are not at all wealthy, except, perhaps, in love. In Washington, we support the Northwest Center and the pregnancy clinic at Providence Hospital, and in every city and town there are similar outreach programs. The Sisters of the Good Shepherd and others have been doing such work for more than a century. But today more and more ordinary lay people are pitching in; it is a very satisfying ministry.

I wish those on the pro-choice side would join in this work. This would give some substance to the word "choice." When consciences are bitterly divided, nothing is so mutually healing as a cooperative effort to help the vulnerable and the needy.

JANA: *I asked my roommate to read what you wrote in this chapter. I know it's a lot more balanced than many of the opinions she and I run into, but I think her comments are very good.*

STEPHANIE: *I believe in a woman's right to choose. I am frightened by the idea of someone taking away the rights I have over a decision such as this. Shouldn't this choice be made by the family, not government? The woman, not the state?*

I have listened to the stories of many women in my work at women's centers during college. The reasons they give for abortion, and the events which transpired to bring them to this decision, are real and anguishing. We must attempt to understand the reasons that would make a woman choose to have an abortion: We need to listen to women more.

It seems to me that much of the abortion issue revolves around how we as a society do not value life. To put a label on me as a hater of life or as an advocate for the death of children, however, is simply wrong. I want to think about the lives of the mother and the child. But I do not want to inhibit women who feel they have no other choice than aborting their child. As women, we are denying much of ourselves, our nature, if we think that an abortion does not go against a woman's intrinsic connection to her child. Nonetheless, many women who have chosen abortion would argue that they were thinking of the future quality of life of the child.

Reproductive freedom is very important and the thought of returning to the days when abortions were not safe is what compels women to fight to keep abortions legal. There is something wrong with an environment in which young teenagers are afraid to tell their parents they are pregnant. Especially for a teenager, it would seem so much easier to abort the child, erasing all trace that it was ever there. How can we change this? How can we teach children to go to teachers for help? And how can we teach adults to be available and understanding?

Furthermore, who is to say that all women should be mothers? Though most women are "designed" to be able to give birth, many are not mentally prepared or do not want to give birth. We desperately need more discussion about the choice of adoption.

I believe this issue has been oversimplified and cut up into sound bites and hatred. We must come together on both sides of the issue and take a good look at what each side is advocating.

DAD: Stephanie's words reinforce my view, Jana, that two separate issues are at stake, and need to be kept separate. The first is the struggle of women to define their own identity in a world of new possibilities—and that means redefining their relations to men, to pregnancy, to work, to being female itself. In these matters, ideology will eventually be shed, burned away by the fires of reality, until only good gold remains.

The other issue is respect for the life of the child in the womb. A mother patting her womb says "my child," never "my fetus." Only extreme alienation, a kind of desperation, can cause her to imagine that her child is not a child. I accept the idea that an abortion is a symptom of a terrible disorder,

271

and that we need to attend to the disorder, not solely to avoiding the abortion.

Jana, for your part, you are thoroughly right in quoting St. Augustine (and the Western religious tradition generally) that it is never right to commit an evil in order to do good. A good purpose does not transmute an evil deed into a just one, but compounds the evil. Those pitiful few who have killed abortion workers have committed a triple evil. The killings in themselves were evil; they have also discredited the pro-life cause and injured the morale of pro-life workers; and they have brutally sullied the pro-life principle, which is the defense of life, in means as well as ends. Each of these three dimensions of evil has done terrible damage. It is the same with torching or bombing abortion clinics. Such raw and violent acts inflame passions and harden hearts; they do not advance the work of persuasion, they dramatically set it back.

Regarding the morning-after pill, I think your own reasoning is on the right track. You are learning the "how to" on your own. If I were to be asked to write something on this or the RU-486 professionally, I'd consult first with a medical ethics specialist, to make sure I was up to snuff on the technical detail. The main lines of the moral argument are clear enough: No direct blowing out of the candle of life; no direct killing as a means to some other end, even a good end.

This so-called "principle of double effect" covers the odd set of cases in which *two* lines of action are at work, but one of those lines has the foreseen but indirect effect of closing off the other. Thus, a doctor might wish with all his might to save both the infant and the mother, but he knows in advance that a necessary attempt to save the mother might indirectly and unintentionally result in the infant's loss of life, even with some high probability. The doctor does not will the death of the child, or kill the infant directly, but recognizes that as a result of the procedures done to save the mother the infant might not survive. No one likes this sort of situation. But it is morally good and noble to save the mother, and morally licit to put the infant at risk—but *not* to kill it directly—in that attempt.

Of course, the principle of double effect can work the other way, too. I read a year or so ago of a brave and good mother in the Washington area who was diagnosed with life-threatening cancer when she was well along in her pregnancy. In her case, she refused chemotherapy which might possibly have saved her (probably not), but would have had the certain effect of killing her child. She gave birth to a healthy child, but yielded to death a short time later. Stephanie told me of a similar case, in which both the mother and the child lived—and the mother went on to have a third child.

As always, the moral life demands extraordinary things of ordinary people. All of us in life face chances to act heroically—with calm self-control, nobility of character, tenderness, regard for the nuances of feeling in the other, love for the *good* of the other (rather than self-assertion at any cost). Heroism is not for other people. All of us are called to it. Even in our failures, the present is always a chance to begin the hard road of heroic freedom all over again. There are heroes everywhere. Life is a school for heroes in small things, on call for heroism in large things, when that call comes. As it will.

Regarding your questions on premarital sex and contraception, I'd rather postpone them for longer treatment in a different context, if that's all right with you. You've already worn me out on this series of questions.

JANA: *I'm afraid, Dad, that I can't let you off the hook so easily. The issue of contraception is tightly woven with the issue of abortion. As you mentioned earlier, Margaret Sanger founded Planned Parenthood in the hope that widely available contraception would prevent—or at the very least, decrease the number of—abortions. Now I don't condone or advise premarital sex (which we discussed in Chapter 9), but let's face it, the reality is that many people are having sex. Therefore, we need to respond to the real, not the ideal. (Isn't that the meaning of "prudence," as you used it above?) It seems to me—I admit to being in favor of contraception, or "family planning" as it is euphemistically called these days—that even a "strict" Christian has to view contraception as the lesser of two evils. While it does allow sex to become detached from its original purpose as an expression of God's love and creation, and does make sex more like—as you put it earlier—"shaking hands," contraception does serve an important purpose in responding to reality as it is: messy, irresponsible, and seemingly lacking in moral direction. And therefore it prevents later abortions.*

DAD: Your assumption is that the widespread use of contraceptives today is preventing abortions. Maybe it is. But twenty-eight thousand abortions per week, four thousand per day suggests that something is wrong. Not all those abortions are the result of not using contraception. In New York City, cops used to say that they had no time for petty crimes like defacing buildings with graffiti, they had to concentrate on stopping crimes of violence. Then Mayor Rudolph Giuliani put in effect the opposite policy—get serious about petty crimes, and pretty soon the big ones will diminish, too. And it worked. Suppose we tried that here, too.

The ultimate cause of most abortions is illicit and disrespectful sex—sex using the other person as a means, not an end. The culture of contraceptives has made that type of sex the new social reality, as you point out. The problem is that new social reality.

I have heard of freshman orientation days at Ivy League universities, at which condoms are thrown out from a stage over the heads of screaming freshmen, who are expected to scramble for them on the floor and to be sure to carry one out of the auditorium. The assumption is that these sons and daughters will have sex with strangers they do not know and to whom they have no commitment. This is to carry impersonality and the objectification of other human beings to an extreme. No wonder campuses have problems with alcohol and drugs; they may be needed just to endure this regime.

I don't expect the secular world to give up its current fixation on sex—as much sex as possible—until the destructiveness of this course becomes ever more obvious. It always does. Ours is not the first era to get drunk on easy sex. During such an era, it is really very hard to resist the tide. Sex is a powerful lure. Perhaps nothing is more powerful—not money, not power. There are too many examples of people throwing those away for the sake of a sexual liaison they have lost their will to resist. This loss of will spreads to other matters. The weakening of the will is the corruption that brings civilizations down.

On contraception, I once argued for its permissibility, under certain limited conditions (within marriage, e.g., when the clear practice was to have children); but I have come to see that this was a mistake. The longer I live, the more vivid become the unintended consequences of a regime and an ethos that make contraception their foundation. Contraceptives begin as a merely functional instrument, a preventative; but they soon become a tyrant. They bypass the human will, to rely upon a technological fix. They fail often. Always they weaken the will, and submit the spirit to the flesh.

Besides, the many changes in a woman's body during ovulation make it possible for science today to determine with accuracy her particular rhythms of fertility. Providing that her husband is willing to respect these rhythms, a couple can "plan" a pregnancy without using contraceptives. The techniques of this so-called "natural family planning" become more advanced with every passing year. *Crisis* magazine and others have published many accounts of the satisfaction the use of these methods brings, especially through the growth of mutual respect between husband and wife, and the sense of wholeness they enjoy. Natural family planning is worth exploring.[1]

Jana, I fear proposing to you a regime too difficult to pursue in this age. But I can at least try to make clear what the stakes are. In my view—I know how old-fashioned and sexist I must seem to your generation—all moral regeneration for the human race begins with women, who establish the boundaries on sex. The burden is not entirely theirs—

---

[1] For information, you can write to: The Couple to Couple League, P.O. Box 111184, Cincinnati, Ohio 45211, or call 1-513-471-2000.

men have, in some ways, the more difficult part. But women, in the nature of the case, inevitably establish the boundaries: their *no* means *no*. Men must then restrain themselves, out of regard for the woman's self-respect.

If sexual urges were not so powerful, there would be less emphasis on *no*. A culture that places more emphasis on the nobility of self-government, mutual respect, and a fuller human relation than one thoroughly tyrannized by the sexual drive would be a more humane culture. Ironically, when sexual love reaches the higher intensity that builds up when it is channeled into commitments that mean permanent union and mutual love on all levels, it gains tremendously in power and meaning. Chaste couples experience heights and depths not accessible through automatic, meaningless coupling. *Meaning* lies at the heart of sexual pleasure. The old joke that chastity is its own punishment is the reverse of the truth. Meaningless sex is its own punishment, making a desert where God intended superabundant joy.

In our time, this may seem hopelessly unrealistic. Yet it is for the return of such a time that we must work. Adults must not renounce their responsibilities, in this matter or any other. It is our task to lay down the moral expectations youngsters must meet to become adults—not the task of youngsters to establish the expectations for adults.

In sum, the key word in Jewish and Christian sexual life is respect: respect for mutual friendship; respect for the mysteries of a woman's body; respect for the sanctity of sex; respect for human life and liberty (including the freedom of the infant to choose, in time, for herself). Once the habit of such respect spreads throughout a population, people may be surprised by how different the visage of our culture will become: a culture of friendship and of life.

12

DO I NEED TO BE MOTHER TERESA?

THE EIGHT STEPS OF LOVE

There are eight degrees or steps in the duty of charity. The first and lowest degree is to give, but with reluctance or regret. This is the gift of the hand, but not of the heart.

The second is to give cheerfully, but not proportionately to the distress of the sufferer.

The third is to give cheerfully, and proportionately, but not until solicited.

The fourth is to give cheerfully, proportionately, and even unsolicited; but to put it in the poor man's hand, thereby exciting in him the painful emotion of shame.

The fifth is to give charity in such a way that the distressed may receive the bounty, and know their benefactor, without their being known to him. Such was the conduct of some of our ancestors, who used to tie up money in the corners of their cloaks, so that the poor might take it unperceived.

The sixth, which rises still higher is to know the objects of our bounty, but remain unknown to them. Such was the conduct of those of our ancestors, who used to convey their charitable gifts into poor people's dwellings, taking care that their own persons and names should remain unknown.

The seventh is still more meritorious, namely to bestow charity in such a way that the benefactor may not know the relieved persons, nor they the name of their benefactors, as was done by our charitable forefathers during the existence of the Temple. For there was in that holy building a place called the Chamber of the Silent, wherein the good deposited secretly whatever their generous hearts suggested, and from which the poor were maintained with equal secrecy.

Lastly, the eighth, and the most meritorious of all, is to anticipate charity, by preventing poverty; namely, to assist the reduced fellowman, either by a considerable gift, or a loan of money, or by teaching him a trade, or by putting him in the way of business, so that he may earn an honest livelihood, and may not be forced to the dreadful alternative of holding out his hand for charity.

To this Scripture alludes when it says: "And if thy brother be waxen poor, and fallen in decay with thee, then thou shalt relieve him; yea, though he be a stranger or a sojourner; that he may live with thee." This is the highest step and the summit of charity's golden ladder.

—Maimonides
(1135–1204)

In order not to believe, my child, you would have to shut your eyes and plug your ears. In order not to see, not to believe.

Unfortunately Charity is obvious. Charity can walk on its own. To love your neighbor you just have to let yourself go, you just have to look around at all the distress. In order not to love you would have to do violence to yourself, torture yourself, torment yourself, frustrate yourself. Harden yourself. Hurt yourself. Distort yourself. Run yourself backwards, turn yourself inside-out. Thwart yourself. Charity is completely natural, simple, overflowing, very easy-coming. It's the first movement of the heart. And the first movement is the right one. Charity is a mother and a sister.

—Charles Péguy
(1873–1914)

JANA: *Earlier I protested that I was not trying to be lazy, but to be honest, I am rather lazy. I am not a truly good person, I'm nowhere near perfect, I can probably only settle on okay. What's more, I don't put as much effort as I should into trying to change my vices and imperfections. I have many faults—far too long to list—but suffice it to say that one of the worst is laziness.*

I do like helping people, but usually I'm not out there doing too much about it. I am not out in the trenches volunteering a lot of my time (sometimes not even any of it), and thus I'm not exactly making a lot of personal effort with individual, face-to-face contact—as I know we are admonished, as Christians, to do.

For example, I don't like giving money to beggars on the street, and I tend to resent the harassment. The Christian side of me would like to help them, but I still worry that my change wouldn't be used to help the recipient out of the situation, but would be used instead to buy alcohol and drugs. For this reason, I opt never to give money to individuals, only to organizations. One such organization is the Salvation Army, which has one of the best records of allocating the majority of donations to helping people, and spending less on administrative costs (something like ninety cents of every dollar goes to helping others).

At the same time, I am still made to feel guilty, and am often yelled at, by the beggars whom I pass on the street and to whom I refuse to give money (although usually, if you just acknowledge that they are human beings, too, and treat them with respect, there isn't a problem). I have resorted to avoiding carrying any cash, so I can honestly respond, "I'm sorry, I don't carry cash." But, I will admit, it angers me that I can't take a peaceful walk down the street without being accosted every few feet. Should I allow beggars to make me feel guilty? Is it "un-Christian" of me to turn away from them and refuse to give money to them as individuals? Or do I need to be like Mother Teresa and personally reach out and try to help people in need? Should I walk them to the nearest shelter and find them food, housing, a job, etc.?

Basically, I am curious about what happens once a person decides to embrace god and a religion. Will life change? Should one's life change? How much? I always have this deep-rooted guilt that to be truly "good" and religious, one should be at the very least trying to be Mother Teresa. But I will admit it: I would never be able to be Mother Teresa, and I really don't think I want to be Mother Teresa.

DAD: It is interesting, isn't it, that when you think of Christian holiness you think of serving the poor? It is a good association. The idea is Jewish—who is the man of true religion? "It is he who sees justice done for the orphan and widow, who loves the stranger and gives him food and clothing." (Deut. 10:18–19). Jesus was so steeped in Jewish understanding that the rabbis who heard him speak in the synagogue wondered at his knowledge. With this idea, Judaism and Christianity have transformed the world, shifting history's center of gravity away from the mighty and the rich and toward the poor and the vulnerable.

From this historical seed followed the sustained building of hospitals, orphanages, and schools for the poor down through the Christian centuries. From this same seed, in due time, sprang the search of the Scottish humanists (Francis Hutcheson, Adam Smith, and David Hume) for a secular system that would raise the poor of this earth to universal plenty; the ethical justification for socialism; and, in general, progressive politics. Down the ages, hundreds of thousands of women and men have consecrated their lives to serving the poor, lepers, and outcasts such as victims of AIDS. Isn't this what the name of Mother Teresa evokes, and what makes all of us feel a bit guilty? We know very well what God is calling us to.

At the very least, we need to unite our hearts with those who are directly helping the poor, sustain them in their necessary work by our generosity, and pray for them and with them. One core principle of Christian and Jewish belief is that we are all bound together in covenant with God. What one person does in our name, all do. Jews and Christians see the world as close-knit; all humans are part of one garment, one body. The link among us is forged in consciousness, but we also enact it when at the end of the Eucharist the priest opens his hands and says: "Go, to love and serve the Lord and one another."

Christian life is a constant effort to alter our consciousness, to lift it out of the ruts of everyday sameness, in order to see what God sees in it. Religious "faith" is not like a level of beliefs added on to the beliefs of reason; it is like seeing *everything* in a different light, from a different angle. It changes the experience of "seeing." Christianity and Judaism remind us that more goes on in everyday life than our eyes see: that there is reality behind reality, abyss beyond abyss. We live within the mystery of God's life. That is the reason for so much attention to humble things—so many blessings, so many prayers—such as bread, food, drink; bells, candles, and incense; the doors of our homes; the clothing we wear and the prayers we breathe to ask blessing on our activities.

In parochial school, for example, the nuns used to teach us to mark each fresh sheet of paper with the tiny letters AMDG or JMJ—"for the greater glory of God" (*ad majorem Dei gloriam)* or "Jesus, Mary, and Joseph." One nun taught us to greet everyone we meet with a smile, to remind ourselves that we are all held within God's love.

Another said that there are too few compliments in the world, and that when we see anything done well we should thank the doer with a compliment, to add to the wave of goodness that circles the world. Yet another told us to raise our hearts in prayer every time we heard a bell ring or a siren sound—to pray for those in pain or at the point of death. Another said that in the dentist's chair or the doctor's office, any time we felt a sharp pain, we should offer it to God as a prayer, so that someone else suffering even worse pain, no matter how faraway, might receive an inner inspiration that would ease their suffering. They tried to teach us that we are tied by invisible cords to the suffering people on earth.

The hard truth is, Jana, that you *are* called to be a Mother Teresa. Every Christian is. But in your own way, in your own place. Not in Mother Teresa's way, but then one never knows what will be asked of one next. God's call is unconditional, even though the dearest hope of most of us is that God will not basically interfere with us, just leave us alone. In your own way, in your own place, you are called to be holy. There is no escaping it. Everyday life is intended to be the arena of holiness.

What we would all like is for God to let us live a normal life like everybody else, not too good, not too bad, just normal. But God almost never lets us do that. There is always sickness and death in the family—sorrow, failure, disappointment, "the cross." We are always being reminded that we do not belong to ourselves. That if we want to live, we must first die. All sorts of plans, all sorts of selves, must die.

It is all right to rage against this, to resist, to go kicking and screaming, to dread the whole thing. Even Jesus did, the night before he suffered. "Father, let this cup pass from my lips," he asked in his torment. Why me? Why not leave me alone? "Nevertheless, not my will, but Thine be done." "Be it done to me, according to thy word" is the archetypal Christian prayer.

What we really want is to hold on to our own will, in our own way. We would like God to be there, but not to interfere. Just let us be. A divine *laissez-faire*.

Alas, it won't happen.

Thank God, it won't happen. God wants us for his own purposes. He made the world, He made us, for his own purposes. I am not the center of the universe, nor was the universe constructed so that I would be at its center. "Thou shalt not have false gods before me!"

This is a hard truth, hard every day. I wish I could give you better news, in a way more likely to please at least part of you (and a large part of me). But you have put me on the spot. It would be horrible for a father to lie to his daughter.

JANA: *So what exactly are you saying? That it is normal for people to want to focus on nothing besides themselves and their own circle of loved ones? In other words, people would prefer to be self-centered and rebel against God and his call for us to be a part of a greater community, a community which we then need to care about and pay attention to; yet God, inevitably, will call us for his purposes, and this requires our sense of self as individual, alone, to die and be replaced by a sense of being a part of something greater? If*

284

I understand you correctly, then I must add that it sounds very hard to be completely "selfless."

DAD: No, I don't think you should be "selfless," and I certainly don't think you should lose your sense of self in trying to belong to something greater. Even in *caritas* (the specific form of Jewish and Christian love that we discussed in Chapter 3), there is a right order. Your first love must be to fulfill what God wants of you, the unique Jana. The "salvation of your own soul" is your first responsibility in rightly ordered love. For this, you might have to leave "father, mother, brother, sister" for the Lord's sake. (I remember leaving home at the age of fourteen to enter the seminary against my parents' wishes; obviously, they permitted that or I couldn't have done it, but they did insist on telling me why it was against their better judgment.) Sometimes, you have to stand alone, against the world, for conscience's sake. I have watched with pride when each of you three children has done this.

The next order of *caritas* is to love well those committed to your care—family first of all, and other dependents. Next come immediate neighbors, before more distant ones. The poor and the needy make the next claim. Your own coreligionists and countrymen have claims in *caritas*, too, before those farther away. In the end, the love of Jews and Christians should encompass the whole world, in participation in the Creator's love for all he has made—but all in right and just and wise order. The mother who is neglecting her own children because she is so active "doing good" for the community is slipping on one of love's inner ordering principles.

And, by the way, the goal is not to be selfless. The goal

is to be, in a rightly ordered way, other-centered. There's quite a difference between those two ways of thinking of things. If you take pleasure in being other-centered, consider it a grace. You don't have to be "selfless," just alert to seeking the good of others as best you can, even if that is your joy. (Those who worry whether they are selfish may be too self-preoccupied; a nice irony.)

Note, too, that doing things well requires focus and concentration. Unlike God, we are finite, not infinite. We need to do one thing at a time, love well one love at a time.

You asked, Jana, what God requires of you, and Judaism and Christianity make three demands upon their members: faith, action, and ritual. Take ritual first.

Ritual binds us physically in communion with others. Judaism and Christianity are not "spiritualizing" religions. They do not treat our spirits as the central reality of life, and cast our bodies aside as unworthy. (Gnostic heresies have always pitted our "pure" spirits against our bodies, and struggled to break free from earth. The mass suicide in the Heaven's Gate community in California in 1997 is a vivid example of gnostic ideas in practice.) The Biblical religions come to us as flesh and blood, bodies and souls together, *inspirited* flesh and blood, one, as we are. The new life that God gives us through his covenant with us is a new life for *both* body and soul. That is why ritual—kosher food, blessings, ceremonies—is crucial to Judaism. That is why the sacraments are crucial to Christians.

What are the "sacraments"? Outward physical actions, instituted by Christ, that infuse communion in God's life (i.e., *grace*) into us. The sacraments grab hold of our bodies, senses, imaginations, and memories, and bring them into our worship. They aid our souls and bodies to act together. They give us a physical sense of communion, so that our sense of belonging to a whole people is not merely ethereal. We enact our unity with our bodies, in public and tangible acts.

Over the centuries, the oldest Christian community, the Orthodox Catholic of the East first, counted seven sacraments instituted by Christ, other more modern Christian communities count fewer. In addition to baptism and the Eucharist (holy communion), the seven included confirmation (the special gift of the Holy Spirit), holy orders, matrimony, the sacrament of the sick and dying, and confession or reconciliation. This last sacrament, the telling of one's sins to an ordained representative of the community, with a resolve to sin no more, and asking forgiveness from God, is perhaps the most objectionable to most Protestants.

In an age like ours, thought by some to be a materialistic age but in reality a highly spiritualizing age, it is especially important to stress the physical side of the sacraments. The constant emphasis on sex in the public media makes our age seem sensuous. Yet, movies and magazines bombard us with idealizations to which no human body and no real sexual relation can measure up. Our age rejects the normal conditions of human life. Our daily schedules drive us away from the natural harmonies of body and soul, their imperfections, their limits.

Down the centuries, Judaism and Christianity have done more than any other religious movement in history to emphasize the central role of the body along with the soul: the embodied person. In addition, Judaism and Christianity are *not* religions of the private person. For them, the strong individual person springs from (and only from) a community—a very public community, a physical community of the here and now, an organized community with canonical sacred rituals for body and mind alike. Further, Christianity is the only world religion that promises eternal life for body as well as soul; a startling claim.

In our age, the liturgy of the synagogue and the church—their public work of adoration and gratitude—is meant to be a dike, protecting quiet pools of contemplation. Today, one finds the liturgy done best among Christians in one of the older religious orders, like the Benedictines, still redolent with the rhythms and tonalities of the early centuries, in places where time stops. (Often, alas, the modern busy liturgy in the suburban parish lacks the majesty and quiet.) In monastic or traditional settings one gets a foretaste of living outside of time, which is what the term *eternity* points to: not a very long time, but a restful point outside the insistent rush of time. In liturgy and ritual, attentively performed, all one's powers are gathered up and shot forward, to rest in a kind of simultaneity, fully active and alert, quivering in the bull's-eye of God's presence.

I am trying to make a practical point, Jana. To be a faithful Jew, you must go through the door of a synagogue with your body, and your body must perform communal acts. To be a serious Christian, you must also take your body into participation in the mysteries of faith, the reenactment of the scriptural narratives of God's actions among his people in human history. Not for nothing is the year 2000 A.D. called the "millennial year." It celebrates the two thousandth anniversary of the most decisive event in history, the appearance of the Creator in the flesh.

It is wrong to think of faith as a "spiritual" reality only, or a "private affair" only. Faith is a historical, public, communal reality carried forward in history. Taking part in ritual is as important to love of God—dare I say it—as lovemaking in the love between wife and husband. It is a sign of the covenant, and a fruitful sign, too. Never approach religion without taking your body and your sense of public history with you. To become a believer is to become one of the history-changers.

JANA: *I have always liked rituals, as I find their consistency comforting. But your response so far still doesn't tell me what I'm supposed to do in daily life.*

DAD: Besides *ritual*, the Christian life demands *faith* and *action*. Faith does not mean a list of beliefs; it means new eyes, a new way of seeing. Faith does not mean seeing "new things" (although one does see new things), so much as seeing all things in a new way.

In a sense, Jana, you share the predicament of all inquisitive young Jews and Christians brought up by birth within a tradition. At a certain point you have to be *converted* to it, on your own. You have to walk by yourself the long path by which the tradition was fashioned in the first place. Having learned the way the world works, you have to make yourself ready for *a new way of seeing the world* through faith and *acting in it* through new deeds. You have to be born a second time.

In faith, one does not see a different world; it is the same world as before. But now one sees in it aspects that one had previously missed. One observes relations within it differently and—so it immediately seems—in their true light. This new light is more penetrating than any light you have experienced before. Faith is as if one sees the *why* of things, in a hidden code that now seems so obvious, and yet before was so unaccountably beyond one's grasp. Everything seems related. Many arrows, shot from many angles, converge on one point: *The Creator had a purpose. Everything speaks of him.* The world is as it was. Yet it is no longer mute.

The believer feels no contradiction between faith and reason; to her, reason seems now more valuable than ever. No contradiction is felt between faith and practicality. In fact, practicality as seen by faith seems now more practical, more open, more achievable. Common sense receives infusions of the grace of perseverance.

I will not linger much more here on belief, since that is the work of every chapter, except again to draw attention to *point of view, horizon, way of seeing:* a power of understanding in a new way. Belief is like putting on a new mind, not damaging to the mind one already has but enhancing it, extending its range and its depth, completing it.

For clarity's sake, I must admit that I have seen faith actually do damage to a good mind. This damage resulted from complacence, an undeserved satisfaction in "explaining" things already known, instead of *ceaselessly inquiring further* into new things. Similarly, a love too early blest prematurely turns to smugness, and loses its alertness, and so its fire. Even in our best strengths, weakness waits. This is the point of C. S. Lewis in *The Screwtape Letters.*

JANA: *But what "action" are you talking about? What am I supposed to do? That's what worries me now.*

DAD: You brought up the question of everyday life earlier, so I did want to point out that ritual and faith are everyday actions. By the way, there is an ancient precedent for treating ritual first, and then faith, as I have done: *Lex orandi, lex credendi: One learns the laws of believing from the laws of worship.* Liturgy teaches belief. Then liturgy *and* belief teach us how to be *doers.*

Yet you are right in your impatience *to do.* To be a *doer* of the Word, not just a hearer, is an ancient injunction. Here is the prayer of a sixteenth-century English reformer:

> We most humbly beg you to give us not only to be hearers of the Word, but doers also of the same; not only to love, but also to live your gospel; not only to favor, but also to follow your godly doctrine; not only to profess, but also to practice your blessed commandments, to the honor of your Holy Name, and the health of our souls.[1]

In medicine, the first law is, Do no harm. Similarly, in Christianity the first law for action is, Go and sin no more. The first thing a new Christian needs to do is, "Obey the laws of the house. Keep the commandments."

Even so, a young woman may still ask, like the rich young man of the gospels: What more do I need to do to in order to enter fully into my new life? "Go, sell what you own, and give the money to the poor," Jesus told him. (Matt. 19:21) An echo of this story may have played in your mind as you began this chapter, for you went immediately to examples about what you should do when beggars accost you in the street. You feel, almost instinctively, that a Christian ought to give to the poor, perhaps even give her whole life to the poor.

---

[1] Thomas Becon (1511–1567), not to be confused with Francis Bacon.

JANA: *You cannot seriously mean you should sell everything you have and give it to the poor.*

DAD: Well, some have done that, and some always will, as long as Christian faith burns in human hearts. Still, as you rightly sense, this is not the vocation of everybody. Not, at least, giving the *whole* of one's life to working with the poor. To be poor in the United States in this era is not what it was in biblical times, or even a hundred years ago. Today there are food stamps from the government and both private and public soup kitchens, and providers of sandwiches and other foods for the poor. You rightly suspect that those who are dunning you in the street are in no danger of starving— although, if you meet one who is in that danger, I have no doubt that you would help instantly. There is ample reason to believe that some will spend their earnings on alcohol or drugs; but some may simply have a sudden (and passing) urgent need.

In some cities, as a way of addressing this problem, a system of coupons has been arranged, so that people who want to can purchase the coupons and give them to the poor, who can in turn cash them in only at soup kitchens or night shelters. In this way, the integrity of the asking and of the giving is protected. The receiver can get basic needs met and the giver can be more certain of not doing more harm than good.

It is obvious from our experience in the streets that many of those who beg have many needs besides those of food and shelter. They need counseling; they need medical attention; they need love and care. At this point of acute human vulnerability, one can give something of some small but necessary value—not just a polite word, but a passing bit of human kindness that is intended to reflect their dignity. You make this point yourself. "I don't have any change now," I can imagine you saying, and then adding a kind wish. Said with a smile, you honor the beggar's request as a reasonable one. I have learned from rough experience that prolonging such a conversation is not a good idea; I would certainly not recommend it for a young woman.

Christians should also volunteer to work among the poor at a shelter or food kitchen as often and as much as they can. More than merely giving money or praying, necessary as those are, it is important for one's own soul, and one's own human experience, to serve the poor, to actually be with them.

JANA: *Yes, but what about daily life? Okay, so we should—if we choose not to dedicate our lives to helping others—help those who help others, both with money and time. But what about the other minutes and hours in the day? Is it simply a matter of always trying to be good, kind, and cheerful? Of always keeping in mind to do unto others what you would have done unto you and that we are all God's creatures? So that how my life has to change is that I need to concentrate on always trying to make myself a better (nicer, less impatient) person, on not doing evil to others, and on utilizing the gifts God gave me to their fullest?*

DAD: I think you're moving in the wrong direction. You're turning Christian faith into a morality tale—religion is niceness, communication, understanding, using your talents well. How would that differ from a high noble paganism? It's good as far as it goes.

The biblical religions have something else in mind: the love of God with your whole heart, your whole mind, and your whole soul. These religions are not you-centered; they are God-centered. Their aim is holiness. Not goodness alone (although that is indispensable), but another dimension: the sense of the holy. The holy is what induces mystery, wonder, awe—a light and love greater than our hearts, minds, or wills, beyond what our eyes see (which is wonderful enough) or our imaginations imagine. *"Allah is great!"* the Muslims say. So, in silence, does every believing Jew and Christian. The Creator of all is great.

If we are right in where our reflections have so far led us, God is present with us in every moment of every day. Therefore, a kind of holiness is possible in everyday life. All you have to do is open your heart to him, invite him to act in you, to guide you, to advise you, to protect you, to make up for your deficiencies. Ask God to show his love to others through your actions. Your smile should be his, your helping hand his, your generosity and calm of spirit his. Let him do the acting.

Among all the saints, Jana, let me tell you one story, the story of a young woman who died in the twenty-fourth year of her life, whose name was Therese Martin. Her father was a doctor in a suburb of Le Mans, and two of her older sisters had entered a Carmelite convent not far away, in Lisieux, in her native Normandy. The Normans are known for hardheaded practicality, clarity, and common sense, and from a very early age (like you) Therese was no exception.

She was born almost exactly one hundred years before you, in 1873, and was dead by the end of September, 1897.

At the age of fourteen Therese set off with her father for a visit to Rome, where her agenda was to ask Pope Leo XIII—whom she later described as so old he looked dead— for permission to enter Carmel the next year, at the unprecedented age of fifteen. She knew what she wanted to do. She didn't want to do anything else. It might be against the rules, but rules are made to be broken when the reasons are good, and she knew that hers were the best possible: She was *sure* that God called her to Carmel. If she could see it so clearly, why couldn't the pope?

From then on for almost nine interminable months she was the first to inspect the morning's mail, but there was never anything there. Finally, just before Christmas she received a letter from the local bishop granting her permission. Her older sister Pauline was prioress of Carmel at the time, and arranged for Therese to arrive at Easter—just after the rigors of Lent. Carmel is a contemplative order, founded by St. Teresa of Avila (and St. John of the Cross) in the middle decades of the 1500s. The mission of the nuns is to pray, night and day, for the good of souls everywhere on earth, and especially for the Church. The sisters live a very bare and simple life consisting of work; the public prayer of the Eucharist and the "hours" of the Church, seven times a day from matins in the morning until vespers and compline at eventide; meditation on the Scriptures; private prayer; and an hour of recreational conversation. They sleep in adequate but spartan rooms, eat a simple diet in a common refectory. Periodically, or as needed, a doctor comes in for their physical care, and a confessor for independent guidance in the ways of the spirit.

For many months, Therese was a postulant, in effect asking the community to judge her worthiness for a life commitment to this small band of twenty or so nuns, bound together for life in the one place. Once admitted to the novitiate year, as a novice in the appropriate habit of the Carmelites—heavy brown robes, with a white veil over her hair—Therese prepared herself for the taking of vows, first vows for a short span of years, then vows for life once that term was complete. In those days, there was much political turmoil in France (again), and anticlerical voices were threatening to empty out the convents and monasteries, so the prioress counseled her sisters to keep their hair reasonably long in case they were of a sudden thrown out into the streets. But the usual custom was to offer up their long tresses to the Lord, in favor of very short hair hidden by the veil. Their communal aim was, like Christ, who being God "emptied Himself" and took the form of a slave, to offer everything of themselves to God as living offerings. For by his life, Jesus established the Christian way: God so loves the world that He sent his only Son to live among us, showing that the point of creation is mercy and love, and that love is suffering love, even unto death.

I know secular people, Jana, who think that this a grisly and terribly repressed view of life, to which they prefer a sunnier view based on happiness. But I note that I have never met one person who has been exempted from suffering, often quite acute suffering, and inner torments of many kinds. So far as "happiness" goes, I have met nuns who are as happy as anyone I know. If happiness is using your mind and will to the fullest extent possible, upon an object infinitely worthy of your efforts to understand and to love, I do not see how a full and total love for God measures less than other loves. And what is love?

Therese Martin had a little picture based on the image of the suffering Christ—beaten, crowned with thorns, streaked with blood, sweaty from the exertion of carrying the cross through the streets of Jerusalem—taken from the Shroud of Turin, purportedly the veil Veronica used when along the way of the cross she stepped forward to wipe his face. The historical validity of that Shroud is not the point. However arrived at, the portrait of that suffering face is unforgettable. Therese loved to look at it, as the face of her Beloved. This was the measure of his love for her. To return commensurate love seemed beyond her. Except that, according to the faith, God endows in us his own love, infuses into us his own life, so that we may love him with his love. All God asks is that we open ourselves to let him act in us. This is the central insight of the life of Therese Martin.

You probably are aware that your sister Tanya was born on the feast day of St. Therese, October 3, and was given as her second baptismal name Therese. Your own name, Jana, is the Slovak form of Jeanne, as in Ste. Jeanne d'Arc. Although Therese died in total obscurity in the convent of Lisieux in 1897, the next year her own notebooks were published in a small edition, and then reprinted again and again, until by the time of the war in 1914 her image was known throughout the French army; and so was her promise that, after her death, she would spend her heaven doing good upon earth, and send a rain of roses (favors) upon earth. For years before she was canonized by the Church, she was regarded as a saint by the people of France and many others. As it was, her canonization occurred in record time, in 1924, and the crowds at the ceremonies in France were immense. With amazing speed, a huge basilica in her honor was built in Lisieux. She was declared the Patroness of all France, coequal with Ste. Jeanne d'Arc. (Both you and Tanya are named for patronesses of France!)

What did Therese Martin do to win such affection? By now there are over twenty-five hundred churches around the world dedicated in her name. Only once in my life have I found a Catholic church anywhere in the world—and I have always looked, from Bangladesh to Eastern Europe—that did not have a statue recalling her name in one corner or another. Along with St. Francis of Assisi, Therese has become the most popular saint in all Christian history. The insight mentioned above, that God wants to offer his love to the world through each of us, if we allow him, is at the heart of her witness.

So also is the conclusion that this bright young woman drew from this insight: in order to be a saint, even a very great saint, one does not have to do great deeds. Rather, one may simply do all the ordinary things of life—like her job in the convent, the laundry—as intently and as deeply steeped in God's love as possible. It is not the greatness of the deed but the intensity of the divine love that packs the power, that is what is really real in life. She called this "the little way," the way for lay persons and ordinary persons divinized (so to speak) in their ordinary tasks by the fire of God's love within them.

Protestants might call this "justification by faith"—the crucial thing is God's action, not ours. Therese thought of it, so to speak, as justification by love. Love is the reality through which God reveals himself in Jesus, in Scriptures, and in daily life. Think of it: What are our best images of God, if not the examples of love we have known in life, in our parents, in our friends, in those most dear to us? And the test of love is the suffering we are willing to endure to be faithful to the one we love. Yet suffering is not only a "test" but the one most reliable way to be imitators of the suffering Christ; it is a privilege. Love means atonement; it means suffering unto death. This turns ordinary liberal piety upside down. It is right of course to try to alleviate suffering in others, as Veronica did in gently wiping Christ's face; compassion is the central Christian virtue. But compassion often entails taking suffering upon ourselves, and in such moments a Christian considers it a privilege to be asked to be like Christ.

What brought about Therese's death at such a young age was tuberculosis, which fairly rapidly destroyed one of her lungs and began eating away at the other. She had fevers, headaches, weariness, and she often felt as though she would suffocate like a drowning person. For years she had found no comfort or sweetness in prayer, only aridity, and for some years terrible doubts that no God was with her as she thought, and that there is no eternal life with him. She welcomed this darkness, so that it could not be said that she prayed and remained faithful to Love because it comforted her; she wanted, she said, to come to her Lover with empty hands, relying solely on his love within her, making up for the feelings she lacked. Most Christians who try to pray sometimes experience this emptiness. For her this was a special trial when she received the Lord in communion; she felt distracted, directionless, empty. This, too, she welcomed, and kept up her outward cheerfulness and good humor as a way of expressing God's love for her sisters, when she felt nothing herself.

Jana, I chose St. Therese as an example because at her death she was just your age, and because her example is so stark, clear, and lucid. You might like her writing: *The Story of a Soul*, her poems, and the record of her last conversations with her sisters. There is a short, somber, but terribly moving movie about her life made by a woman (and non-Christian) director in France, *Thérèse*. Unlike her namesake, St. Teresa of Avila (1515–1582) or Mother Teresa of Calcutta (1910–1997), who took her name, Therese never left her suburban convent, never founded a great community of nuns or made visits to them all over the then-known world, never was a missionary or martyr or preacher. She lived in solitude, and yet she changed the way in which scores of millions have seen the Christian vocation: to do ordinary things in extraordinary ways, channeling God's own love to others. She knew that God could touch others in all parts of the world through her, and he did. She knew that her own insignificance didn't matter, and it didn't. God is great.

What you said about everyday life, Jana—to do everything as well as you can—needs to be supplemented by a sense of God acting within you. This requires more time on your part dedicated to spiritual reading, prayer, meditation, quiet time. The trick is to keep your attention "gathered up," not scattered and dispersed in a thousand directions. The idea is to nourish an inner life as attentive and active as your outer life. That requires a continuous conversation with God.

I like to use sounds that break in on my consciousness—a bell, a fire siren, the screech of a car's wheels, even the song of a bird or the buzz of a fly in the room—to remind myself of God's presence in the things of this world. God attends lovingly to each detail. Why don't we?

Most people think of the Creator as distant—distant in time (back then) and in space (up there). That is all wrong! By "Creator" we mean Sustainer. Even if the world had no beginning (no "big bang"), God has always held it in existence (however long its life span). God is in all things, holding them in being in their vitality and glory.

The other night at dinner our host had the most marvelous huge bowl of flowers as a centerpiece: roses and carnations and whites and pinks I did not recognize, an abundance of flowers, a richness and profusion of (it seemed) more than a hundred flowers tightly and beautifully packed in the shape of a round mound. All the guests kept looking at this amazing outburst of color. "I have never looked at flowers before," the woman next to me said, "and felt *elevated*." This was the Mozart of floral arrangements. We wondered at it. We were in awe of it. The artist knew how to express love and beauty and truth through it, a unity of being, a kind of purity, virtually the essence of floral possibilities. I don't know what the florist's intentions were, but if she did it with the love of God in her heart, this was a work of holiness.

The beauty of her creation honored the Creator.

That's what your life should do, by his grace. A testimonial from seven centuries ago by one thought to be the most Christ-like of all Christians, expresses this well:

A SIMPLE PRAYER
Lord, make me an instrument of your peace
Where there is hatred . . . let me sow love.

Where there is injury . . . pardon.
Where there is discord . . . unity.
Where there is doubt . . . faith.
Where there is error . . . truth.
Where there is despair . . . hope.
Where there is sadness . . . joy.
Where there is darkness . . . light.

O Divine Master, grant that I may not so much seek
To be consoled . . . as to console.
To be understood . . . as to understand.
To be loved . . . as to love.
For
It is in giving . . . that we receive,
It is in pardoning . . . that we are pardoned,
It is in dying . . . that we are born to eternal life.

—St. Francis of Assisi (1182–1226)

THE LAST WORD: JANA

JANA: *I have read this manuscript so many times now that I fear it is difficult to remember exactly how I thought before we started. Each time I read these pages, I react to them as I once did to my older brother: I wrestle with them, fight with them, talk back to them, quote their authority, look up to them, and, ultimately, appreciate and love them. Most important, though, I think about them.*

I haven't been to church regularly since grade school. There were periods of church-going, such as mandatory attendance at my Catholic boarding school and when I had a religious boyfriend during college. But on the whole, I neither saw the purpose nor felt the desire. After some difficult times, when it seemed the church and God were not there to help, I had abandoned them as useless. It was with this history that I began this project with my father. I had come to a crossroads in my life and was curious about the parts of my heritage that I had dropped by the wayside. I had come to terms with the concept of God—although "agnodeist" probably described my beliefs best: I believed there was some sort of higher being, but wasn't so sure about anything else, or even that we could know anything else. Yet perhaps there was something to this God thing, this religion thing.

What do I think now? Well, first of all, instead of the

concepts of God and religion being at the periphery of my mind, they now dominate my thoughts. A year or so ago it began to seem worthwhile to explore a subject that I used to believe had no relevance to my life. I now see that it has more relevance than my choice of what to do with my life, or whom to pick as a significant other (dilectio, I think my father called that), concerns that had previously dominated my time.

In our human relationships we need to call attention to our suffering and ask others to help us; we can't assume that other people are mindreaders, able to sense our pain (although some people do like to claim they can do so). Why can't this be true of our relationship with God? and church? It is a challenge to learn to open ourselves to others and ask for help—at least for me it is—but we end up stronger and richer in our relationships and in ourselves as a result of such momentary "weakness." (Is it really a weakness to be honest with yourself, and admit that you cannot do it all?)

From my understanding, it seems that our relationship with God is like that, too; He seeks us out, as we should Him. It has become a cliché, but I've always loved this story:

FOOTPRINTS

One night a man had a dream. He dreamed he was walking along the beach with the Lord. Across the sky flashed scenes from his life. For each scene, he noticed two sets of footprints in the sand: one belonging to him, and the other to the Lord.

When the last scene of his life flashed before him, he looked back at the footprints in the sand. He noticed that many times along the path of his life there was only one set of footprints. He also noticed that it happened at the very lowest and saddest times in his life.

This really bothered him and he questioned the Lord about it. "Lord, you said that once I decided to follow you, you'd walk with me all the way. But I have noticed that during the most troublesome times in my life, there is only one set of footprints. I don't understand why when I needed you most you would leave me."

The Lord replied, "My precious, precious child, I love you and I would never leave you. During your times of trial and suffering, when you see only one set of footprints, it was then that I carried you."

—Anonymous

If I am honest with myself, then God is there. If I am honest with my successes, my abilities, and especially my failings, then I am open to love and to being loved. By another person, and by God.

So I need to learn how to be honest with myself. Which is the simplest yet most difficult thing to do. It requires a lot of effort, and it requires that I also—as my father complained was the kicker in the commandment—love myself. (I really do find that hard at times.) Mostly, it requires that I reflect. If there is one thing that—in my tendency to make sweeping, grandiose statements—I believe would be a cure for many of today's problems, it is reflection. I tend to be so busy that I don't take the time to think: about the big picture; about consequences; about other people; about their feelings; about myself; about my soul; about life; about truth; about God.

Recently, my father suggested that I spend two hours alone on my knees. I have begun to try that, as the first step toward changing my life (okay, the knees part isn't necessary). Turn off the television and sit quietly—my favorite time is twilight, when the harsh artificial lights are not quite necessary, and the sun's glare is no longer blinding; or eve-ning, when a flickering candle in a dark room provides such a calming effect. Just sit and reflect. Don't think of work or problems with my significant other or the ball game. Think of nothing. Sometimes I feel silly, and imagine nothing is being accomplished. But if I stay quiet, that blank mind allows my soul to come pouring out, and suddenly I feel in touch with myself. Truly in touch. This is because I am in the context of a truth greater than myself.

This is my first step toward change and toward living better: When I am in touch with myself, I am then a little more able to focus on others, such as my loved ones, such as God.

It all sounds very "New Age" I know, but a part of New Age actually has its roots in "old age" traditions. "Know thyself." "The unexamined life is not worth living." "To thine own self be true." These are not sayings from the last few decades of pop psychology. I learned the first two from the philosopher Socrates, who lived in ancient Greece be-fore Christ, and the latter from a sixteenth-century play. They got it right, a long time ago.

"New Age"—which claims to be an improvement over these "old age" ideas and over the traditions of Judaism and Christianity—still can't get it right, though. Pantheism or "touchy-feely" body-focused "religions" can't compare to the truths that spring from a Creator and the succor offered by a Redeemer. Sin, evil, and pain need to be confronted, not just covered up.

What have I learned from this book? Humans crave community and traditions, and a church provides this; and it's all right to be human. Religion offers tangible benefits and support. God may be intangible, but he offers us the chance to participate in something greater than ourselves. He offers us the sorrows and pains of the millions of others around us. He also offers us the joy and love of himself and everyone else.

Not all of my questions have been answered. Each reply my father gave made me think of several other points I was curious about. This book could have stretched to a thousand pages and I probably would not have been satisfied. But these additional questions will have to wait; Dad needs to catch his breath before I start interrogating him again.

In the meantime, I will continue on the path he has started me down: I will examine my life, God, religion. I will continue searching.

DAD'S READING LIST
FOR JANA

To learn about Christianity, there is no substitute for reading the New Testament. It is not a long book; it is accessible and absorbing. The new *Introduction to the New Testament* by Raymond E. Brown may well become the new standard in the field. My favorite life of Christ is Romano Guardini's *The Lord*. The generation-old works of Fulton Oursler, *The Greatest Book Ever Written*, *The Greatest Story Ever Told*, and *The Greatest Faith Ever Known*, are written from a Protestant point of view, are wonderfully approachable, and may be read by a Catholic with great profit. For contemporary help in understanding the historical setting of the Jewish Testament, the particular characteristics of its authors, and traditions of interpretation, I found helpful as a beginner John L. McKenzie's *The Two-Edged Sword*. But the best introduction is no doubt Rabbi Abraham Joshua Heschel's *The Prophets*.

Regarding particular questions about Christianity, among the best books I have ever read are those by G. K. Chesterton and C. S. Lewis. Chesterton's *Orthodoxy, An Outline of Sanity* and *The Everlasting Man* inspired C. S. Lewis to deal with similar questions in *Mere Christianity*, *The Abolition of Man*, *The Problem of Pain*, *Surprised by Joy*, and *The Screwtape Letters*. More than twenty million copies of Lewis's books have been sold, and they are available these days in multiple editions. Chesterton is the most quoted author in the English language next to Samuel Johnson, and his collected works have been published by Ignatius Press in San Francisco. Many readers will already have read some of his Father Brown mystery stories, and of course the Narnia stories of C. S. Lewis.

I'm a great fan of fiction and biography, and so I strongly recommend the novels of Sigrid Undset, especially the *Kristin Lavransdatter* trilogy; Georges Bernanos, especially *Under the Sun of Satan*; and Léon Bloy, *The Woman Who Was Poor*. I love the poetry of Charles Péguy, too, especially the little collection *God Speaks*. The novels of Louis de Wohl about St. Thomas Aquinas (*The Quiet Light*) and St. Augustine (*The Restless Flame*) bring entire eras to life.

Among biographies of the saints, my favorites are *Saint Teresa of Avila*, by Marcelle Auclair; the autobiography of St. Therese of Lisieux, *The Story of a Soul;* and two little introductions to St. Thomas Aquinas by Josef Pieper, *The Silence of St. Thomas* and *A Guide to St. Thomas Aquinas*. Ralph McInerny's introductions to Aquinas are crystal clear; I especially like *A First Glance at St. Thomas Aquinas: A Handbook for Peeping Thomists*.

For church history, I very much admire *A Popular History of the Catholic Church*, by Philip Hughes; the energetic *History of Christianity*, by Paul Johnson; and *Saints and Sinners*, a beautifully illustrated history of the papacy by Oxford's Eamon Duffy.

Since I was not raised as an evangelical, I have found two or three books written by evangelicals who have become Catholics extremely helpful, not for what they say about Catholicism but for insight into how ugly they found aspects of Catholicism as they grew up, and the obstacles they met in it. Such books simultaneously shed light on *both* traditions, evangelical and Catholic. I have learned a greater respect for and appreciation of evangelical churches through books by Thomas Howard, Peter Kreeft, David Currie, and Scott Hahn particularly. (Currie comments that when John F. Kennedy was shot, he felt very sorry as a nine-year-old that poor Kennedy, as a Catholic lacking justification by faith, must be in hell.) Currie also reports being surprised that Catholics tend to believe that Evangelicals share 70 or 80 percent of Catholic life and faith.

On Judaism, I have been greatly helped by the writings of Dennis Prager in his newsletter *Ultimate Issues;* Naomi Rosenblatt's reflections on the Book of Genesis, *Wrestling with Angels;* Elliott Abrams's wonderfully illuminating book *Faith or Fear: How Jews Can Survive in a Christian America;* and David Novak's *The Election of Israel.*

I also like to learn about each tradition through key magazines and journals of opinion, and their commentaries on passing events, personalities, and books. The best general religious review in English is *First Things;* my favorite general review from a Jewish standpoint is *Commentary;* among Protestant magazines, I keep an eye on *Christianity Today, Christian Century,* and, on the left, *Sojourners.* It's probably unfair of me to list first among Catholic periodicals the monthly *Crisis,* since I helped to found it. In any case, the most respected standbys for many years have been *Commonweal* and *America. Catholic World Report, The Vatican Today,* and *Dossier* (a monthly survey of disputed questions) are new entries in the field.

ACKNOWLEDGMENTS

First off, the authors must thank Eerdmans Press for permission to quote from the wonderful collection of prayers, *The Communion of Saints*, edited by Horton Davies, and from *The Portal of the Mystery of Hope*, by Charles Péguy, newly translated by David Louis Schindler, Jr.; also, Dennis Prager, president of the Micah Center for Ethical Monotheism, for permission to quote from his brave and groundbreaking essay, "Why Judaism Rejected Homosexuality, Judaism's Sexual Revolution" in *Crisis* (September 1993).

The authors also wish to thank Brian Anderson, formerly a Research Associate at the American Enterprise Institute, and his wife, Amy, for many good suggestions, constant scrutiny of succeeding drafts, and early and persistent encouragement. If they had not responded so enthusiastically to the first pages assembled in Kraków, this book might not have appeared.

Thanks are also due to Cathie Love in Michael Novak's office, who managed the flow of paper, E-mails, and faxes, not to mention telephone calls and correspondence, and made irreverent comments along the way.

Jana would especially like to thank her roommate, Stephanie Kristich, who was kind enough to read through many of the drafts of the book and offer her comments and criticism; her patience, listening ability, and understanding taught Jana "the true meaning of friendship—*amicitia.*"

Our literary agent, Loretta Barrett, not only contributed many good suggestions but also introduced us to a most encouraging, affectionate, and acute editor, Jane Cavolina at Pocket Books, who was a dream to work with. Both Loretta and Jane have become our friends.

We are also very grateful to those who sacrificed their time to criticize early versions of our questions and replies (especially the replies), pointing out ambiguities, errors, lapses, and omissions, and sometimes raising questions of their own. Their efforts helped us, particularly Michael, to rethink many passages. We are particularly grateful to Catherine Cox; Michael Cromartie; T. M. Moore; Avery Dulles, S.J.; Richard John Neuhaus; and William F. Buckley, Jr. At the office, intern Wasfi Bsisu offered guidance regarding Muslim sources; at home, Karen Laub Novak made several strategic suggestions about the order of chapters.

Finally, after Brian Anderson left us to become senior editor of *The City Journal* in New York, Steven Long stepped in to help us through the final stages of publication, including the index, and Tom Kilroy helped, too.

JANA NOVAK
MICHAEL NOVAK

INDEX